Gareth Moore writes the monthly magazine Sudoku Pro. His previous books include *The 10-Minute Brain Workout*, *Kid's 10-Minute Brain Workout*, and *The Book of Kakuro*. He is an expert in language modelling and a Ph.D-qualified scientist from Cambridge University.

Also available
The Mammoth Book of 20th Century Science Fiction
The Mammoth Book of Best New Erotica 7
The Mammoth Book of Best New Horror 18
The Mammoth Book of Best New Manga 2
The Mammoth Book of Best New SF 20
The Mammoth Book of Best War Comics
The Mammoth Book of Bikers
The Mammoth Book of Celtic Myths and Legends
The Mammoth Book of Comic Fantasy
The Mammoth Book of Comic Quotes
The Mammoth Book of CSI
The Mammoth Book of the Deep
The Mammoth Book of Dickensian Whodunnits
The Mammoth Book of Dirty, Sick, X-Rated & Politically Incorrect Jokes
The Mammoth Book of the Edge
The Mammoth Book of Erotic Women
The Mammoth Book of Extreme Science Fiction
The Mammoth Book of the Funniest Cartoons of All Time
The Mammoth Book of Great Detective Stories
The Mammoth Book of Great Inventions
The Mammoth Book of Haunted House Stories
The Mammoth Book of Insults
The Mammoth Book of International Erotica
The Mammoth Book of IQ Puzzles
The Mammoth Book of Jacobean Whodunnits
The Mammoth Book of Jokes
The Mammoth Book of Killers at Large
The Mammoth Book of King Arthur
The Mammoth Book of Lesbian Erotica
The Mammoth Book of Modern Ghost Stories
The Mammoth Book of Monsters
The Mammoth Book of Mountain Disasters
The Mammoth Book of New Jules Verne Adventures
The Mammoth Book of New Terror
The Mammoth Book of On the Road
The Mammoth Book of Perfect Crimes and Impossible Mysteries
The Mammoth Book of Pirates
The Mammoth Book of Polar Journeys
The Mammoth Book of Roaring Twenties Whodunnits
The Mammoth Book of Roman Whodunnits
The Mammoth Book of Secret Code Puzzles
The Mammoth Book of Sex, Drugs & Rock 'n' Roll
The Mammoth Book of Sorcerers' Tales
The Mammoth Book of Space Exploration and Disasters
The Mammoth Book of Special Forces
The Mammoth Book of Special Ops
The Mammoth Book of Sudoku
The Mammoth Book of Travel in Dangerous Places
The Mammoth Book of True Crime
The Mammoth Book of True War Stories
The Mammoth Book of Unsolved Crimes
The Mammoth Book of Vampires
The Mammoth Book of Wild Journeys
The Mammoth Book of Women Who Kill
The Mammoth Book of the World's Greatest Chess Games

THE MAMMOTH BOOK OF BRAIN WORKOUTS

RUNNING PRESS
PHILADELPHIA · LONDON

9 8 7 6 5 4 3 2 1
Digit on the right indicates the number of this printing

Library of Congress Cataloging-in-Publication Data is available on file

ISBN 978-0-7624-3375-9

This book may be ordered by mail from the publisher.
Please include $2.50 for postage and handling.
But try your bookstore first!

Running Press Book Publishers
2300 Chestnut Street
Philadelphia, PA 19103–4371

Visit us on the web!
www.runningpress.com

Contents

Introduction

Challenge yourself to improve your brain power! With well over 400 mental conundrums to stimulate your grey matter, this month-long programme of brain gymnastics is a fantastic step on the way to a sharper and smarter you.

Physical workouts can make you sweat, but the mental challenges in this book are much more fun. You won't even need to worry about your weight or heartbeat rate or any absolute assessment of how you're doing. The book allows you to keep track of your improvement.

But why should you care? The answer is simple: use it or lose it! The synaptic connections between neurons in your brain degenerate with lack of use, and exercising as much of your brain as you can helps keep it in tip-top condition, just like physical exercise helps look after the rest of your body.

It's important to exercise all of your brain, not just a small part. That's why this book features such a wide range of mental tasks broken down into various categories, each designed to target different areas.

Mind Power workouts help hone your visual analysis and visual manipulation skills, along with more basic counting and observation processes.

Memory workouts challenge you to remember lists of words and visual information in a range of different ways. Both ordered and unordered information, with a variety of cues, are used to help you improve this important mental asset.

Your **Problem-Solving** skills are put to the test by a wide range of logical reasoning and deduction challenges. Helping you improve everything from your number and word skills through to analysis and inference, these puzzles work on many key abilities.

Creativity puzzles focus on exercising the right-hand side of your brain, working on your skills of intuition and your ability to consider the entirety of a problem all at once. Requiring you to think outside normal parameters, these workouts provide vigorous exercise for your imagination.

Concentration workouts are directed at improving your ability to focus on one specific task for a couple of minutes, tested by providing a series of time or arithmetical challenges to complete as quickly as possible.

The book is divided into 31 chapters or days, each day containing a new set of workouts that require thorough and entertaining mental exercise. You'll find 13 workouts for each day, carefully selected to provide the necessary variety that your brain needs to help it stay in great condition.

All you need is a pencil – if you're pulling out a calculator for any of the number puzzles then you've probably missed an easier method of working out the answer, and if you find yourself rotating the book or using a mirror to solve the visual puzzles then you're missing the point! (but full marks for creative thinking!)

You can of course take this book with you anywhere – you may want to do your daily workout on the way to work, in a break during the day, or simply whenever you can fit them in – but try to do them as regularly as you can. You'll find it most rewarding if you do them somewhere you can concentrate.

Don't worry if you find some of the workouts a bit tricky – if you found them all easy then you would not be exercising enough parts of your brain. But it's your book, so if you want to cover up half of each memory puzzle and work on remembering fewer items, until you feel more comfortable with longer lists, then by all means do that. And if the concentration puzzles take you a particularly long time, try doing only half of them until you get faster – and so on.

One thing you shouldn't do is miss out the workouts you don't like so much. If you do this then you'll be missing the balanced benefit they provide. At least try each puzzle for a couple of minutes before moving on – these are almost certainly the workouts that will bring the most improvement the most quickly!

Finally, remember that whilst a healthy brain is extremely important so is a healthy body – your brain needs regular supplies of a wide range of vitamins, minerals and other chemicals in order to function to the best of its ability, so it helps to make sure that you consume a wide and varied diet. Studies often indicate that fish is particularly good, but the best general advice is to have as wide a diet as you possibly can. A recent study summarizing a vast range of dietary research concluded that this was the only piece of eating advice that could be proven beyond all reasonable doubt.

Good luck – and have fun!

Scoring

To keep track of your progress as you work through the book, use this simple scoring system to log your performance each day. You can then compare the results as a guide to see how you're improving.

Time
Each time you complete a workout in the book, keep a note of how long you spend on it. Write this down in the 'Time taken' box at the bottom of each page, and then work out how many sets of 30 seconds you used and write this number in the 'Time points' box. For example if you spend 1 minute 10 seconds on a workout then you have gone into your third set of 30 seconds, so you would write '3' in the 'Time points' box.

The memory workouts don't have these time boxes – that's because a fixed amount of time is already assigned to memorize the words or diagrams. You can take as long as you like to try and recall them!

Accuracy
Once you've completed each day's worth of workouts, check your answers against the given solutions. Each time you've made a mistake score 1 point, and then write the total number of points in the 'Incorrect answers' box.

Totals
For each workout, add together the 'Time points' and 'Incorrect answers' scores and write the total in the 'Total score' box at the bottom of each page.

Add up the total in all of the 'Total score' boxes for that day, and write the overall result in the table on the following two pages. As the days progress, check back here to see how you're improving.

Your workout results

DAY 1	DAY 2	DAY 3
DAY 4	**DAY 5**	**DAY 6**
DAY 7	**DAY 8**	**DAY 9**
DAY 10	**DAY 11**	**DAY 12**
DAY 13	**DAY 14**	**DAY 15**
DAY 16	**DAY 17**	**DAY 18**

DAY 19	DAY 20	DAY 21
DAY 22	DAY 23	DAY 24
DAY 25	DAY 26	DAY 27
DAY 28	DAY 29	DAY 30
DAY 31		

DAY
1

Observation and Counting

Look at these overlapping circles and see how long it takes you to answer the observation questions below.

How many circles are there in this diagram?

What is the maximum number of circles that overlap at any point?

How many line intersections are there, where one circle crosses another?

TIME TAKEN:	INCORRECT ANSWERS:
TIME POINTS:	**TOTAL SCORE:**

Logical Puzzlers

Try to solve these problems – each requires only simple logic to solve, but you might find that making notes with a pencil will help!

A ball is dropped from 100cm above the ground. It bounces twice straight back up, and then stops dead on the ground. How far has it travelled, given that each bounce peaks at half the ball's previous maximum height?

Two dogs are racing to meet the postman. If the first dog has 50 metres to run and the second has 25 metres to run, but runs at less than half the speed of the first, which dog will get there first?

If I cut a large cake into 27 pieces and eat a third of the cake, and then a third of what is left, and finish off all but a third of the remaining amount, how many pieces of cake remain?

TIME TAKEN:	INCORRECT ANSWERS:
TIME POINTS:	**TOTAL SCORE:**

DAY: 1	WORKOUT: 3	CONCENTRATION

Time Elapsed

Work out how many hours and minutes have passed between each of these pairs of times.

12:05am to 4:15pm =	:	2:45am to 9:30pm =	:
5:55pm to 11:15pm =	:	10:55am to 4:25pm =	:
4:50am to 10:25am =	:	9:05am to 2:05pm =	:
1:55pm to 7:30pm =	:	3:35am to 7:20am =	:
2:00pm to 3:55pm =	:	1:00pm to 11:25pm =	:
2:00am to 11:20am =	:	11:40am to 12:10pm =	:
5:35am to 6:00pm =	:	3:20pm to 9:05pm =	:
12:55pm to 1:45pm =	:	11:05am to 6:10pm =	:
3:10am to 4:50pm =	:	10:25am to 10:00pm =	:
10:15am to 12:05pm =	:	11:50am to 4:50pm =	:
12:50pm to 2:40pm =	:	10:20am to 10:55am =	:
10:55am to 5:50pm =	:	8:20pm to 9:25pm =	:
2:15am to 8:25pm =	:	2:40am to 9:20am =	:
9:55am to 7:00pm =	:	11:10am to 5:10pm =	:
10:25am to 3:50pm =	:	6:35am to 1:40pm =	:

TIME TAKEN:	INCORRECT ANSWERS:
TIME POINTS:	**TOTAL SCORE:**

Odd One Out

Look at each of these sets of words. Can you work out which word is the odd one out in each case?

Dog
Cat
Mouse
Gerbil
Lizard

Athens
Beijing
Warsaw
Milan
Tokyo

Red
Green
White
Orange
Violet

Bitter
Cool
Biting
Frosty
Rainy

TIME TAKEN:	INCORRECT ANSWERS:
TIME POINTS:	**TOTAL SCORE:**

Matchstick Thinking

The picture below shows 8 matchsticks arranged in a square.

Can you add 4 more matchsticks within the square in order to make 2 shapes only of exactly the same size and shape? There must be no left-over matches, and matches may not overlap or be broken into pieces.

TIME TAKEN:	INCORRECT ANSWERS:
TIME POINTS:	**TOTAL SCORE:**

Missing Words

Study each of these 3 lists of words for a total of 2 minutes. Then cover the top half of the page and see if you can identify which word is missing from each list below.

Monkey	Chimpanzee	Orang-utan	Llama
Camel	Lemur	Leopard	Panther

Scalene	Isosceles	Perfect	Regular
Acute	Equilateral	Obtuse	Right-angle

Diamond	Topaz	Opal	Ruby
Emerald	Sapphire	Pearl	Amber

Now try to spot the missing word from each list:

Leopard, Panther, Chimpanzee, Orang-utan, Llama, Camel, Lemur

MISSING:

Obtuse, Isosceles, Perfect, Acute, Scalene, Regular, Equilateral

MISSING:

Diamond, Amber, Sapphire, Topaz, Ruby, Emerald, Opal

MISSING:

INCORRECT ANSWERS:	TOTAL SCORE:

Missing Signs

Insert the missing sign into each of these arithmetic expressions in order to make the equation true. You will need to add, subtract, multiply, or divide.

20	☐	27 = 47		5	☐	10 = 50		11	☐	11 = 1	
3	☐	3 = 1		5	☐	12 = 17		65	☐	15 = 50	
20	☐	5 = 4		140	☐	16 = 156		29	☐	9 = 20	
29	☐	7 = 36		5	☐	5 = 1		43	☐	35 = 8	
4	☐	2 = 8		29	☐	18 = 11		18	☐	4 = 14	
5	☐	7 = 35		7	☐	7 = 49		111	☐	16 = 127	
107	☐	3 = 104		5	☐	5 = 10		25	☐	108 = 133	
7	☐	11 = 77		2	☐	10 = 20		4	☐	5 = 20	
143	☐	11 = 13		5	☐	8 = 40		80	☐	36 = 44	
30	☐	28 = 58		31	☐	13 = 44		59	☐	40 = 19	
12	☐	2 = 24		6	☐	3 = 18		86	☐	8 = 78	
2	☐	9 = 18		11	☐	12 = 132		9	☐	3 = 3	
29	☐	2 = 31		90	☐	10 = 9		22	☐	39 = 61	

TIME TAKEN:	INCORRECT ANSWERS:
TIME POINTS:	**TOTAL SCORE:**

Reflective Power

Look at each of the figures on the left-hand side of the vertical "mirror". Work out which of the figures on the right-hand side corresponds to the figure reflected in the mirror line.

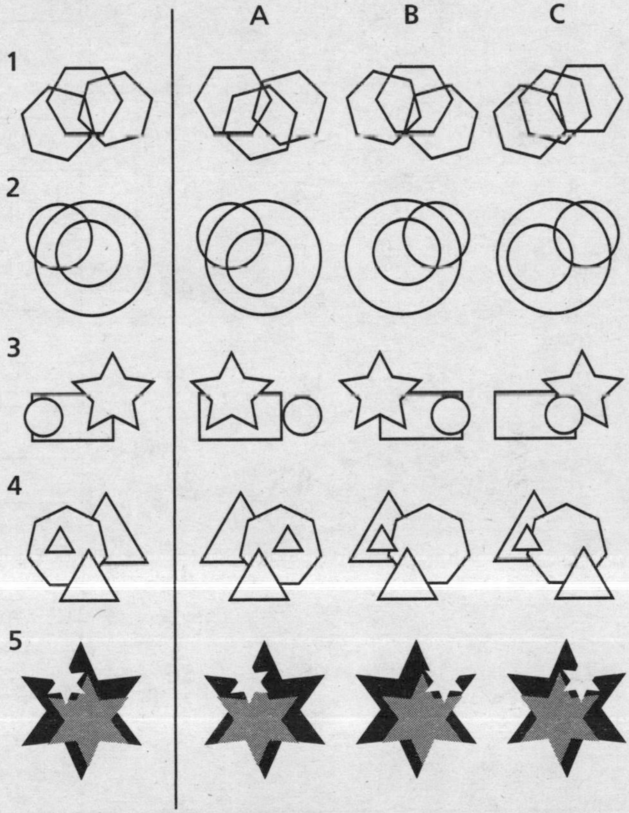

A B C

1

2

3

4

5

TIME TAKEN:	INCORRECT ANSWERS:
TIME POINTS:	**TOTAL SCORE:**

Number Sequences

Look at each of these number sequences and see if you can deduce which number comes next in the series.

4	7	10	13	16	
2	4	8	16	32	
2	3	5	7	11	
3	6	12	24	48	
21	19	16	12	7	
3	4	6	9	13	
2	2	4	12	48	
12	23	34	45	56	

TIME TAKEN:	INCORRECT ANSWERS:
TIME POINTS:	**TOTAL SCORE:**

Visual Memory

Spend 1 minute studying this path. Then cover the top half of this page and try to redraw it accurately on the empty grid below.

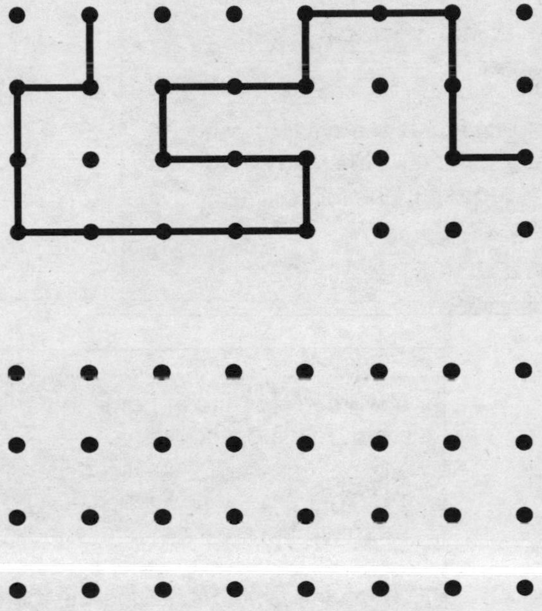

INCORRECT ANSWERS:	**TOTAL SCORE:**

Creative Thinking

See if you can solve each of the following conundrums. If you get stuck then try thinking laterally – they all have logical solutions, but the logic might not be what you expect!

A man walks into a bar and asks for a glass of water.

Instead of handing him a glass of water, the barman suddenly turns and screams at him as loud as he possibly can.

Why?

A woman is sitting at home in her living room, reading a book.

It is night and suddenly there is a power cut, plunging the room into complete darkness. She has no other light but carries on reading, without leaving the room.

How does she do this?

TIME TAKEN:	INCORRECT ANSWERS:
TIME POINTS:	**TOTAL SCORE:**

Counting and Perception

Spend no more than 10 seconds looking at each group of symbols in turn, then try to sort them into order of increasing frequency. Write "1" in the "Order" column for the shape that occurs least often, and so on.

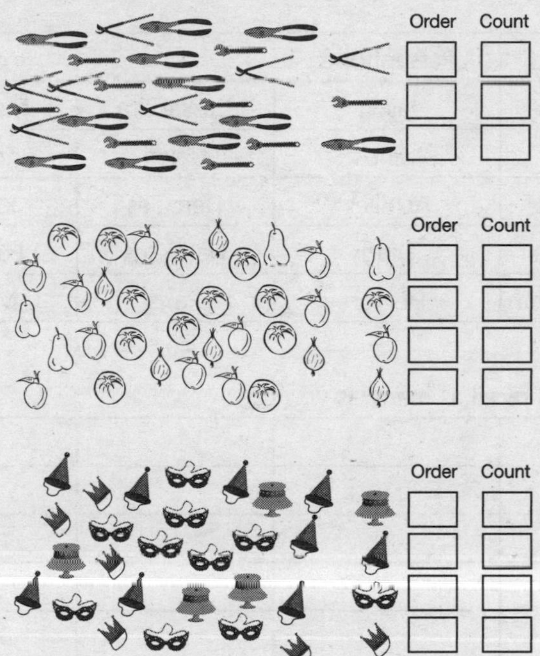

Now take as long as you think you need to write in the second column the precise number of each symbol.

TIME TAKEN:	INCORRECT ANSWERS:
TIME POINTS:	**TOTAL SCORE:**

Word List

Try to memorize these 24 mythological characters.

After 2 minutes, cover the table and write as many as you can in the boxes below. You do not need to remember the correct order.

Orpheus	Persephone	Io	Romulus
Ulysses	Jason	Cassandra	Medusa
Atlas	Minos	Helen	Adonis
Ajax	Achilles	Hercules	Icarus
Ariadne	Dido	Narcissus	Europa
Ganymede	Hector	Paris	Midas

Now try to recall as many as you can:

INCORRECT ANSWERS:	TOTAL SCORE:

Solutions

1: Observation and Counting

10 circles in total.
4 circles is the maximum overlap.
32 line intersections.

2: Logical Puzzlers

250cm. This is 100cm (drop) + 50cm (1st bounce back up) + 50cm (drop) + 25cm (2nd bounce back up) + 25cm (drop).
The first dog.
4 pieces are left. First I eat 9 pieces, leaving 18. Then I eat 6 pieces, leaving 12. Finally I eat 8 pieces, leaving 4.

3: Time Elapsed

12:05am to 4:15pm =	**16:10**	2:45am to 9:30pm =	**18:45**
5:55pm to 11:15pm =	**5:20**	10:55am to 4:25pm =	**5:30**
4:50am to 10:25am =	**5:35**	9:05am to 2:05pm =	**5:00**
1:55pm to 7:30pm =	**5:35**	3:35am to 7:20am =	**3:45**
2:00pm to 3:55pm =	**1:55**	1:00pm to 11:25pm =	**10:25**
2:00am to 11:20am =	**9:20**	11:40am to 12:10pm =	**0:30**
5:35am to 6:00pm =	**12:25**	3:20pm to 9:05pm =	**5:45**
12:55pm to 1:45pm =	**0:50**	11:05am to 6:10pm =	**7:05**
3:10am to 4:50pm =	**13:40**	10:25am to 10:00pm =	**11:35**
10:15am to 12:05pm =	**1:50**	11:50am to 4:50pm =	**5:00**
12:50pm to 2:40pm =	**1:50**	10:20am to 10:55am =	**0:35**
10:55am to 5:50pm =	**6:55**	8:20pm to 9:25pm =	**1:05**
2:15am to 8:25pm =	**18:10**	2:40am to 9:20am =	**6:40**
9:55am to 7:00pm =	**9:05**	11:10am to 5:10pm =	**6:00**
10:25am to 3:50pm =	**5:25**	6:35am to 1:40pm =	**7:05**

4: Odd One Out

Lizard – the only one that is not a mammal.
Milan – the rest are capital cities.
White – not a colour of the rainbow.
Rainy – all the other words can be synonyms for 'cold'.

5: Matchstick Thinking

7: Missing Signs

20	+	27	=	47	5	×	10	=	50	11	÷	11	=	1
3	÷	3	=	1	5	+	12	=	17	65	–	15	=	50
20	÷	5	=	4	140	+	16	=	156	29	–	9	=	20
29	+	7	=	36	5	÷	5	=	1	43	–	35	=	8
4	×	2	=	8	29	–	18	=	11	18	–	4	=	14
5	×	7	=	35	7	×	7	=	49	111	+	16	=	127
107	–	3	=	104	5	+	5	=	10	25	+	108	=	133
7	×	11	=	77	2	×	10	=	20	4	×	5	=	20
143	÷	11	=	13	5	×	8	=	40	80	–	36	=	44
30	+	28	=	58	31	+	13	=	44	59	–	40	=	19
12	×	2	=	24	6	×	3	=	18	86	–	8	=	78
2	×	9	=	18	11	×	12	=	132	9	÷	3	=	3
29	+	2	=	31	90	÷	10	=	9	22	+	39	=	61

8: Reflective Power

1B, 2B, 3B, 4A, 5C

9: Number Sequences

4, 7, 10, 13, 16, **19**
Rule: add 3

2, 4, 8, 16, 32, **64**
Rule: multiply by 2

2, 3, 5, 7, 11, **13**
Rule: prime numbers

3, 6, 12, 24, 48, **96**
Rule: multiply by 2

21, 19, 16, 12, 7, **1**
Rule: subtract 2, 3, 4, 5 etc

3, 4, 6, 9, 13, **18**
Rule: add 1, 2, 3, 4 etc

2, 2, 4, 12, 48, **240**
Rule: multiply by 1, 2, 3, 4 etc

12, 23, 34, 45, 56, **67**
Rule: add 11

11: Creative Thinking

The man had hiccoughs and wanted the glass of water to help cure them, but the barman gave him a fright instead (which cured his hiccoughs right away!).

The woman is blind and is reading a Braille book, so it does not affect her when the light goes out.

12: Counting and Perception

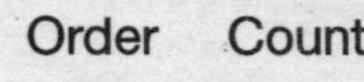

	Order	Count
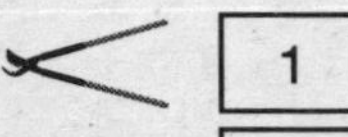	1	6
	2	8
	3	10

	Order	Count
	1	3
	4	12
	3	10
	2	5

	Order	Count
	1	4
	3	8
	4	9
	2	5

DAY
2

Rotation

If you were to rotate each of these three pictures as indicated by the arrow beneath, which of the set of figures below would be the result?

A B C

1

2

3

TIME TAKEN:	INCORRECT ANSWERS:
TIME POINTS:	**TOTAL SCORE:**

Odd One Out

Look at each of these sets of words. Can you work out which word is the odd one out in each case?

Relating
Triangle
Alerting
Trailing
Integral

Pluto
Mars
Venus
Sun
Earth

Copper
Bronze
Silver
Gold
Platinum

Radish
Orange
Lettuce
Sprout
Bean

TIME TAKEN:	INCORRECT ANSWERS:
TIME POINTS:	**TOTAL SCORE:**

Visual Memory

Spend 1 minute studying this path. Then cover the top half of this page and try to redraw it accurately on the empty grid below.

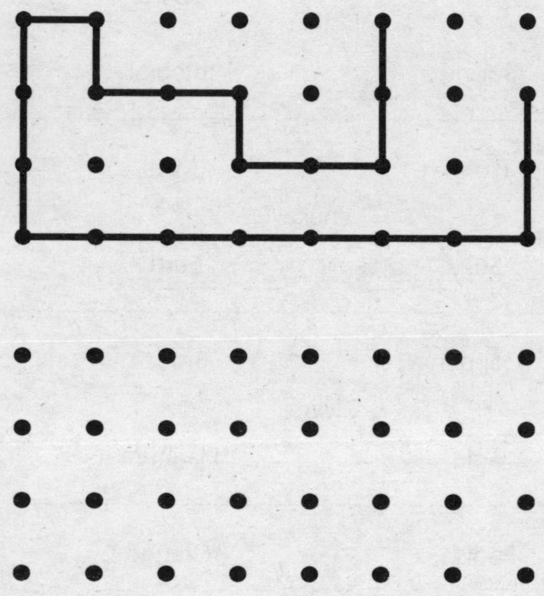

INCORRECT ANSWERS:	**TOTAL SCORE:**

Observation and counting

Look at these overlapping triangles and see how long it takes you to answer the observation questions below.

How many triangles can you count? [ ]

How many places are there where 3 or more straight lines intersect? [ ]

If you were to colour each area in so that no two areas of the same colour touched on any side, how many colours would you need? [ ]

TIME TAKEN:	INCORRECT ANSWERS:
TIME POINTS:	**TOTAL SCORE:**

Creative Thinking

See if you can solve each of the following conundrums. If you get stuck then try thinking laterally – they all have logical solutions, but the logic might not be what you expect!

At the end of a long hike you struggle up the side of a hill into an empty cabin in order to spend the night. You look at the fireplace piled high with wood, but then discover you have only one match. Next to the fireplace is a sheet of paper, a candle, and a small piece of tinder. What do you light first?

Which 7-letter word is longer when its third letter is removed?

TIME TAKEN:	INCORRECT ANSWERS:
TIME POINTS:	**TOTAL SCORE:**

Missing Signs

Insert the missing sign into each of these arithmetic expressions in order to make the equation true. You will need to add, subtract, multiply, or divide.

56 ☐ 8 = 7	5 ☐ 7 = 35	4 ☐ 10 = 40
84 ☐ 12 = 7	55 ☐ 11 = 5	36 ☐ 12 = 3
70 ☐ 10 = 7	8 ☐ 12 = 96	8 ☐ 5 = 13
3 ☐ 11 = 33	63 ☐ 9 = 7	45 ☐ 5 = 9
36 ☐ 23 = 13	11 ☐ 8 = 88	109 ☐ 8 = 101
5 ☐ 6 = 30	3 ☐ 12 = 36	132 ☐ 10 = 142
91 ☐ 27 = 64	30 ☐ 6 = 5	41 ☐ 37 = 78
60 ☐ 16 = 44	5 ☐ 2 = 10	87 ☐ 37 = 50
11 ☐ 6 = 66	67 ☐ 15 = 52	14 ☐ 1 = 13
96 ☐ 8 = 12	31 ☐ 9 = 40	2 ☐ 9 = 18
90 ☐ 9 = 10	9 ☐ 4 = 36	76 ☐ 22 = 54
39 ☐ 3 = 13	105 ☐ 17 = 88	77 ☐ 20 = 97
33 ☐ 10 = 43	55 ☐ 1 = 56	100 ☐ 17 = 83

TIME TAKEN:	INCORRECT ANSWERS:
TIME POINTS:	**TOTAL SCORE:**

Cryptograms

Decode each of these quotations by replacing A with P, B with Q, C with R and so on through to replacing Y with N and Z with O.

Bxcsh pgt axzt epgprwjith – iwtn dcan ujcrixdc lwtc detc.

Iwdbph Stlpg

Ndj lxaa ctktg uxcs ixbt udg pcniwxcv. Xu ndj lpci ixbt ndj bjhi bpzt xi.

Rwpgath Qjmidc

Iwt apsstg du hjrrthh xh qthi raxbqts qn hiteexcv dc iwt gjcvh du deedgijcxin.

Hxg Lpaitg Hrdii

Lwpi ldjcs sxs tktg wtpa qji qn stvgtth?

Lxaaxpb Hwpzthetpgt

TIME TAKEN:	INCORRECT ANSWERS:
TIME POINTS:	**TOTAL SCORE:**

Word List

Try to memorize these 24 breeds of dog.

After 2 minutes cover the table and write as many as you can in the boxes below. You do not need to remember the correct order.

Bulldog	Spaniel	Deerhound	Harrier
Husky	Terrier	Retriever	Alsatian
Setter	Labrador	Pekingese	Rottweiler
Wolfhound	Chihuahua	Beagle	Foxhound
Collie	Mastiff	Whippet	Staghound
Greyhound	Doberman	Dane	Bloodhound

Now try to recall as many as you can:

INCORRECT ANSWERS:	**TOTAL SCORE:**

Speed Arithmetic

Complete the following set of arithmetic equations as quickly as possible. You should be able to do them all in your head without using a calculator or making notes.

8 × 6 =	41 − 8 =	19 + 16 =
93 − 2 =	45 + 8 =	15 + 28 =
8 × 3 =	70 − 11 =	10 × 4 =
69 − 5 =	15 + 19 =	96 − 1 =
23 − 2 =	45 + 20 =	9 × 9 =
101 − 4 =	35 + 4 =	11 + 8 =
12 × 2 =	9 + 10 =	48 + 14 =
17 + 99 =	77 − 8 =	27 + 17 =
23 − 18 =	9 × 12 =	18 + 58 =
74 + 12 =	8 + 25 =	33 − 16 =
42 − 1 =	47 + 17 =	1 + 75 =
37 − 17 =	7 × 12 =	5 + 26 =
40 − 9 =	91 − 12 =	8 × 10 =

TIME TAKEN:	INCORRECT ANSWERS:
TIME POINTS:	**TOTAL SCORE:**

Logical Puzzlers

Try to solve these problems – each requires only simple logic to solve, but you might find that making notes with a pencil will help!

Tomorrow is Tuesday, which is 3 days after the day before I went to the dentist. On what day did I go to the dentist?

If the greenhouse effect causes the average temperature of the earth to increase by half a degree over the next year, with this rate doubling every year, by how many degrees will the temperature have risen 5 years from now?

If a bicycle wheel consists of 15 spokes, how many gaps are formed between those spokes?

TIME TAKEN:	INCORRECT ANSWERS:
TIME POINTS:	**TOTAL SCORE:**

Reflective Power

Look at each of these figures on the left-hand side of the vertical "mirror". Work out which of the figures on the right-hand side corresponds to the same figure when reflected in the mirror line.

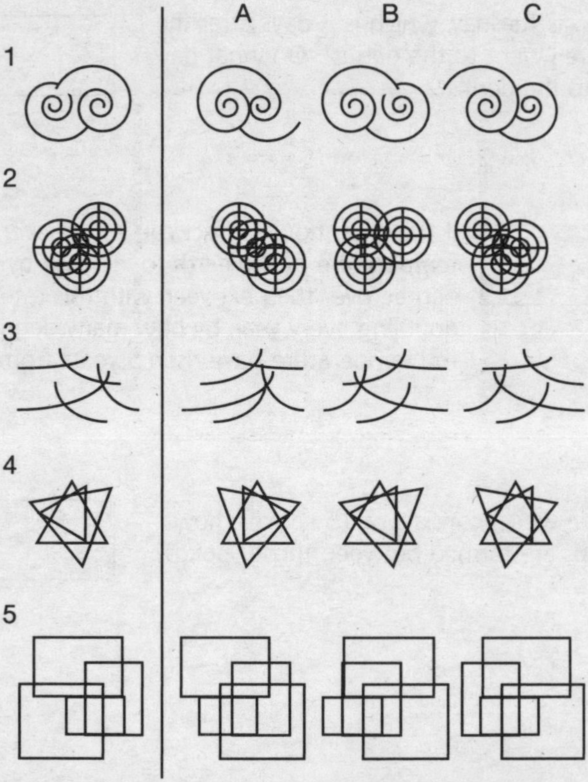

A B C

1

2

3

4

5

TIME TAKEN:	INCORRECT ANSWERS:
TIME POINTS:	**TOTAL SCORE:**

Matchstick Thinking

The picture below shows 12 matchsticks arranged into 1 large and 4 small squares.

Can you move 2 matchsticks in order to make precisely 7 squares?

TIME TAKEN:	INCORRECT ANSWERS:
TIME POINTS:	**TOTAL SCORE:**

Missing Words

Study each of these 3 lists of words for a total of 2 minutes. Then cover the top half of the page and see if you can identify which word is missing from each list below.

Copper	Silver	Magnesium	Sodium
Mercury	Gold	Iron	Lead

Red	Green	Violet	Yellow
White	Indigo	Black	Brown

Grub	Bee	Spider	Fly
Earthworm	Wasp	Ant	Woodlouse

Now try to spot the missing word from each list:

Silver, Sodium, Iron, Copper, Gold, Lead, Mercury

MISSING:

Violet, Yellow, Black, Red, Green, White, Indigo

MISSING:

Fly, Earthworm, Bee, Grub, Woodlouse, Spider, Wasp

MISSING:

INCORRECT ANSWERS:	TOTAL SCORE:

Solutions

1: Rotation
A1, B2, C2

2: Odd One Out
Trailing – the rest are all anagrams of one another.
Sun – the only one that is not a planet.
Bronze – these metals are all elements, except bronze which is an alloy.
Orange – the rest are vegetables.

4: Observation and Counting
13 triangles in total.

7 places where 3 or more lines intersect.

2 colours are needed.

5: Creative Thinking
You should light the match first!

The word is 'lounger'.

6: Missing Signs

56	÷	8	=	7	5	×	7	=	35	4	×	10	=	40
84	÷	12	=	7	55	÷	11	=	5	36	÷	12	=	3
70	÷	10	=	7	8	×	12	=	96	8	+	5	=	13
3	×	11	=	33	63	÷	9	=	7	45	÷	5	=	9
36	–	23	=	13	11	×	8	=	88	109	–	8	=	101
5	×	6	=	30	3	×	12	=	36	132	+	10	=	142
91	–	27	=	64	30	÷	6	=	5	41	+	37	=	78
60	–	16	=	44	5	×	2	=	10	87	–	37	=	50
11	×	6	=	66	67	–	15	=	52	14	–	1	=	13
96	÷	8	=	12	51	–	3	=	48	2	×	9	=	18
90	÷	9	=	10	9	×	4	=	36	76	–	22	=	54
39	÷	3	=	13	105	–	17	=	88	77	+	20	=	97
33	+	10	=	43	55	+	1	=	56	100	–	17	=	83

7: Cryptograms

Minds are like parachutes – they only function when open.

Thomas Dewar

You will never find time for anything. If you want time you must make it.

Charles Buxton

The ladder of success is best climbed by stepping on the rungs of opportunity.

Sir Walter Scott

What wound did ever heal but by degrees?

William Shakespeare

9: Speed Arithmetic

8 × 6 = **48**	41 − 8 = **33**	19 + 16 = **35**
93 − 2 = **91**	45 + 8 = **53**	15 + 28 = **43**
8 × 3 = **24**	70 − 11 = **59**	10 × 4 = **40**
69 − 5 = **64**	15 + 19 = **34**	96 − 1 = **95**
23 − 2 = **21**	45 + 20 = **65**	9 × 9 = **81**
101 − 4 = **97**	35 + 4 = **39**	11 + 8 = **19**
12 × 2 = **24**	9 + 10 = **19**	48 + 14 = **62**
17 + 99 = **116**	77 − 8 = **69**	27 + 17 = **44**
23 − 18 = **5**	9 × 12 − **108**	18 + 58 = **76**
74 + 12 = **86**	8 + 25 = **33**	33 − 16 = **17**
42 − 1 = **41**	47 + 17 = **64**	1 + 75 = **76**
37 − 17 = **20**	7 × 12 = **84**	5 + 26 = **31**
40 − 9 = **31**	91 − 12 = **79**	8 × 10 = **80**

10: Logical Puzzlers

Sunday.

15½ degrees. ½ + 1 + 2 + 4 + 8 = 15½

15 gaps. The wheel is circular, so the answer is not 14.

11: Reflective Power

1B, 2C 3B, 4A, 5C

12: Matchstick Thinking

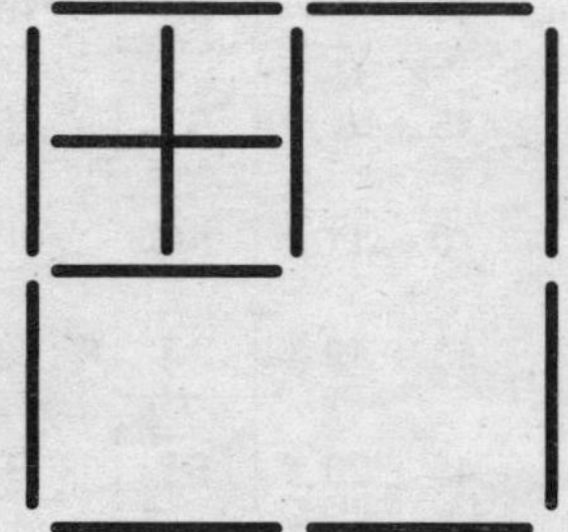

DAY
3

Speed Arithmetic

Complete the following set of arithmetic equations as quickly as possible. You should be able to do them all in your head without using a calculator or making notes.

51 − 6 =	49 − 19 =	70 + 10 =
13 + 81 =	42 + 13 =	12 + 64 =
3 × 10 =	24 − 14 =	12 + 72 =
89 + 2 =	28 − 9 =	94 + 8 =
66 + 19 =	17 − 3 =	68 − 16 =
5 + 97 =	37 − 12 =	44 − 18 =
14 + 87 =	24 + 6 =	75 − 6 =
6 × 3 =	76 + 15 =	108 − 4 =
66 − 13 =	5 + 12 =	6 × 8 =
94 + 6 =	92 − 20 =	24 + 3 =
7 + 34 =	59 − 7 =	22 + 14 =
18 − 12 =	94 + 15 =	13 + 31 =
15 + 10 =	51 + 9 =	45 − 2 =

TIME TAKEN:	INCORRECT ANSWERS:
TIME POINTS:	**TOTAL SCORE:**

Missing Words

Study each of these 3 lists of words for a total of 2 minutes. Then cover the top half of the page and see if you can identify which word is missing from each list below.

Laugh	Joke	Smile	Grin
Chuckle	Chortle	Giggle	Titter

Ordinary	Dull	Common	Nothing
Inferior	Poor	Vague	Unknown

Harsh	Extreme	Rough	Austere
Stern	Strict	Tough	Hard

Now try to spot the missing word from each list:

Chortle, Joke, Titter, Giggle, Chuckle, Smile, Grin

MISSING:

Vague, Poor, Dull, Nothing, Common, Ordinary, Inferior

MISSING:

Hard, Harsh, Stern, Extreme, Rough, Tough, Strict

MISSING:

INCORRECT ANSWERS:	TOTAL SCORE:

Logical Puzzlers

Try to solve these problems – each requires only simple logic or arithmetic to solve, but you might find that making notes with a pencil will help!

If a straight fence consists of 20 posts, each spaced 2 metres apart, what is the total length of the fence?

In my living room I have a clock which chimes on the hour. If it chimes once a second when it sounds, how long will it take to chime 6pm? Assume that each chime itself is of negligible length.

If you plant two trees this year, three next year and then twice as many as you have already planted for each of the following two years, how many trees will you have at the end of that period?

TIME TAKEN:	INCORRECT ANSWERS:
TIME POINTS:	**TOTAL SCORE:**

Counting and Perception

Spend no more than 10 seconds looking at each group of symbols in each turn, then try to sort them into order of increasing frequency. Write "1" in the "Order" column for the shape that occurs least often, and so on.

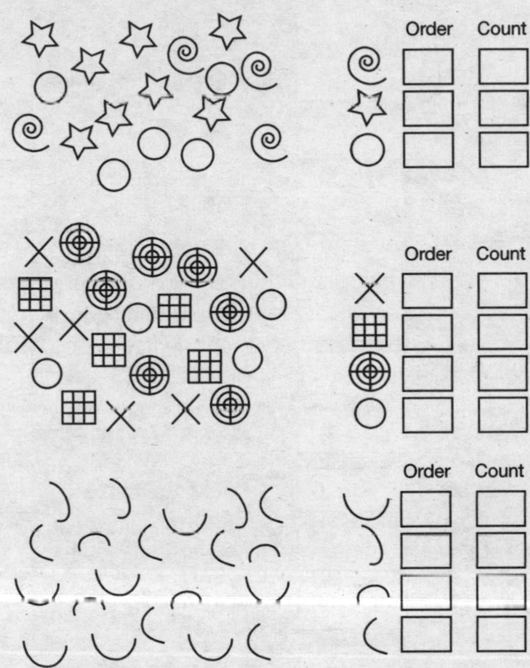

Now take as long as you think you need to write in the second column the precise count of each symbol.

TIME TAKEN:	INCORRECT ANSWERS:
TIME POINTS:	**TOTAL SCORE:**

DAY: 3 | WORKOUT: 5 | CONCENTRATION

Time Elapsed

Work out how many hours and minutes have passed between each of these pairs of times.

12:40am to 11:15pm =	:	6:25am to 4:10pm =	:
7:00am to 10:30pm =	:	12:50am to 2:50am =	:
6:55am to 8:55am =	:	2:30am to 5:40am =	:
6:35am to 8:00pm =	:	3:10pm to 7:30pm =	:
4:45am to 3:55pm =	:	12:25pm to 5:35pm =	:
12:45am to 4:15pm =	:	1:40am to 4:05pm =	:
3:35am to 8:00pm =	:	12:35am to 1:00am =	:
12:10pm to 9:25pm =	:	4:55pm to 9:15pm =	:
2:00pm to 2:05pm =	:	6:05am to 9:00pm =	:
12:20am to 1:50pm =	:	4:40am to 5:40am =	:
4:05am to 9:15pm =	:	9:55am to 8:05pm =	:
12:15am to 3:40am =	:	1:35pm to 10:45pm =	:
4:40am to 1:35pm =	:	5:55am to 7:10am =	:
4:10am to 9:50pm =	:	7:25am to 12:40pm =	:
8:45am to 8:25pm =	:	4:35am to 10:00pm =	:

TIME TAKEN:	INCORRECT ANSWERS:
TIME POINTS:	**TOTAL SCORE:**

Shape Dividing

Draw two straight lines in order to divide the box into three separate areas. Each area must contain precisely one of each size of circle. The two lines may touch but they must not cross.

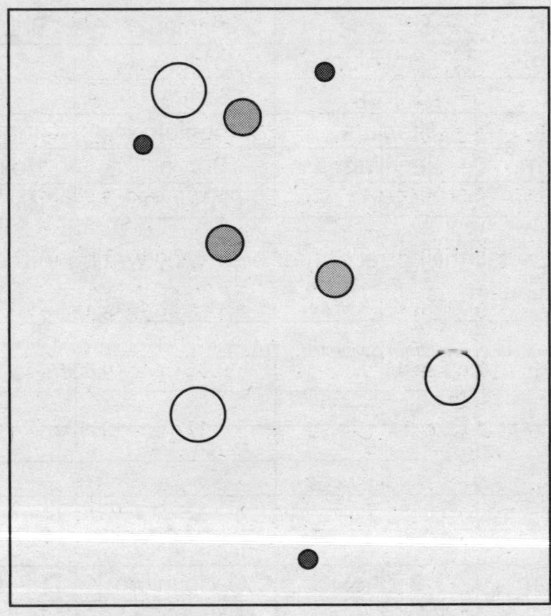

TIME TAKEN:	INCORRECT ANSWERS:
TIME POINTS:	**TOTAL SCORE:**

Ordered List

Can you memorize the order of these 24 elements?

Spend 2 minutes studying the top list, then cover the table and look at the list at the bottom of the page. Use the alphabetical labels to help recall the precise order of the words in the covered table.

Copper	Sodium	Selenium	Rubidium
Cadmium	Gadolinium	Erbium	Cobalt
Arsenic	Silicon	Barium	Tin
Zinc	Niobium	Rhenium	Tungsten
Titanium	Beryllium	Boron	Holmium
Cerium	Lead	Platinum	Mercury

Now try to recall the correct order below, by writing in the corresponding letters:

A Cadmium	**B** Zinc	**C** Gadolinium	**D** Rubidium
E Tin	**F** Beryllium	**G** Niobium	**H** Erbium
I Rhenium	**J** Sodium	**K** Holmium	**L** Barium
M Platinum	**N** Titanium	**O** Copper	**P** Cobalt
Q Arsenic	**R** Mercury	**S** Selenium	**T** Cerium
U Silicon	**V** Lead	**W** Tungsten	**X** Boron

INCORRECT ANSWERS:	**TOTAL SCORE:**

Observation and Counting

Look at these overlapping squares and see how long it takes you to answer the observation questions below.

How many squares can you count?

How many rectangles, excluding squares, can you count?

How many separate areas are formed between the lines?

TIME TAKEN:	INCORRECT ANSWERS:
TIME POINTS:	**TOTAL SCORE:**

Anagrammatic

Look at each of these sets of 12 words. How many pairs of anagrams can you spot in each set, and what are they?

UMPIRING	LISTENER	SKEINING
PRUDENCE	SITUATES	SILENTER
MALADIES	EMBRACES	COMEDIES
ELECTION	BOOKINGS	BLASTOFF

SUMMER	PANTED	STRAPS
FLOATS	TENTED	RULING
RULERS	PEDANT	NETTED
MONKEY	THEIST	LURING

FILLER	COALED	REFILL
DURESS	RISKED	THREES
INSERT	IRONED	DRONES
LIABLE	SNORED	INTERS

SOLOED	OODLES	GRUDGE
SIDLES	SLIDES	PHASES
PALLED	RESCUE	SECURE
RUGGED	SHAPES	NICETY

TIME TAKEN:	INCORRECT ANSWERS:
TIME POINTS:	**TOTAL SCORE:**

Rotation

If you were to rotate each of these three pictures as indicated by its neighbouring arrow, which of each set of figures would be the result?

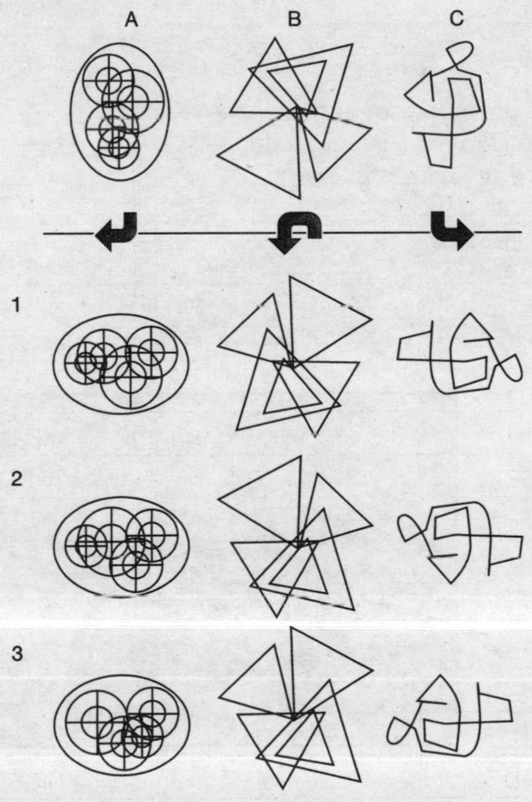

TIME TAKEN:	INCORRECT ANSWERS:
TIME POINTS:	**TOTAL SCORE:**

Creative Thinking

See if you can solve each of the following conundrums. If you get stuck then try thinking laterally – they all have logical solutions, but the logic might not be what you expect!

Wandering down the street you notice that two couples are sharing an umbrella between them. Remarkably, none of them are getting wet.
How is this possible?

There is something which occurs just once in a minute but twice in a week; it also occurs just once in a year.
What is that something?

TIME TAKEN:	INCORRECT ANSWERS:
TIME POINTS:	**TOTAL SCORE:**

Word List

Try to memorize these 24 theatre terms.

After 2 minutes cover the table and recall as many as you can in the boxes below. You do not need to remember the correct order.

Overact	Prompter	Thespian	Entrance
Nerves	Monologue	Exit	Cue
Curtain	Wings	Backstage	Act
Stage	Offstage	Scene	Lines
Gallery	Understudy	Gods	Orchestra
Script	Soliloquy	Chorus	Prompt

Now try to recall as many as you can:

INCORRECT ANSWERS:	**TOTAL SCORE:**

Number Sequences

Look at each of these number sequences and see if you can deduce which number comes next in the series.

374	226	148	78	70	
267	161	106	55	51	
2	2	4	8	32	
585	507	429	351	273	
9	10	19	29	48	
5	15	45	135	405	
34	21	13	8	5	
103	63	40	23	17	

TIME TAKEN:	INCORRECT ANSWERS:
TIME POINTS:	**TOTAL SCORE:**

Solutions

1: Speed Arithmetic

51 – 6 = **45**	49 – 19 = **30**	70 + 10 = **80**
13 + 81 = **94**	42 + 13 = **55**	12 + 64 = **76**
3 × 10 = **30**	24 – 14 = **10**	12 + 72 = **84**
89 + 2 = **91**	28 – 9 = **19**	94 + 8 = **102**
66 + 19 = **85**	17 – 3 = **14**	68 – 16 = **52**
5 + 97 = **102**	37 – 12 = **25**	44 – 18 = **26**
14 + 87 = **101**	24 + 6 = **30**	75 – 6 = **69**
6 × 3 = **18**	76 + 15 = **91**	108 – 4 = **104**
66 – 13 = **53**	5 + 12 = **17**	6 × 8 = **48**
94 + 6 = **100**	92 – 20 = **72**	24 + 3 = **27**
7 + 34 = **41**	59 – 7 = **52**	22 + 14 = **36**
18 – 12 = **6**	94 + 15 = **109**	13 + 31 = **44**
15 + 10 = **25**	51 + 9 = **60**	45 – 2 = **43**

3: Logical Puzzlers

38m. The final post has no fence section following it, so it is not 40m.

5 seconds, for a similar reason.

45 trees.

4: Counting and Perception

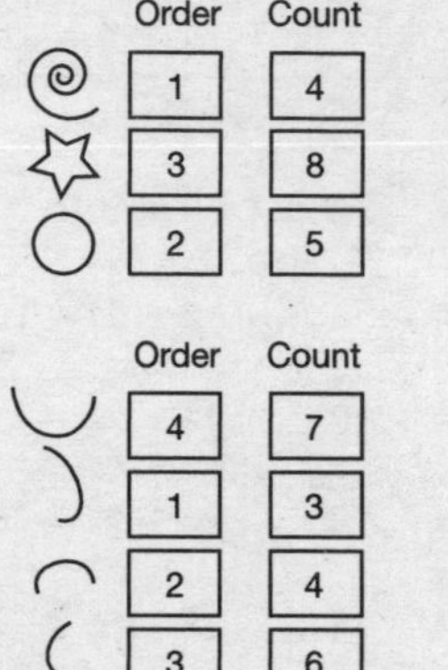

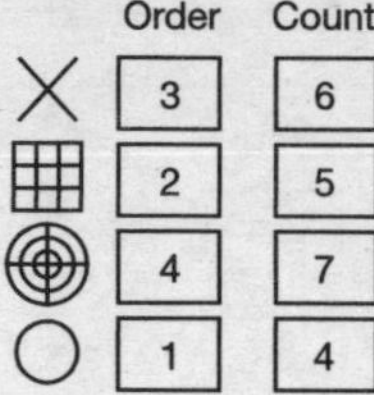

Order	Count
1	4
3	8
2	5

Order	Count
3	6
2	5
4	7
1	4

Order	Count
4	7
1	3
2	4
3	6

5: Time Elapsed

12:40am to 11:15pm =	22:35	6:25am to 4:10pm =	9:45
7:00am to 10:30pm =	15:30	12:50am to 2:50am =	2:00
6:55am to 8:55am =	2:00	2:30am to 5:40am =	3:10
6:35am to 8:00pm =	13:25	3:10pm to 7:30pm =	4:20
4:45am to 3:55pm =	11:10	12:25pm to 5:35pm =	5:10
12:45am to 4:15pm =	15:30	1:40am to 4:05pm =	14:25
3:35am to 8:00pm =	16:25	12:35am to 1:00am =	0:25
12:10pm to 9:25pm =	9:15	4:55pm to 9:15pm =	4:20
2:00pm to 2:05pm =	0:05	6:05am to 9:00pm =	14:55
12:20am to 1:50pm =	13:30	4:40am to 5:40am =	1:00
4:05am to 9:15pm =	17:10	9:55am to 8:05pm =	10:10
12:15am to 3:40am =	3:25	1:35pm to 10:45pm =	9:10
4:40am to 1:35pm =	8:55	5:55am to 7:10am =	1:15
4:10am to 9:50pm =	17:40	7:25am to 12:40pm =	5:15
8:45am to 8:25pm =	11:40	4:35am to 10:00pm =	17:25

6: Shape Dividing

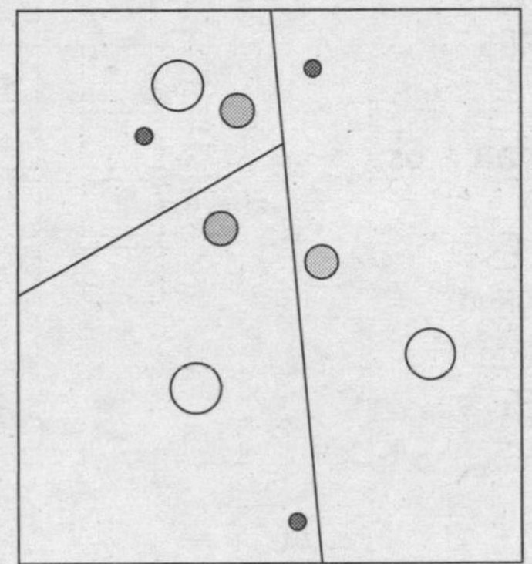

7: Ordered List

O	J	S	D
A	C	H	P
Q	U	L	E
B	G	I	W
N	F	X	K
T	V	M	R

8: Observation and Counting

11 squares in total.

13 rectangles, excluding squares.

9 separate areas.

9: Anagrammatic

Set 1: 1 pair of anagrams:
LISTENER and SILENTER

Set 2: 3 pairs of anagrams:
LURING and RULING
PANTED and PEDANT,
NETTED and TENTED

Set 3: 3 pairs of anagrams:
INSERT and INTERS
SNORED and DRONES
FILLER and REFILL

Set 4: 5 pairs of anagrams:
SIDLES and SLIDES
SOLOED and OODLES
RESCUE and SECURE
GRUDGE and RUGGED
PHASES and SHAPES

10: Rotation
A2, B2, C1

11: Creative Thinking
It simply isn't raining!

The letter 'e'.

13: Number Sequences
374, 226, 148, 78, 70, **8**
Rule: subtract the previous number from the one before it

4, 51, 55, 106, 161, **267**
Rule: add the previous two numbers

256, 32, 8, 4, 2, **2**
Rule: divide each number by the number following it

195, 273, 351, 429, 507, **585**
Rule: add 78 to previous number

77, 48, 29, 19, 10, **9**
Rule: subtract the previous number from the one before it

1215, 405, 135, 45, 15, **5**
Rule: divide previous number by 3

3, 5, 8, 13, 21, **34**
Rule: add the previous two numbers

103, 63, 40, 23, 17, **6**
Rule: subtract the previous number from the one before it

DAY
4

Odd One Out

Look at each of these sets of words. Can you work out which word is the odd one out in each case?

Dodo
Buffalo
Mastodon
Moa
Mammoth

Butler
Subtle
Bluest
Bustle
Sublet

Bath
Bottle
Chair
Sink
Mug

Summary
Hijack
Bends
Giant
Tombola

TIME TAKEN:	INCORRECT ANSWERS:
TIME POINTS:	**TOTAL SCORE:**

Rotation

If you were to rotate each of these three pictures as indicated by the arrow beneath, which of the figures below would be the result?

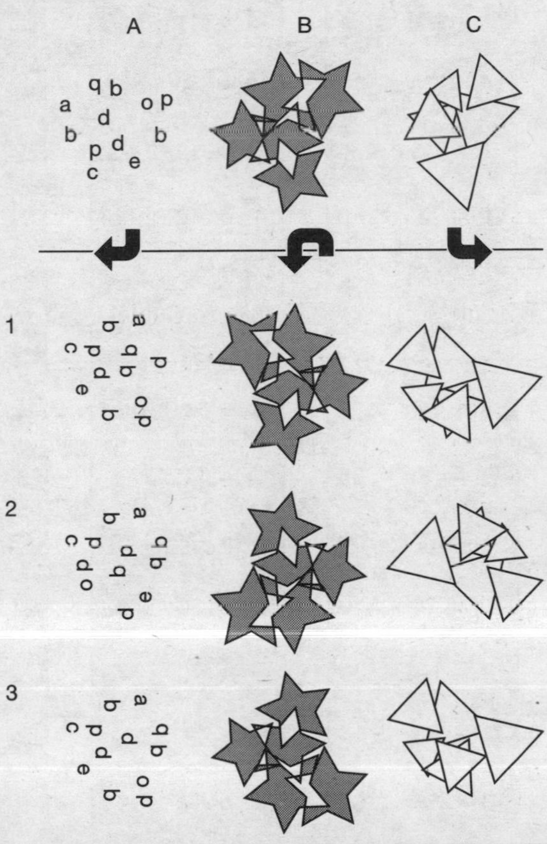

TIME TAKEN:	INCORRECT ANSWERS:
TIME POINTS:	**TOTAL SCORE:**

Missing Signs

Insert the missing sign into each of these arithmetic expressions in order to make the equation true. You will need to add, subtract, multiply, or divide.

15		5	= 3	132		11	= 12	98		35	= 133
7		10	= 70	72		12	= 6	45		23	= 22
3		5	= 15	3		4	= 12	135		24	= 159
20		10	= 2	50		1	= 49	19		97	= 116
115		36	= 151	3		10	= 30	56		36	= 20
3		3	= 1	2		12	= 24	66		11	= 6
10		12	= 120	24		6	= 4	78		4	= 74
64		8	= 8	98		14	= 112	7		3	= 21
66		11	= 77	49		25	= 24	109		13	= 96
10		2	= 20	8		10	= 80	63		24	= 87
12		12	= 144	30		3	= 10	79		18	= 61
90		9	= 10	4		23	= 27	3		13	= 39
48		10	= 58	56		4	= 14	94		5	= 89

TIME TAKEN:	INCORRECT ANSWERS:
TIME POINTS:	**TOTAL SCORE:**

Observation and Counting

Look at this set of spirals and see how long it takes you to answer the observation questions below.

How many spirals can you count?

If you are not allowed to go over the same line twice in a single stroke, what is the minimum number of pen strokes it would take to draw this figure?

How many clockwise spirals are there?

TIME TAKEN:	INCORRECT ANSWERS:
TIME POINTS:	**TOTAL SCORE:**

Number Sequences

Look at each of these number sequences and see if you can deduce which number comes next in the series.

498	440	392	354	326	
19	75	94	169	263	
3	12	48	192	768	
1098	1027	971	930	904	
5	5	10	30	120	
325	322	319	316	313	
598	605	617	634	656	
1701	567	189	63	21	

TIME TAKEN:	INCORRECT ANSWERS:
TIME POINTS:	**TOTAL SCORE:**

Word List

Try to memorize these 24 types of alcoholic drink.

After 2 minutes cover the table and recall as many as you can in the boxes below. You do not need to remember the correct order.

Tequila	Absinthe	Rum	Vodka
Gin	Brandy	Bitter	Rum
Vermouth	Firewater	Mescal	Sambucca
Schnapps	Anisette	Cider	Beer
Ale	Mead	Wine	Snakebite
Pastis	Amaretto	Advocaat	Raki

Now try to recall as many as you can:

INCORRECT ANSWERS:	**TOTAL SCORE:**

Missing Numbers

Insert the missing number into each of these arithmetic expressions in order to make the equations true. You should not need a calculator to do this!

10 + ☐ = **110**	20 + ☐ = **65**	3 × ☐ = **21**
95 − ☐ = **89**	40 − ☐ = **38**	☐ + 52 = **71**
☐ + 9 = **30**	☐ + 6 = **8**	☐ + 6 = **72**
☐ × 6 = **30**	☐ − 7 = **8**	56 + ☐ = **58**
81 + ☐ = **96**	9 + ☐ = **77**	2 + ☐ = **9**
2 × ☐ = **20**	☐ × 2 = **24**	☐ + 14 = **71**
10 + ☐ = **65**	☐ + 16 = **83**	84 − ☐ = **72**
☐ + 4 = **56**	20 + ☐ = **103**	☐ + 16 = **53**
☐ + 18 = **33**	8 + ☐ = **54**	☐ − 20 = **6**
6 + ☐ = **10**	☐ + 36 = **45**	☐ × 5 = **35**
☐ + 3 = **93**	9 × ☐ = **18**	84 + ☐ = **88**
☐ − 18 = **57**	28 − ☐ = **18**	☐ − 16 = **3**
☐ × 4 = **36**	5 × ☐ = **20**	☐ − 14 = **35**

TIME TAKEN:	INCORRECT ANSWERS:
TIME POINTS:	**TOTAL SCORE:**

Matchstick Thinking

The picture below shows 8 matchsticks arranged in the shape of a fish.

Can you move 3 matchsticks only in order to reverse the direction the fish is facing?

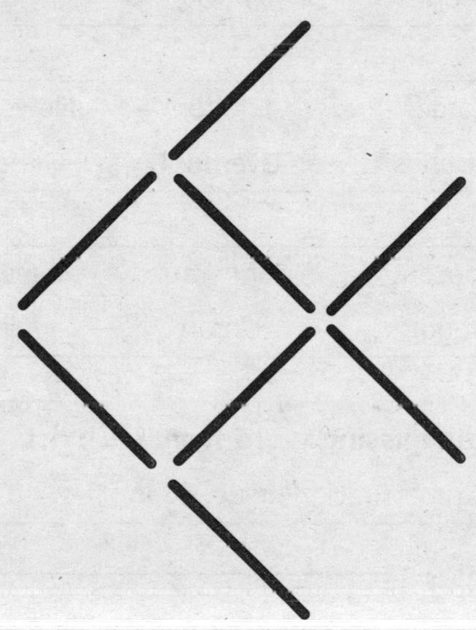

TIME TAKEN:	INCORRECT ANSWERS:
TIME POINTS:	**TOTAL SCORE:**

Missing Words

Study each of these 3 lists of words for 2 minutes. Then cover the top half of the page and see if you can identify which word is missing from each list below.

Drag	Chase	Pursue	Follow
Hound	Hunt	Track	Tail

Bristol	Cardiff	London	Newcastle
Boston	Hastings	Liverpool	Glasgow

Pius	Innocent	John Paul	Benedict
Alexander	Gregory	Urban	Julius

Now try to spot the missing word from each list:

Follow, Tail, Hunt, Chase, Track, Pursue, Drag

MISSING:

Glasgow, Newcastle, Boston, Hastings, Bristol, Liverpool, London

MISSING:

Innocent, Gregory, Benedict, Alexander, Urban, Pius, John Paul

MISSING:

INCORRECT ANSWERS:	TOTAL SCORE:

Reflective Power

Look at each of the figures on the left-hand side of the vertical "mirror". Work out which of the figures on the right-hand side corresponds to the figure reflected in the mirror line.

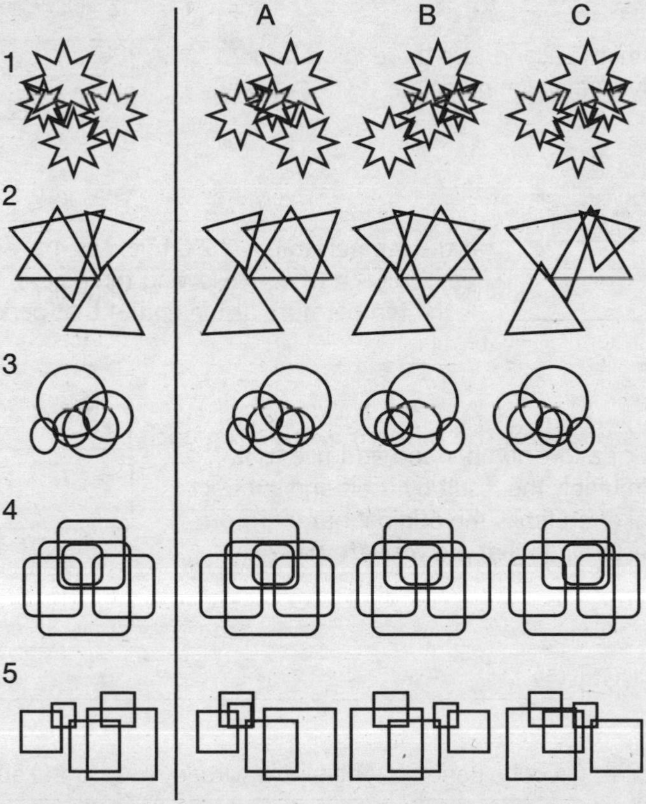

A B C

1

2

3

4

5

TIME TAKEN:	INCORRECT ANSWERS:
TIME POINTS:	**TOTAL SCORE:**

Logical Puzzlers

Try to solve these problems – each requires only simple logic to solve, but you might find that making notes with a pencil will help!

How many seconds are there in an hour? And how many minutes are there in a day?

If the temperature is 23°C but rises 4°C every day for each of the following three days, what is the temperature at the end of that period?

Think of a low number and add five to it. Now multiply the result by itself and subtract 25. Take ten times the original number from this result and what are you left with?

TIME TAKEN:	INCORRECT ANSWERS:
TIME POINTS:	**TOTAL SCORE:**

Creative Thinking

See if you can solve each of the following conundrums. If you get stuck then try thinking laterally – they all have logical solutions, but the logic might not be what you expect!

To live under the veil of evil is a vile thing.

What is remarkable about this particular sentence?

I learnt an interesting fact at the zoo today. What is it that giraffes can make that no other animal can make?

TIME TAKEN:	INCORRECT ANSWERS:
TIME POINTS:	**TOTAL SCORE:**

Visual Memory

Spend 1 minute studying this path. Then cover the top half of this page and try to redraw it accurately on the empty grid below.

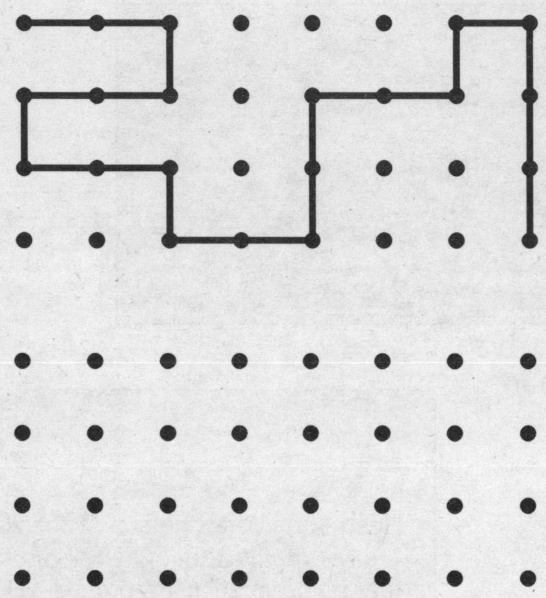

INCORRECT ANSWERS:	**TOTAL SCORE:**

Solutions

1: Odd One Out

Buffalo – the rest are extinct
Butler – the rest are anagrams of each other
Chair – the rest are designed to hold water or liquids
Summary – has a girl's name in it (Mary); the rest have boys in

2: Rotation

A3, B3, C1

3: Missing Signs

15 ÷ 5 = 3	132 ÷ 11 = 12	98 + 35 = 133
7 × 10 = 70	72 ÷ 12 = 6	45 – 23 = 22
3 × 5 = 15	3 × 4 = 12	135 + 24 = 159
20 ÷ 10 = 2	50 – 1 = 49	19 + 97 = 116
115 + 36 = 151	3 × 10 = 30	56 – 36 = 20
3 ÷ 3 = 1	2 × 12 = 24	66 ÷ 11 = 6
10 × 12 = 120	24 ÷ 6 = 4	78 – 4 = 74
64 ÷ 8 = 8	98 + 14 = 112	7 × 3 = 21
66 + 11 = 77	49 – 25 = 24	109 – 13 = 96
10 × 2 = 20	8 × 10 = 80	63 + 24 = 87
12 × 12 = 144	30 ÷ 3 = 10	79 – 18 = 61
90 ÷ 9 = 10	4 + 23 = 27	3 × 13 = 39
48 + 10 = 58	56 ÷ 4 = 14	94 – 5 = 89

4: Observation and Counting

6 spirals in total.

5 pen strokes.

0 clockwise spirals.

5: Number Sequences

308, 326, 354, 392, 440, **498**
Rule: difference between numbers increases by 10 each time

432, 263, 169, 94, 75, **19**
Rule: subtract the previous number from the one before it

3072, 768, 192, 48, 12, **3**
Rule: divide previous number by 4

893, 904, 930, 971, 1027, **1098**
Rule: difference between numbers increases by 15 each time

5, 5, 10, 30, 120, **600**
Rule: multiply by 1, 2, 3 etc – multiplier increases by 1 each time

310, 313, 316, 319, 322, **325**
Rule: add 3 to previous number

683, 656, 634, 617, 605, **598**
Rule: difference between numbers decreases by 5 each time

7, 21, 63, 189, 567, **1701**
Rule: multiply previous number by 3

7: Missing Numbers

10 + 100 = **110**	20 + 45 = **65**	3 ∝ 7 = **21**
95 − 6 = **89**	40 − 2 = **38**	19 + 52 = **71**
21 + 9 = **30**	2 + 6 = **8**	66 + 6 = **72**
5 ∝ 6 = **30**	15 − 7 = **8**	56 + 2 = **58**
81 + 15 = **96**	9 + 68 = **77**	2 + 7 = **9**
2 ∝ 10 = **20**	12 ∝ 2 = **24**	57 + 14 = **71**
10 + 55 = **65**	67 + 16 = **83**	84 − 12 = **72**
52 + 4 = **56**	20 + 83 = **103**	37 + 16 = **53**
15 + 18 = **33**	8 + 46 = **54**	26 − 20 = **6**
6 + 4 = **10**	9 + 36 = **45**	7 ∝ 5 = **35**
90 + 3 = **93**	9 ∝ 2 = **18**	84 + 4 = **88**
75 − 18 = **57**	28 − 10 = **18**	19 − 16 = **3**
9 ∝ 4 = **36**	5 ∝ 4 = **20**	49 − 14 = **35**

8: Matchstick Thinking

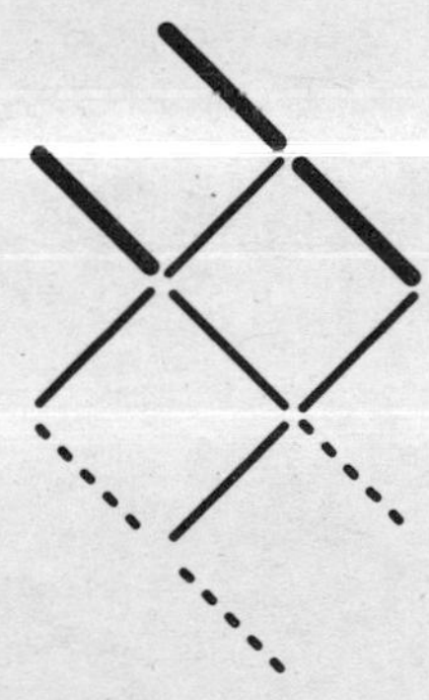

10: Reflective Power

1C, 2B, 3C, 4A, 5B

11: Logical Puzzlers

3600 seconds, and 1440 minutes respectively.

35°C.

The original number squared – i.e. multiplied by itself once.
So if you thought of 3, the result will be 3 x 3 = 9.

12: Creative Thinking

The four words live, veil, evil and veil are all anagrams of one another.

Baby giraffes!

DAY
5

Visual Sequences

Can you work out which pattern comes next in each of these two visual sequences?

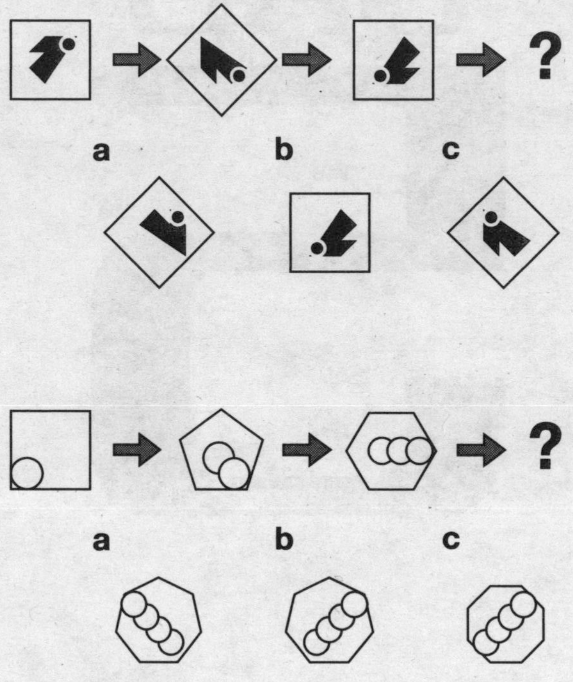

TIME TAKEN:	INCORRECT ANSWERS:
TIME POINTS:	**TOTAL SCORE:**

Speed Arithmetic

Complete the following set of arithmetic equations as quickly as possible. You should be able to do them all in your head without using a calculator or making notes.

97 + 10 =	83 − 11 =	19 + 49 =
6 + 42 =	3 × 9 =	28 + 20 =
85 − 4 =	59 − 8 =	2 + 1 =
60 − 6 =	7 + 27 =	89 + 9 =
5 + 45 =	60 + 10 =	58 + 13 =
63 + 12 =	16 + 20 =	12 × 7 =
6 × 9 =	49 + 12 =	6 + 73 =
4 + 29 =	9 × 10 =	80 − 8 =
50 + 18 =	13 − 4 =	97 − 4 =
71 + 12 =	3 × 3 =	24 − 5 =
10 + 32 =	104 − 1 =	2 + 69 =
6 + 87 =	14 + 7 =	72 − 14 =
5 × 7 =	95 + 16 =	19 + 65 =

TIME TAKEN:	INCORRECT ANSWERS:
TIME POINTS:	**TOTAL SCORE:**

Cryptogram

Decode each of these quotations by replacing A with K, B with L, C with M, and so on through to replacing Y with I and Z with J.

Grkdofob sc gybdr nysxq kd kvv sc gybdr nysxq govv.

Vybn Mrocdobpsovn

Dro wybo go qsfo yp kxidrsxq, dro wybo go crkvv qod lkmu.

Qbkmo Czokbo

Dro ezcsno sc iyeb pedebo sc sx iyeb rkxnc.
Kxn dro nygxcsno sc iyeb pedebo sc sx iyeb rkxnc.

Becc Wiobc

Rkzzsxocc sc dro coxco drkd yxo wkddobc.

Ckbkr Dbswwob

TIME TAKEN:	INCORRECT ANSWERS:
TIME POINTS:	**TOTAL SCORE:**

Visual Memory

Spend 1 minute studying this path. Then cover the top half of this page and try to redraw it accurately on the empty grid below.

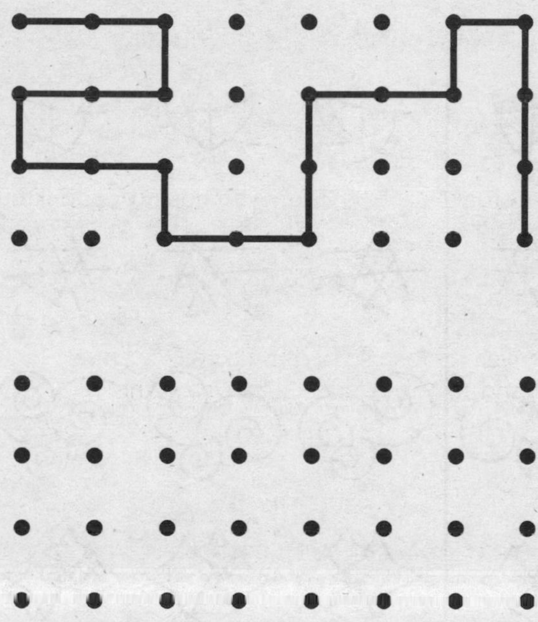

INCORRECT ANSWERS:	TOTAL SCORE:

Reflective Power

Look at each of the figures on the left-hand side of the vertical "mirror". Work out which of the figures on the right-hand side corresponds to the figure reflected in the mirror line.

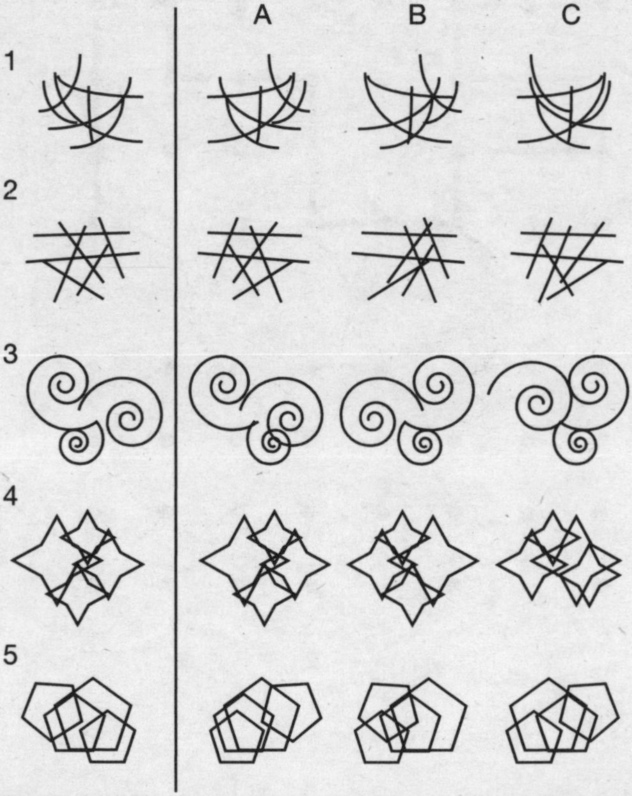

A B C

1

2

3

4

5

TIME TAKEN:	INCORRECT ANSWERS:
TIME POINTS:	**TOTAL SCORE:**

Coin Conundrum

The picture below shows 6 coins. Each coin is touching at least two other coins.

Can you rearrange the coins into a hexagon in precisely 3 moves? At the end of each individual move it must be the case that each coin is still touching at least two other coins.

TIME TAKEN:	INCORRECT ANSWERS:
TIME POINTS:	**TOTAL SCORE:**

Logical Puzzlers

Try to solve these problems – each requires only simple logic to solve, but you might find that making notes with a pencil will help!

If bamboo, the world's fastest-growing grass, grows half a foot every day, how many feet will it have grown by the end of a 31-day month?

Andrew only takes a bath on even-numbered days of the month. How many baths does he take in a year?

A traffic signal that I drive through on the way to work every day spends twice as long on red as it does on green. Assuming there is no amber light, how long does it spend on red each day?

TIME TAKEN:	INCORRECT ANSWERS:
TIME POINTS:	**TOTAL SCORE:**

Counting and Perception

Spend no more than 10 seconds looking at each group of symbols in each turn, then try to sort them into order of increasing frequency. Write "1" in the "Order" column for the shape that occurs least often, and so on.

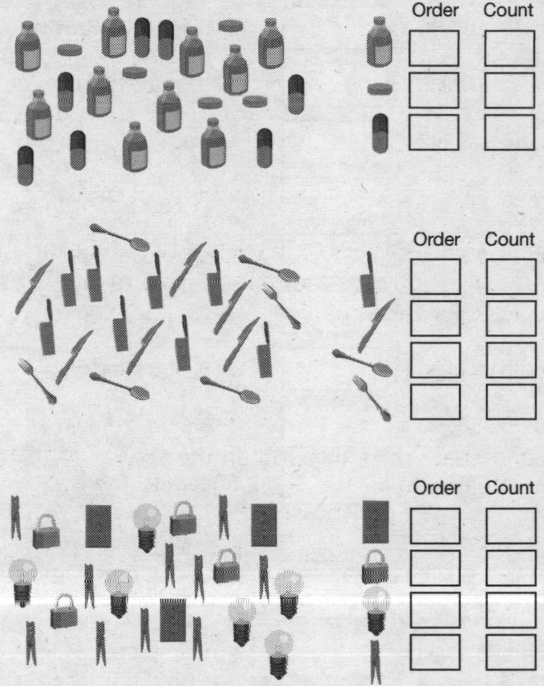

Now take as long as you think you need to write in the second column the precise count of each symbol.

TIME TAKEN:	INCORRECT ANSWERS:
TIME POINTS:	**TOTAL SCORE:**

Time Elapsed

Work out how many hours and minutes have passed between each of these pairs of times.

9:25am to 3:45pm =	:	8:10am to 9:35am =	:
8:45am to 2:15pm =	:	8:00am to 3:35pm =	:
1:15am to 6:10pm =	:	2:40am to 11:00am =	:
3:15am to 10:35pm =	:	2:15am to 3:40am =	:
4:45pm to 7:50pm =	:	8:35pm to 11:35pm =	:
5:40pm to 6:55pm =	:	5:40pm to 11:25pm =	:
8:05am to 9:50am =	:	3:15pm to 5:55pm =	:
6:25am to 11:15am =	:	5:30pm to 7:45pm =	:
11:30am to 2:05pm =	:	1:05am to 6:10pm =	:
4:45pm to 8:35pm =	:	5:10am to 8:30am =	:
2:45pm to 8:50pm =	:	6:30am to 10:55pm =	:
8:30am to 9:25pm =	:	3:00am to 10:50pm =	:
5:30am to 6:35am =	:	9:10am to 11:00pm =	:
12:25am to 5:20pm =	:	11:10am to 5:35pm =	:
9:30am to 5:10pm =	:	12:25pm to 10:35pm =	:

TIME TAKEN:	INCORRECT ANSWERS:
TIME POINTS:	**TOTAL SCORE:**

Ordered List

Can you memorize the order of these 24 items of furniture?

Spend 2 minutes studying the top list, then cover the table and look at the second copy of the list at the bottom of the page. Use the alphabetical labels to help recall the precise order of the words in the covered table.

Lowboy	Settee	Chest	Couch
Whatnot	Secretaire	Armchair	Stool
Tallboy	Dresser	Cradle	Divan
Futon	Desk	Cot	Bureau
Hammock	Cabinet	Bookcase	Wardrobe
Davenport	Sideboard	Berth	Bench

Now try to recall the correct order below, by writing in the corresponding letters:

A Cradle	**B** Desk	**C** Sideboard	**D** Stool
E Secretaire	**F** Cabinet	**G** Bench	**H** Settee
I Futon	**J** Divan	**K** Bookcase	**L** Hammock
M Davenport	**N** Wardrobe	**O** Berth	**P** Couch
Q Cot	**R** Tallboy	**S** Dresser	**T** Whatnot
U Bureau	**V** Lowboy	**W** Armchair	**X** Chest

INCORRECT ANSWERS:	**TOTAL SCORE:**

Word List

Try to memorize these 24 types of dwelling.

After 2 minutes, cover the table and write as many as you can in the boxes below. You do not need to remember the correct order.

House	Tent	Shack	Hut
Villa	Wigwam	Hostel	Hotel
Lodge	Cabin	Bunker	Barrack
Apartment	Teepee	Trailer	Inn
Mansion	Motel	Mud hut	Cottage
Croft	Bungalow	Embassy	Farmhouse

Now try to recall as many as you can:

INCORRECT ANSWERS:	**TOTAL SCORE:**

Observation and Counting

Look at these overlapping stars and see how long it takes you to answer the observation questions below.

How many separate areas are there between the lines?

How many stars are wholly contained within another star?

If you were to colour each area in so that no two areas of the same colour touched on a side, how many colours would you need?

TIME TAKEN:	INCORRECT ANSWERS:
TIME POINTS:	**TOTAL SCORE:**

Creative Thinking

See if you can solve each of the following conundrums. If you get stuck then try thinking laterally – they all have logical solutions, but the logic might not be what you expect!

A monkey and its particularly vocal child are going for a stroll in the monkey park. The child pipes up "I am your daughter but you are not my mother!" How can this be true?

To the nearest thousand, how many animals do you think Moses had on board the Ark?

TIME TAKEN:	INCORRECT ANSWERS:
TIME POINTS:	**TOTAL SCORE:**

Solutions

1: Visual Sequences
a, b

2: Speed Arithmetic

97 + 10 = **107**	83 − 11 = **72**	19 + 49 = **68**
6 + 42 = **48**	3 × 9 = **27**	28 + 20 = **48**
85 − 4 = **81**	59 − 8 = **51**	2 + 1 = **3**
60 − 6 = **54**	7 + 27 = **34**	89 + 9 = **98**
5 + 45 = **50**	60 + 10 = **70**	58 + 13 = **71**
63 + 12 = **75**	16 + 20 = **36**	12 × 7 = **84**
6 × 9 = **54**	49 + 12 = **61**	6 + 73 = **79**
4 + 29 = **33**	9 × 10 = **90**	80 − 8 = **72**
50 + 18 = **68**	13 − 4 = **9**	97 − 4 = **93**
71 + 12 = **83**	3 × 3 = **9**	24 − 5 = **19**
10 + 32 = **42**	104 − 1 = **103**	2 + 69 = **71**
6 + 87 = **93**	14 + 7 = **21**	72 − 14 = **58**
5 × 7 = **35**	95 + 16 = **111**	19 + 65 = **84**

3: Cryptogram
Whatever is worth doing at all is worth doing well.

Lord Chesterfield

The more we give of anything, the more we shall get back.

Grace Speare

The upside is your future is in your hands. And the downside is your future is in your hands.

Russ Myers

Happiness is the sense that one matters.

Sarah Trimmer

5: Reflective Power
1A, 2A, 3B, 4B, 5C

6: Coin Conundrum

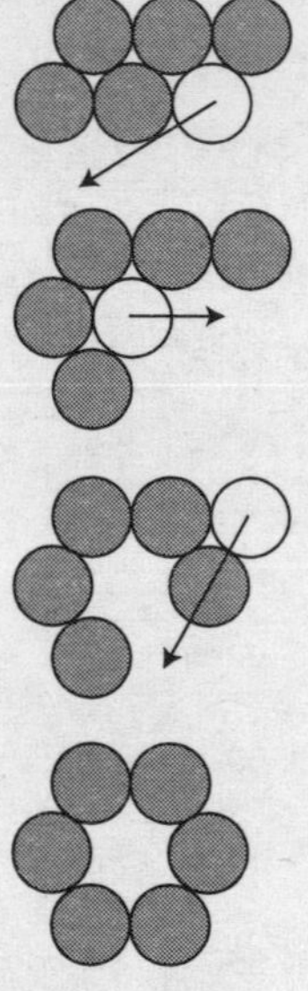

7: Logical Puzzlers
15½ feet.

179 baths. 15 in months with 30 days, 15 in months with 31 days, and 14 in February.

16 hours.

8: Counting and Perception

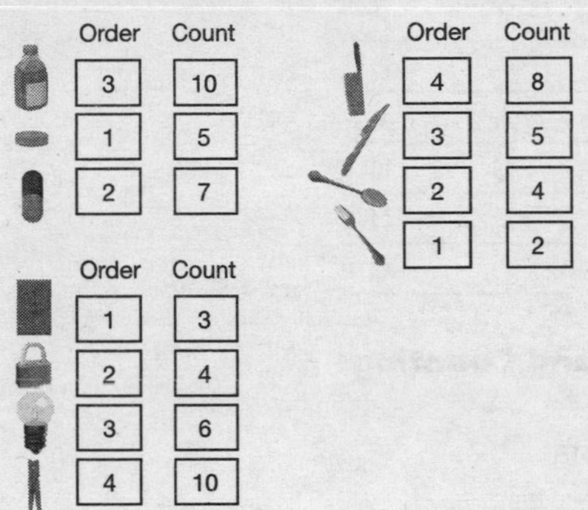

Order	Count
3	10
1	5
2	7

Order	Count
1	3
2	4
3	6
4	10

Order	Count
4	8
3	5
2	4
1	2

9: Time Elapsed

9:25am to 3:45pm =	**6:20**	8:10am to 9:35am =	**1:25**
8:45am to 2:15pm =	**5:30**	8:00am to 3:35pm =	**7:35**
1:15am to 6:10pm =	**16:55**	2:40am to 11:00am =	**8:20**
3:15am to 10:35pm =	**19:20**	2:15am to 3:40am =	**1:25**
4:45pm to 7:50pm =	**3:05**	8:35pm to 11:35pm =	**3:00**
5:40pm to 6:55pm =	**1:15**	5:40pm to 11:25pm =	**5:45**
8:05am to 9:50am =	**1:45**	3:15pm to 5:55pm =	**2:40**
6:25am to 11:15am =	**4:50**	5:30pm to 7:45pm =	**2:15**
11:30am to 2:05pm =	**2:35**	1:05am to 6:10pm =	**17:05**
4:45pm to 8:35pm =	**3:50**	5:10am to 8:30am =	**3:20**
2:45pm to 8:50pm =	**6:05**	6:30am to 10:55pm =	**16:25**
8:30am to 9:25pm =	**12:55**	3:00am to 10:50pm =	**19:50**
5:30am to 6:35am =	**1:05**	9:10am to 11:00pm =	**13:50**
12:25am to 5:20pm =	**16:55**	11:10am to 5:35pm =	**6:25**
9:30am to 5:10pm =	**7:40**	12:25pm to 10:35pm =	**10:10**

10: Ordered List

V	H	X	P
T	E	W	D
R	S	A	J
I	B	Q	U
L	F	K	N
M	C	O	G

12: Observation and Counting

11 separate areas.

1 wholly-contained star.

2 colours are needed.

13: Creative Thinking

The parent monkey is the father.

It was Noah who had an Ark, not Moses, so the answer is zero.

DAY
6

Time Elapsed

Work out how many hours and minutes have passed between each of these pairs of times.

4:25am to 8:20pm =	:	3:45am to 10:10pm =	:
4:00am to 8:45am =	:	11:45am to 5:50pm =	:
3:25am to 9:35pm =	:	2:45pm to 9:20pm =	:
8:30am to 8:55am =	:	3:50am to 10:30pm =	:
7:20am to 1:50pm =	:	10:35am to 10:50am =	:
1:20am to 8:15am =	:	12:20am to 5:40am =	:
6:50pm to 10:15pm =	:	7:10am to 11:35am =	:
10:10pm to 11:30pm =	:	1:20am to 2:30pm =	:
1:55am to 4:40am =	:	3:00pm to 9:45pm =	:
5:00am to 10:55am =	:	2:10am to 12:05pm =	:
4:10am to 8:40am =	:	1:45pm to 2:15pm =	:
1:45am to 8:30am =	:	1:30am to 9:15pm =	:
11:25am to 5:40pm =	:	10:55am to 2:30pm =	:
8:10am to 1:55pm =	:	3:25am to 9:00am =	:
4:15am to 1:15pm =	:	8:45am to 8:10pm =	:

TIME TAKEN:	INCORRECT ANSWERS:
TIME POINTS:	**TOTAL SCORE:**

Matchstick Thinking

The picture below shows 12 matchsticks arranged into 1 large and 4 small squares.

Can you remove 2 matchsticks only in order to leave precisely 2 squares?

TIME TAKEN:	INCORRECT ANSWERS:
TIME POINTS:	**TOTAL SCORE:**

Logical Puzzlers

Try to solve these problems – each requires only simple logic to solve, but you might find that making notes with a pencil will help!

A warehouse contains a 64 litre tank which unfortunately leaks half of its contents every day. If it is completely filled, how long will it take to empty until just 1 litre is left?

If the population of the UK is 60 million people, and grows by 10% every 5 years, what will the population be in 10 years?

A particularly attractive daisy in my garden happens to have 24 petals on it. Each week, however, half of the petals fall off. How many petals will be left after 3 weeks?

TIME TAKEN:	INCORRECT ANSWERS:
TIME POINTS:	**TOTAL SCORE:**

Missing Words

Study each of these 3 lists of words for 2 minutes. Then cover the top half of the page and see if you can identify which word is missing from each list below.

Drag	Chase	Pursue	Follow
Hound	Hunt	Track	Tail

Bristol	Cardiff	London	Newcastle
Boston	Hastings	Liverpool	Glasgow

Pius	Innocent	John Paul	Benedict
Alexander	Gregory	Urban	Julius

Now try to spot the missing word from each list:

Follow, Tail, Hunt, Chase, Track, Pursue, Drag

MISSING:

Glasgow, Newcastle, Boston, Hastings, Bristol, Liverpool, London

MISSING:

Innocent, Gregory, Benedict, Alexander, Urban, Pius, John Paul

MISSING:

INCORRECT ANSWERS:	TOTAL SCORE:

Cryptogram

Decode each of these quotations by replacing A with Z, B with A, C with B, and so on through to replacing Y with X and Z with Y.

Xnt bzmmns ad qdzkkx ehqrs-qzsd zs xntq vnqj he xntq vnqj hr zkk xnt zqd.

Zmmz Pthmckdm

Vd zkk rszqs vhsg zkk sgdqd hr. Hs'r gnv vd trd hs sgzs lzjdr sghmfr onrrhakd.

Gdmqx Enqc

Vgdm rnqqnvr bnld, sgdx bnld mns rhmfkd rohdr, ats hm azsszkhnmr.

Vhkkhzl Rgzjdrodzqd

Sgd nmkx okzbd xnt'kk ehmc rtbbdrr adenqd vnqj hr hm sgd chbshnmzqx.

Lzx A Rlhsg

TIME TAKEN:	INCORRECT ANSWERS:
TIME POINTS:	**TOTAL SCORE:**

Rotation

If you were to rotate each of these three pictures as indicated by the arrow beneath, which of the figures below would be the result?

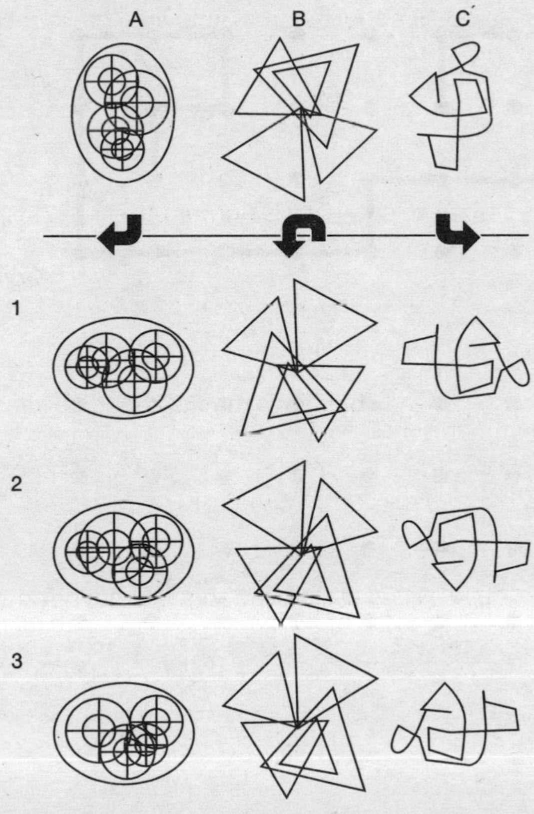

TIME TAKEN:	INCORRECT ANSWERS:
TIME POINTS:	**TOTAL SCORE:**

Visual Memory

Spend 1 minute studying this path. Then cover the top half of this page and try to redraw it accurately on the empty grid below.

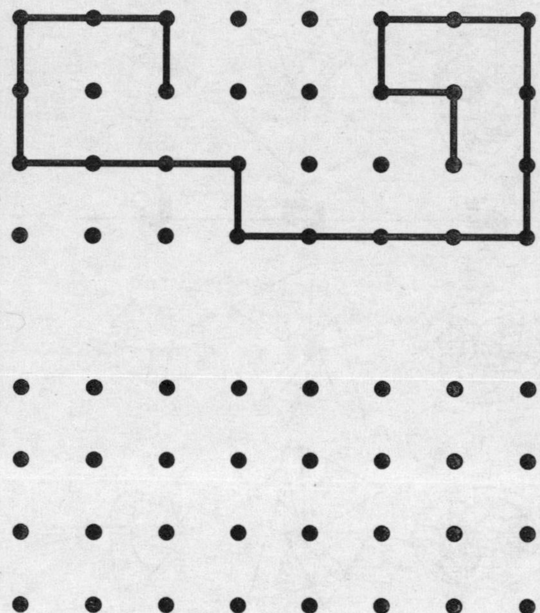

TIME TAKEN:	TOTAL SCORE:

Shape Dividing

Draw two straight lines in order to divide the box into three separate areas. Each area must contain precisely one of each size of circle. The two lines may touch but they must not cross.

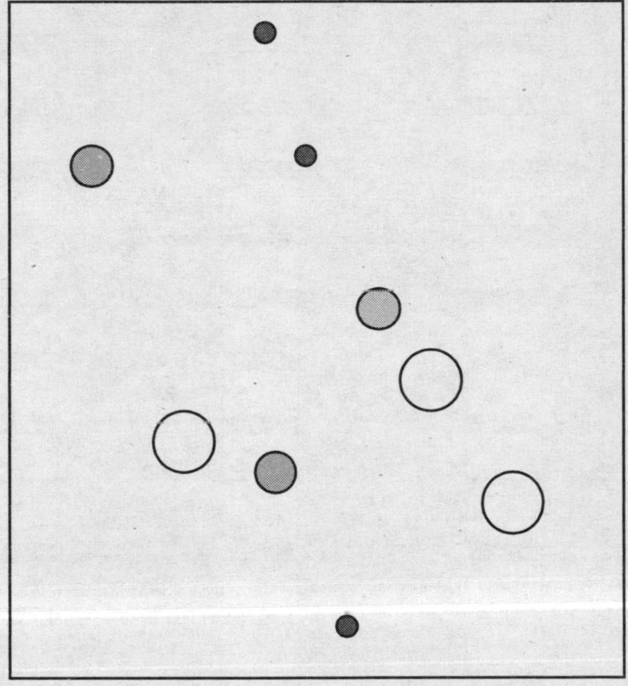

TIME TAKEN:	INCORRECT ANSWERS:
TIME POINTS:	**TOTAL SCORE:**

Speed Arithmetic

Complete the following set of arithmetic equations as quickly as possible. You should be able to do them all in your head without using a calculator or making notes.

6 × 5 =	7 × 10 =	29 − 10 =
10 × 4 =	36 − 14 =	91 − 13 =
4 + 14 =	20 − 16 =	9 × 2 =
73 − 18 =	5 + 17 =	12 × 7 =
68 − 19 =	30 − 15 =	77 − 3 =
16 + 28 =	53 − 5 =	87 + 8 =
10 − 6 =	25 − 20 =	98 − 7 =
10 + 11 =	12 × 12 =	72 + 15 =
16 − 14 =	16 + 82 =	31 − 20 =
64 + 20 =	1 + 57 =	95 − 20 =
98 − 13 =	4 × 3 =	10 × 7 =
66 − 15 =	54 + 4 =	48 − 10 =
83 + 17 =	6 × 10 =	83 + 2 =

TIME TAKEN:	INCORRECT ANSWERS:
TIME POINTS:	**TOTAL SCORE:**

Observation and Counting

Look at these overlapping hexagons and see how long it takes you to answer the observation questions below.

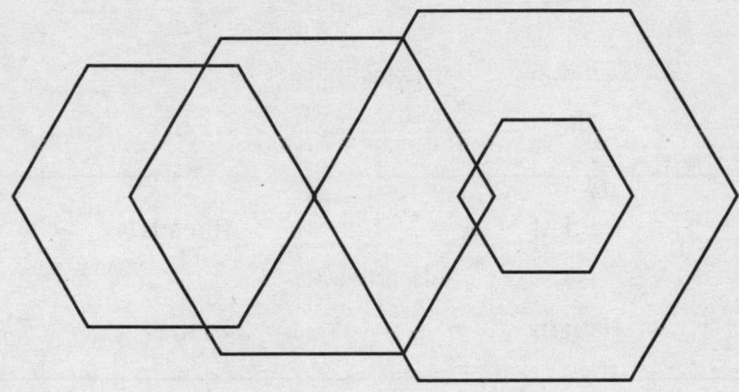

How many hexagons can you count?

Can you draw all of the hexagons in one stroke, without taking the pen off the paper and without going over any line twice? You may, however, cross over a line.

How many diamonds are there?

TIME TAKEN:	INCORRECT ANSWERS:
TIME POINTS:	**TOTAL SCORE:**

Odd One Out

Look at each of these sets of words. Can you work out which word is the odd one out in each case?

List
Sun
Mail
Bird
Out

Hardest
Threads
Hearths
Hatreds
Trashed

Bridge
Dominoes
Croquet
Poker
Chess

Picture
Painting
Portrait
Palette
Print

TIME TAKEN:	INCORRECT ANSWERS:
TIME POINTS:	**TOTAL SCORE:**

Ordered List

Can you memorize the order of these 24 trees and shrubs?

Spend 2 minutes studying the top list, then cover the table and look at the second list at the bottom of the page. Use the alphabetical labels to try to recall the precise order of the words in the covered table.

Poplar	Moolar	Rowan	Yucca
Camellia	Blackbox	Palmyra	Juniper
Euphorbia	Stinkwood	Kalanchoe	Gomuti
Cottonwood	Saltbush	Rambutan	Arbutus
Ebony	Elder	Erica	Maple
Gardenia	Jarrah	Ironwood	Sassafras

Now try to recall the correct order below, by writing in the corresponding letters:

A Arbutus	**B** Cottonwood	**C** Blackbox	**D** Elder
E Ebony	**F** Gomuti	**G** Kalanchoe	**H** Gardenia
I Jarrah	**J** Erica	**K** Maple	**L** Camellia
M Sassafras	**N** Ironwood	**O** Juniper	**P** Yucca
Q Stinkwood	**R** Palmyra	**S** Rowan	**T** Saltbush
U Moolar	**V** Euphorbia	**W** Rambutan	**X** Poplar

INCORRECT ANSWERS:	**TOTAL SCORE:**

Shape Folding

If you were to cut out this shape and fold it into a cube, which of the three pictures below would br the result?

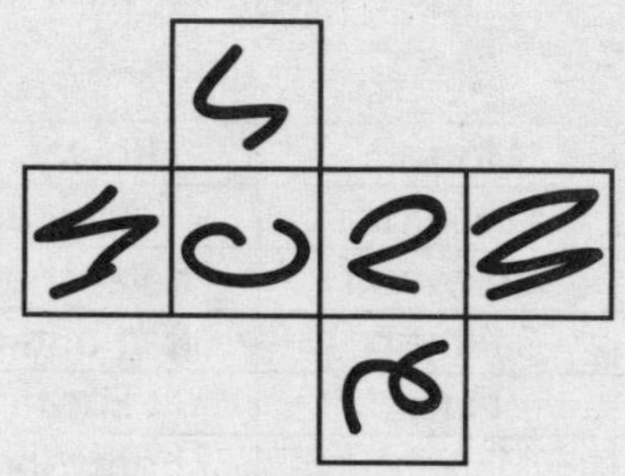

a b c

TIME TAKEN:	INCORRECT ANSWERS:
TIME POINTS:	**TOTAL SCORE:**

Solutions

1: Time Elapsed

4:25am to 8:20pm =	15:55	3:45am to 10:10pm =	18:25
4:00am to 8:45am =	4:45	11:45am to 5:50pm =	6:05
3:25am to 9:35pm =	18:10	2:45pm to 9:20pm =	6:35
8:30am to 8:55am =	0:25	3:50am to 10:30pm =	18:40
7:20am to 1:50pm =	6:30	10:35am to 10:50am =	0:15
1:20am to 8:15am =	6:55	12:20am to 5:40am =	5:20
6:50pm to 10:15pm =	3:25	7:10am to 11:35am =	4:25
10:10pm to 11:30pm =	1:20	1:20am to 2:30pm =	13:10
1:55am to 4:40am =	2:45	3:00pm to 9:45pm =	6:45
5:00am to 10:55am =	5:55	2:10am to 12:05pm =	9:55
4:10am to 8:40am =	4:30	1:45pm to 2:15pm =	0:30
1:45am to 8:30am =	6:45	1:30am to 9:15pm =	19:45
11:25am to 5:40pm =	6:15	10:55am to 2:30pm =	3:35
8:10am to 1:55pm =	5:45	3:25am to 9:00am =	5:35
4:15am to 1:15pm =	9:00	8:45am to 8:10pm =	11:25

2: Matchstick Thinking

3: Logical Puzzlers
6 days.

72.6 million. 60 + 6 = 66; 66 + 6.6 = 72.6.

3 petals.

5: Cryptogram
You cannot be really first-rate at your work if your work is all you are.

Anna Quindlen

We all start with all there is. It's how we use it that makes things possible.

Henry Ford

When sorrows come, they come not single spies, but in battalions.
William Shakespeare

The only place you'll find success before work is in the dictionary.
May B Smith

6: Rotation
A1, B1, C2

8: Shape Dividing

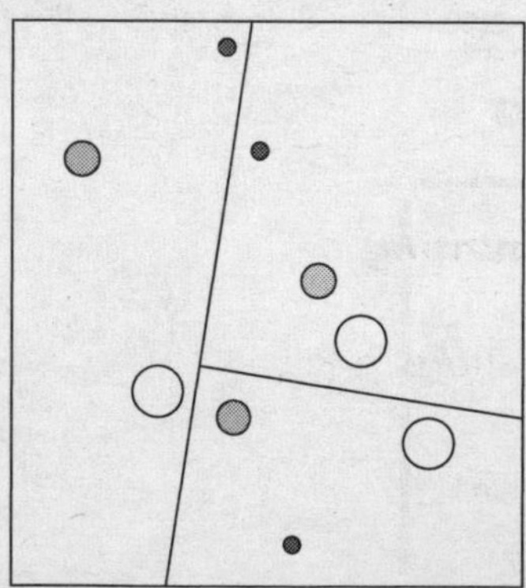

9: Speed Arithmetic

6 × 5 = **30**	7 × 10 = **70**	29 − 10 = **19**
10 × 4 = **40**	36 − 14 = **22**	91 − 13 = **78**
4 + 14 = **18**	20 − 16 = **4**	9 × 2 = **18**
73 − 18 = **55**	5 + 17 = **22**	12 × 7 = **84**
68 − 19 = **49**	30 − 15 = **15**	77 − 3 = **74**
16 + 28 = **44**	53 − 5 = **48**	87 + 8 = **95**
10 − 6 = **4**	25 − 20 = **5**	98 − 7 = **91**
10 + 11 = **21**	12 × 12 = **144**	72 + 15 = **87**
16 − 14 = **2**	16 + 82 = **98**	31 − 20 = **11**
64 + 20 = **84**	1 + 57 = **58**	95 − 20 = **75**
98 − 13 = **85**	4 × 3 = **12**	10 × 7 = **70**
66 − 15 = **51**	54 + 4 = **58**	48 − 10 = **38**
83 + 17 = **100**	6 × 10 = **60**	83 + 2 = **85**

10: Observation and Counting

4 hexagons in total.

Yes, you can draw it in one stroke.

2 diamonds.

11: Odd One Out

Sun – the rest make new words when prefixed with 'black'
Hearths – the rest are anagrams of each other
Croquet – the rest are table sports
Palette – the rest can be art works

12: Ordered List

X	U	S	P
L	C	R	O
V	Q	G	F
B	T	W	A
E	D	J	K
H	I	N	M

13: Shape Folding

b

DAY
7

Counting and Perception

Spend no more than 10 seconds looking at each group of symbols in each turn, then try to sort them into order of increasing frequency. Write "1" in the "Order" column for the shape that occurs least often, and so on.

Now take as long as you think you need to write in the second column the precise count of each symbol.

TIME TAKEN:	INCORRECT ANSWERS:
TIME POINTS:	**TOTAL SCORE:**

Creative Thinking

See if you can solve each of the following conundrums. If you get stuck then try thinking laterally – they all have logical solutions, but the logic might not be what you expect!

Write this number down: 14 million, 14 thousand, 14 hundred, and 14.

Whilst taking a walk through the countryside I spy a field full of long grass with a mummy cow, daddy cow, and baby cow. They're drinking from a fast-flowing stream near an old wooden fence, but then I realize that something is not quite right. What is it?

TIME TAKEN:	INCORRECT ANSWERS:
TIME POINTS:	**TOTAL SCORE:**

Odd One Out

Look at each of these sets of words. Can you work out which word is the odd one out in each case?

Reserve
Reverse
Versier
Reveres
Severer

November
July
September
April
June

Drift
Down
Ball
Man
Storm

Net
Safety
Blackout
Iron
Cloak

TIME TAKEN:	INCORRECT ANSWERS:
TIME POINTS:	**TOTAL SCORE:**

Missing Words

Study each of these 3 lists of words for a total of 2 minutes. Then cover the top half of the page and see if you can identify which word is missing from each list below.

Ban	Forbid	Prevent	Stop
Discourage	Disallow	Outlaw	Exclude

Matthew	Mark	John	David
Simon	Stephen	Jason	Daniel

November	September	July	April
October	August	December	March

Now try to spot the missing word from each list:

Outlaw, Exclude, Discourage, Prevent, Forbid, Ban, Stop

MISSING:

John, David, Jason, Matthew, Mark, Daniel, Stephen

MISSING:

October, July, November, December, September, August, March

MISSING:

INCORRECT ANSWERS:	TOTAL SCORE:

Observation and Counting

Look at this path, made up of a series of arcs (single curves), and see how long it takes you to answer these observation questions.

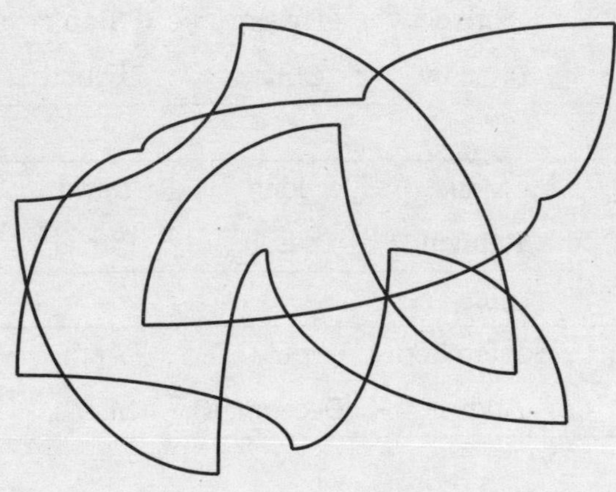

Is it possible to draw this entire figure in one stroke, without taking the pen off the paper or going over any line twice? You may cross over a line, however.

What is the minimum number of arcs you need to draw this picture?

If you were to colour in each area so that no two areas of the same colour touched on any side, how many colours would you need?

TIME TAKEN:	INCORRECT ANSWERS:
TIME POINTS:	**TOTAL SCORE:**

Number Sequences

Look at each of these number sequences and see if you can deduce which number comes next in the series.

661	600	553	520	501	
9	9	18	54	216	
1200	240	60	20	10	
265	162	103	59	44	
764	674	603	551	518	
0	9	27	54	90	
188	116	72	44	28	
665	672	696	737	795	

TIME TAKEN:	INCORRECT ANSWERS:
TIME POINTS:	**TOTAL SCORE:**

DAY: 7 | WORKOUT: 7 | CONCENTRATION

Missing Signs

Insert the missing sign into each of these arithmetic expressions in order to make the equation true. You will need to add, subtract, multiply, or divide.

3	☐	112 = 115	108	☐	9 = 12	6	☐	4 = 24
10	☐	3 = 30	2	☐	12 = 24	7	☐	5 = 35
41	☐	11 = 30	12	☐	12 = 144	15	☐	9 = 6
50	☐	37 = 13	27	☐	9 = 3	22	☐	2 = 11
55	☐	25 = 30	84	☐	12 = 7	33	☐	23 = 56
29	☐	18 = 11	71	☐	11 = 82	4	☐	2 = 8
18	☐	3 = 6	24	☐	18 = 42	84	☐	7 = 12
2	☐	3 = 6	7	☐	10 = 70	22	☐	32 = 54
86	☐	16 = 102	61	☐	8 = 69	11	☐	12 = 132
52	☐	4 = 13	68	☐	4 = 64	4	☐	11 = 44
129	☐	9 = 138	6	☐	2 = 12	1	☐	111 = 112
28	☐	131 = 159	31	☐	7 = 24	6	☐	2 = 3
42	☐	3 = 14	87	☐	15 = 102	21	☐	3 = 7

TIME TAKEN:	INCORRECT ANSWERS:
TIME POINTS:	**TOTAL SCORE:**

Word List

Try to memorize these 24 economic terms.

After 2 minutes cover the table, and write as many as you can in the boxes below. You do not need to remember the correct order.

Assets	Exchange	Consumer	Barter
Bank	Insurance	Interest	Deposit
Yield	Tax	Balance	Slump
Withdrawal	Tariff	Residual	Future
Share	Pension	Payroll	Invoice
Merger	Income	Insolvency	Employees

Now try to recall as many as you can:

INCORRECT ANSWERS:	**TOTAL SCORE:**

Matchstick Thinking

The picture below shows 12 matchsticks arranged into a crossed grid pattern with a single square in the middle.

Can you move only 3 matchsticks in order to make precisely 3 squares? There must be no left-over matches which do not form part of one of the squares.

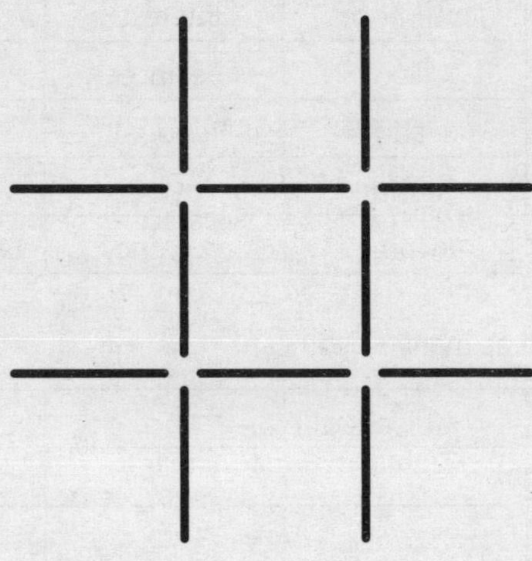

TIME TAKEN:	INCORRECT ANSWERS:
TIME POINTS:	**TOTAL SCORE:**

Logical Puzzlers

Try to solve these problems – each requires only simple logic to solve, but you might find that making notes with a pencil will help!

If you count how many dots there are on a normal 6-sided dice, what is the total number?

If I spend eight hours sleeping every night, how many hours in total do I sleep each week?

A book in my library has 512 pages, and is made from a stack of pieces of paper which have been sewn through across the middle to make the final book. How many pieces of paper were necessary to make the book?

TIME TAKEN:	INCORRECT ANSWERS:
TIME POINTS:	**TOTAL SCORE:**

Speed Arithmetic

Complete the following set of arithmetic equations as quickly as possible. You should be able to do them all in your head without using a calculator or making notes.

44 − 19 =	100 − 12 =	106 − 19 =
7 × 11 =	14 + 50 =	52 − 16 =
39 − 20 =	12 × 7 =	52 − 11 =
5 × 6 =	6 × 9 =	56 − 18 =
1 + 14 =	60 + 3 =	42 − 16 =
13 + 19 =	30 − 11 =	70 − 14 =
17 + 7 =	109 − 4 =	10 × 9 =
18 + 3 =	67 − 20 =	92 + 9 =
2 × 7 =	2 × 3 =	53 − 7 =
108 − 14 =	21 − 3 =	19 + 27 =
12 × 8 =	2 × 8 =	55 − 5 =
27 + 5 =	48 − 13 =	90 − 6 =
49 − 7 =	33 + 3 =	100 + 13 =

TIME TAKEN:	INCORRECT ANSWERS:
TIME POINTS:	**TOTAL SCORE:**

Reflective Power

Look at each figure on the left-hand side of the vertical "mirror". Work out which of the figures on the right-hand side corresponds to the figure reflected in the mirror line.

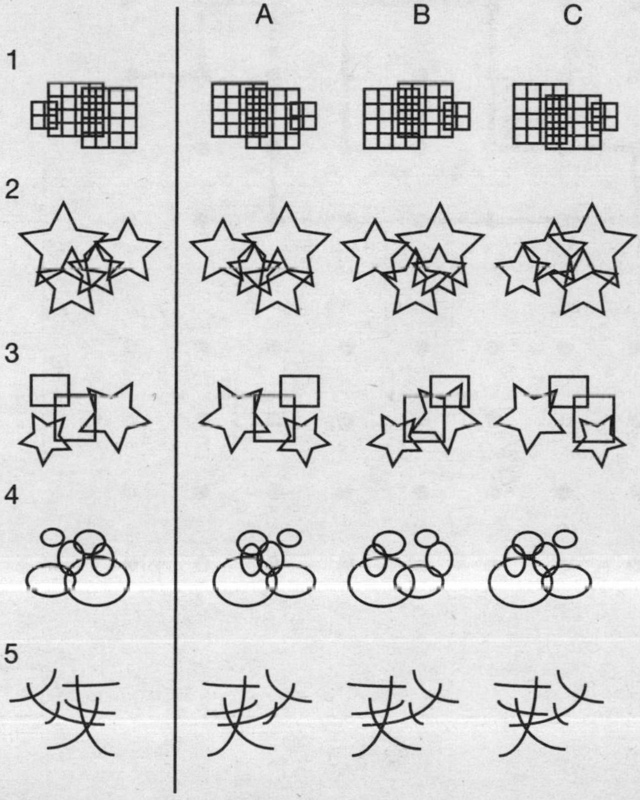

A B C

1

2

3

4

5

TIME TAKEN:	INCORRECT ANSWERS:
TIME POINTS:	**TOTAL SCORE:**

Visual Memory

Spend 1 minute studying this path. Then cover the top half of this page and try to redraw it accurately on the empty grid below.

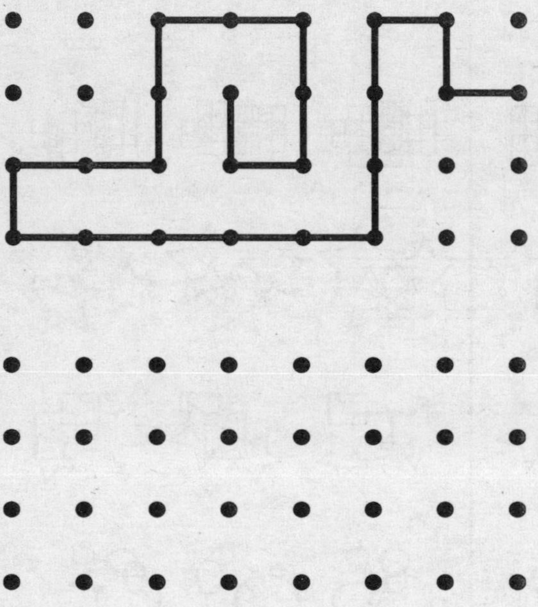

INCORRECT ANSWERS:	**TOTAL SCORE:**

Solutions

1: Counting and Perception

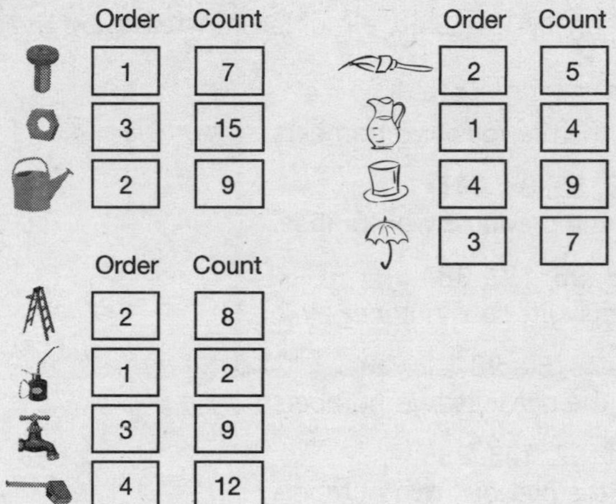

2: Creative Thinking

14,015,414.

There's no such thing as a daddy cow! Cows are always female.

3: Odd One Out

Versier – the rest are anagrams of each other
July – all the other months have 30 days
Down – the rest make new words when prefixed with 'snow'
Cloak – the rest are types of curtain

5: Observation and Counting

Yes, you can draw it in one stroke.

15 arcs is the minimum.

2 colours are needed.

6: Number Sequences

9, 27, 81, 243, 729, **2187**
Rule: multiply previous number by 3

1, 1, 2, 6, 24, **120**
Rule: multiply by 1, 2, 3 etc – multiplier increases by 1 each time

18, 18, 36, 54, 90, **144**
Rule: add the previous two numbers

11, 22, 33, 55, 88, **143**
Rule: add the previous two numbers

12, 24, 48, 96, 192, **384**
Rule: multiply previous number by 2

6, 16, 22, 38, 60, **98**
Rule: add the previous two numbers

10, 41, 51, 92, 143, **235**
Rule: add the previous two numbers

14, 22, 39, 65, 100, **144**
Rule: difference between numbers increases by 9 each time

7: Missing Signs

3 + 112 = 115		108 ÷ 9 = 12		6 × 4 = 24	
10 × 3 = 30		2 × 12 = 24		7 × 5 = 35	
41 – 11 = 30		12 × 12 = 144		15 – 9 = 6	
50 – 37 = 13		27 ÷ 9 = 3		22 ÷ 2 = 11	
55 – 25 = 30		84 ÷ 12 = 7		33 + 23 = 56	
29 – 18 = 11		71 + 11 = 82		4 × 2 = 8	
18 ÷ 3 = 6		24 + 18 = 42		84 ÷ 7 = 12	
2 × 3 = 6		7 × 10 = 70		22 + 32 = 54	
86 + 16 = 102		61 + 8 = 69		11 × 12 = 132	
52 ÷ 4 = 13		68 – 4 = 64		4 × 11 = 44	
129 + 9 = 138		6 × 2 = 12		1 + 111 = 112	
28 + 131 = 159		31 – 7 = 24		6 ÷ 2 = 3	
42 ÷ 3 = 14		87 + 15 = 102		21 ÷ 3 = 7	

9: Matchstick Thinking

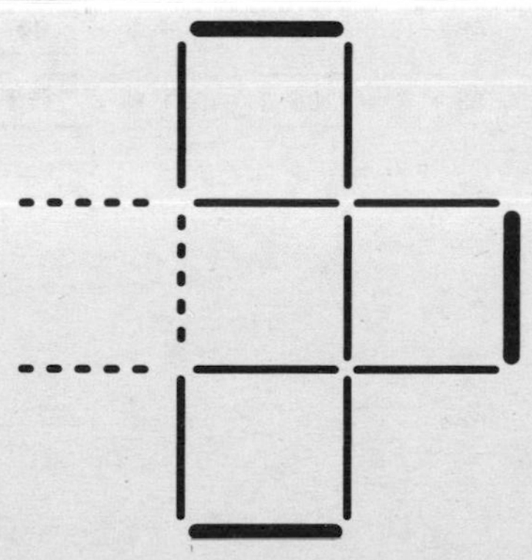

10: Logical Puzzlers

21.

56 hours.

128 pieces of paper (half of each piece of paper on each side of the seam, and then printed on both sides).

11: Speed Arithmetic

44 − 19 = **25**	100 − 12 = **88**	106 − 19 = **87**
7 × 11 = **77**	14 + 50 = **64**	52 − 16 = **36**
39 − 20 = **19**	12 × 7 = **84**	52 − 11 = **41**
5 × 6 = **30**	6 × 9 = **54**	56 − 18 = **38**
1 + 14 = **15**	60 + 3 = **63**	42 − 16 = **26**
13 + 19 = **32**	30 − 11 = **19**	70 − 14 = **56**
17 + 7 = **24**	109 − 4 = **105**	10 × 9 = **90**
18 + 3 = **21**	67 − 20 = **47**	92 + 9 = **101**
2 × 7 = **14**	2 × 3 = **6**	53 − 7 = **46**
108 − 14 = **94**	21 − 3 = **18**	19 + 27 = **46**
12 × 8 = **96**	2 × 8 = **16**	55 − 5 = **50**
27 + 5 = **32**	48 − 13 = **35**	90 − 6 = **84**
49 − 7 = **42**	33 + 3 = **36**	100 + 13 = **113**

12: Reflective Power

1B, 2A, 3A, 4C, 5B

DAY
8

Balancing

Looking at these two weighing scales. Can you say which of these three objects is the heaviest?

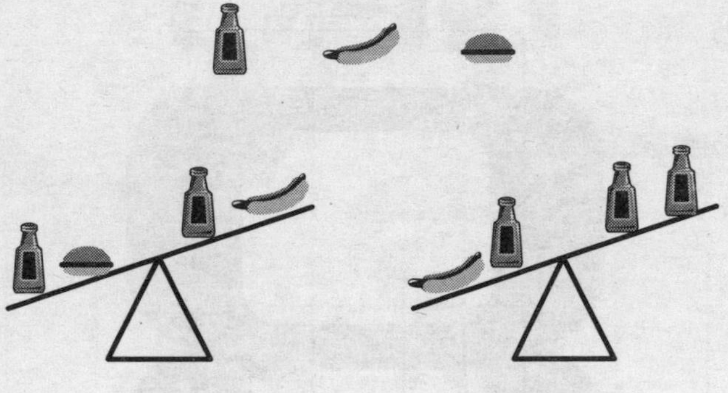

And which of these three objects is the heaviest?

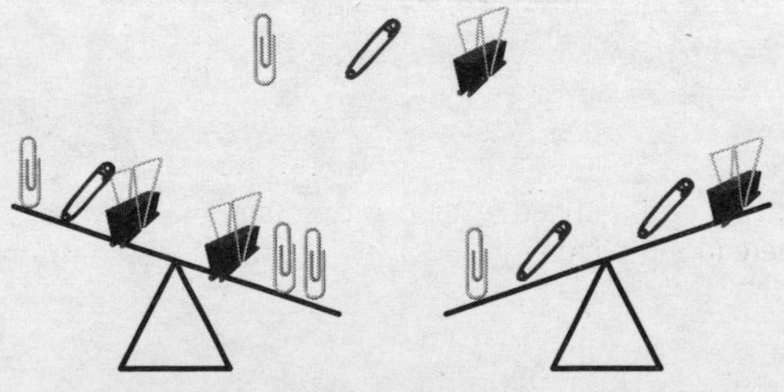

TIME TAKEN:	INCORRECT ANSWERS:
TIME POINTS:	**TOTAL SCORE:**

Observation and Counting

Look at these rounded rectangles and see how long it takes you to answer the observation questions below.

How many enclosed areas are formed by two overlapping rounded rectangles?

How many rounded rectangles are there in total?

How many non-rounded rectangles or squares are there in this picture?

TIME TAKEN:	INCORRECT ANSWERS:
TIME POINTS:	**TOTAL SCORE:**

Speed Arithmetic

Complete the following set of arithmetic equations as quickly as possible. You should be able to do them all in your head without using a calculator or making notes.

69 + 19 =	45 − 2 =	30 + 14 =
3 × 10 =	98 − 5 =	9 × 3 =
44 + 2 =	85 − 19 =	6 × 8 =
84 + 18 =	32 − 1 =	60 − 20 =
36 − 5 =	4 + 50 =	6 + 13 =
13 − 4 =	90 + 13 =	43 − 15 =
89 − 14 =	78 + 10 =	82 − 14 =
26 − 5 =	101 − 17 =	12 + 90 =
9 + 1 =	8 + 15 =	9 + 21 =
3 × 4 =	18 + 92 =	65 − 4 =
5 × 3 =	26 − 6 =	5 + 62 =
16 + 89 =	99 − 11 =	7 × 3 =
5 × 11 =	19 + 88 =	57 − 19 =

TIME TAKEN:	INCORRECT ANSWERS:
TIME POINTS:	**TOTAL SCORE:**

Shape Dividing

Draw three straight lines in order to divide the shape into four separate areas. Each area must contain precisely one of each size of circle. The three lines may touch but they must not cross.

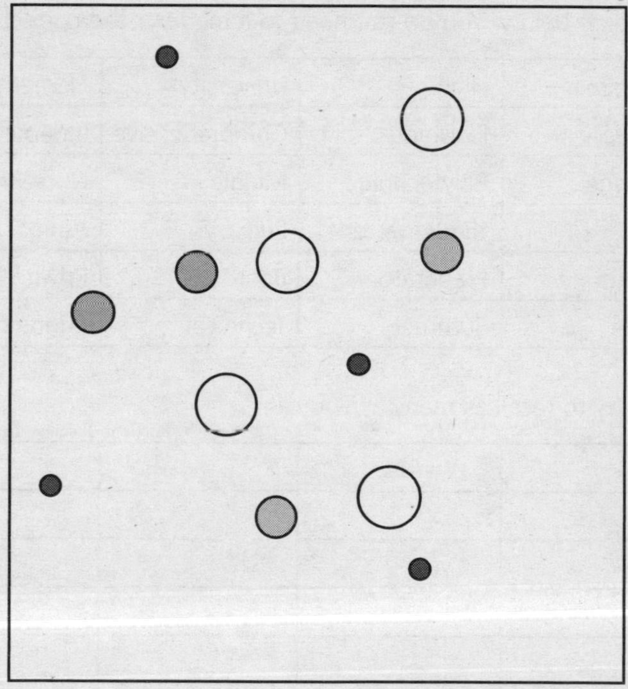

TIME TAKEN:	INCORRECT ANSWERS:
TIME POINTS:	**TOTAL SCORE:**

Word List

Try to memorize these 24 types of school and other educational institution.

After 2 minutes cover the table and write as many as you can in the boxes below. You do not need to remember the correct order.

Grammar	High	University	Elementary
Grade	Finishing	Comprehensive	Independent
College	Polytechnic	Middle	Nursery
Day	Kindergarten	Primary	Junior
Public	Preparatory	Boarding	Private
State	Summer	Technical	Sunday

Now try to recall as many as you can:

INCORRECT ANSWERS:	**TOTAL SCORE:**

Visual Memory

Spend 1 minute studying this path. Then cover the top half of this page and try to redraw it accurately on the empty grid below.

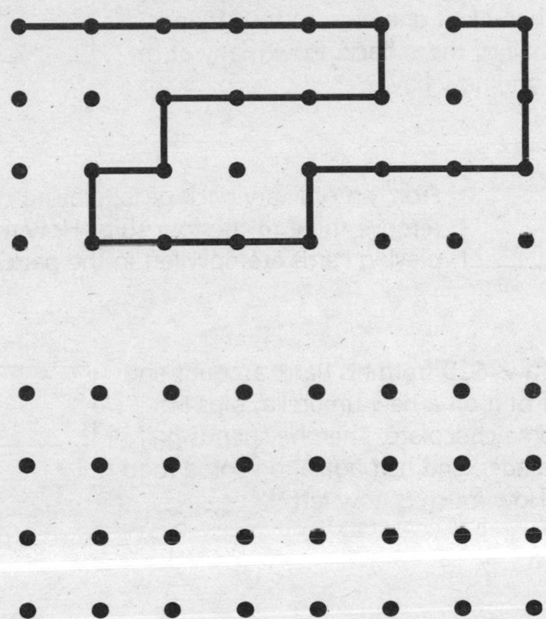

INCORRECT ANSWERS:	TOTAL SCORE:

Logical Puzzlers

Try to solve these problems – each requires only simple logic to solve, but you might find that making notes with a pencil will help!

I went to the stationery store and bought eight pens, but then I lent one each to four friends. I then got half of these back. How many of my eight pens do I now have?

From an ordinary pack of 52 playing cards I remove three of the four suits. How many playing cards are now left in the pack?

Pete withdraws $25 from his bank account and spends half of it on a new umbrella, plus 50 cents on some chocolate. Then he spends half of the remainder, and half again, on some food and drink. How much is now left?

TIME TAKEN:	INCORRECT ANSWERS:
TIME POINTS:	**TOTAL SCORE:**

Reflective Power

Look at each figure on the left-hand side of the vertical "mirror". Work out which of the figures on the right-hand side corresponds to the figure reflected in the mirror line.

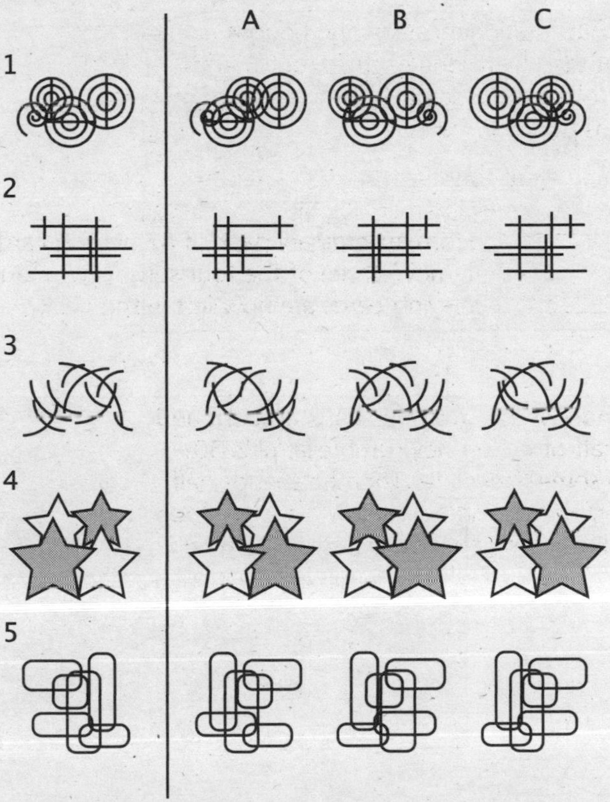

	A	B	C
1			
2			
3			
4			
5			

TIME TAKEN:	INCORRECT ANSWERS:
TIME POINTS:	**TOTAL SCORE:**

Creative Thinking

See if you can solve each of the following conundrums. If you get stuck then try thinking laterally – they all have logical solutions, but the logic might not be what you expect!

I went into a hardware store and to my delight I found exactly what I was looking for. Each item cost exactly £1. I picked up 472 and went to the counter and paid, where I was only charged £3. This was the correct amount. How can this be true?

Every time you eat you're eating over at least an inch of dirt. How is this so?

TIME TAKEN:	INCORRECT ANSWERS:
TIME POINTS:	**TOTAL SCORE:**

DAY: 8	WORKOUT: 10	CONCENTRATION

Time Elapsed

Work out how many hours and minutes have passed between each of these pairs of times.

5:50am to 12:00pm =	:	7:45am to 6:10pm =	:
8:10am to 11:35am =	:	9:50am to 5:10pm =	:
1:00am to 12:30pm =	:	1:50am to 8:15pm =	:
5:25am to 6:20pm =	:	10:20am to 3:15pm =	:
6:55am to 7:15am =	:	6:25am to 2:50pm =	:
6:35am to 6:25pm =	:	5:40am to 4:40pm =	:
3:30am to 7:25pm =	:	12:05am to 2:20am =	:
5:10am to 5:20pm =	:	9:35am to 11:00pm =	:
6:00am to 6:30pm =	:	3:20pm to 8:30pm =	:
3:45am to 9:50am =	:	2:35am to 3:35am =	:
6:35am to 7:55am =	:	5:40am to 3:20pm =	:
7:30pm to 11:55pm =	:	6:35am to 8:25am =	:
4:40am to 11:15pm =	:	12:50am to 3:55pm =	:
4:30am to 2:05pm =	:	7:10am to 11:35pm =	:
11:35am to 9:40pm =	:	8:05pm to 9:10pm =	:

TIME TAKEN:	INCORRECT ANSWERS:
TIME POINTS:	**TOTAL SCORE:**

Shape Folding

If you were to cut out this shape and fold it into a cube, which of the three pictures below would result?

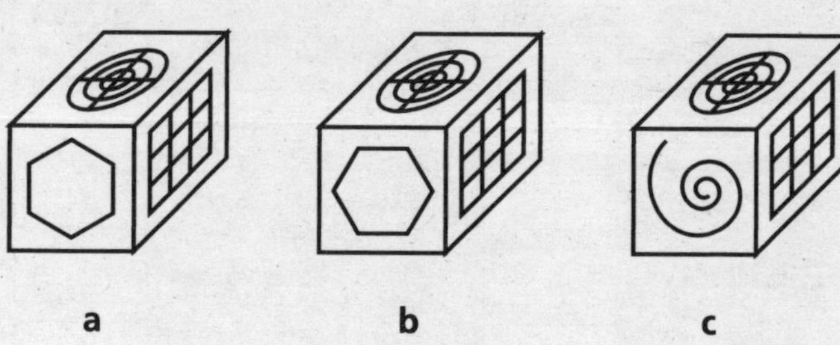

a **b** **c**

TIME TAKEN:	INCORRECT ANSWERS:
TIME POINTS:	**TOTAL SCORE:**

Missing Words

Study each of these 3 lists of words for 2 minutes. Then cover the top half of the page and see if you can identify which word is missing from each list below.

Laugh	Joke	Smile	Grin
Chuckle	Chortle	Giggle	Titter

Ordinary	Dull	Common	Nothing
Inferior	Poor	Vague	Unknown

Harsh	Extreme	Rough	Austere
Stern	Strict	Tough	Hard

Now try to spot the missing word from each list:

Chortle, Joke, Titter, Giggle, Chuckle, Smile, Grin

MISSING:

Vague, Poor, Dull, Nothing, Common, Ordinary, Inferior

MISSING:

Hard, Harsh, Stern, Extreme, Rough, Tough, Strict

MISSING:

INCORRECT ANSWERS:	TOTAL SCORE:

Odd One Out

Look at each of these sets of words. Can you work out which word is the odd one out in each case?

Earth
Wind
Fire
Air
Water

Valiant
Heroic
Bold
Italic
Daring

Beta
Alpha
Neuter
Iota
Zeta

Proton
Boson
Atom
Electron
Neutron

TIME TAKEN:	INCORRECT ANSWERS:
TIME POINTS:	**TOTAL SCORE:**

Solutions

1: Balancing

The heaviest items are: 

2: Observation and Counting

10 enclosed areas.

9 rounded rectangles.

6 non-rounded rectangles or squares.

3: Speed Arithmetic

69 + 19 =	88	45 − 2 =	43	30 + 14 =	44
3 × 10 =	30	98 − 5 =	93	9 × 3 =	27
44 + 2 =	46	85 − 19 =	66	6 × 8 =	48
84 + 18 =	102	32 − 1 =	31	60 − 20 =	40
36 − 5 =	31	4 + 50 =	54	6 + 13 =	19
13 − 4 =	9	90 + 13 =	103	43 − 15 =	28
89 − 14 =	75	78 + 10 =	88	82 − 14 =	68
26 − 5 =	21	101 − 17 =	84	12 + 90 =	102
9 + 1 =	10	8 + 15 =	23	9 + 21 =	30
3 × 4 =	12	18 + 92 =	110	65 − 4 =	61
5 × 3 =	15	26 − 6 =	20	5 + 62 =	67
16 + 89 =	105	99 − 11 =	88	7 × 3 =	21
5 × 11 =	55	19 + 88 =	107	57 − 19 =	38

4: Shape Dividing

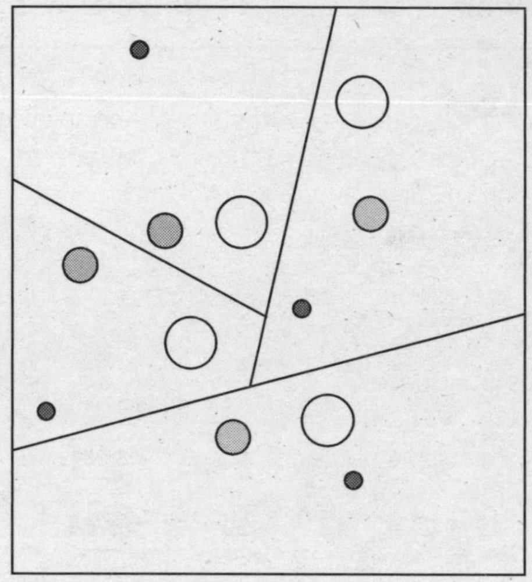

7: Logical Puzzlers

6 pens.

13 cards.

$3.

8: Reflective Power:

1C, 2B, 3B, 4C, 5C

9: Creative Thinking

I was buying numbers for the outside of my house. I bought a '4', a '7' and a '2'.

Somewhere beneath you is the ground, and somewhere in that ground is at least an inch of dirt. So every time you eat you're eating over at least an inch of dirt.

10: Time Elapsed

5:50am to 12:00pm =	**6:10**	7:45am to 6:10pm =	**10:25**
8:10am to 11:35am =	**3:25**	9:50am to 5:10pm =	**7:20**
1:00am to 12:30pm =	**11:30**	1:50am to 8:15pm =	**18:25**
5:25am to 6:20pm =	**12:55**	10:20am to 3:15pm =	**4:55**
6:55am to 7:15am =	**0:20**	6:25am to 2:50pm =	**8:25**
6:35am to 6:25pm =	**11:50**	5:40am to 4:40pm =	**11:00**
3:30am to 7:25pm =	**15:55**	12:05am to 2:20am =	**2:15**
5:10am to 5:20pm =	**12:10**	9:35am to 11:00pm =	**13:25**
6:00am to 6:30pm =	**12:30**	3:20pm to 8:30pm =	**5:10**
3:45am to 9:50am =	**6:05**	2:35am to 3:35am =	**1:00**
6:35am to 7:55am =	**1:20**	5:40am to 3:20pm =	**9:40**
7:30pm to 11:55pm =	**4:25**	6:35am to 8:25am =	**1:50**
4:40am to 11:15pm =	**18:35**	12:50am to 3:55pm =	**15:05**
4:30am to 2:05pm =	**9:35**	7:10am to 11:35pm =	**16:25**
11:35am to 9:40pm =	**10:05**	8:05pm to 9:10pm =	**1:05**

11: Shape Folding
a

13: Odd One Out
Air – not an Ancient Greek element
Italic – the rest all mean 'courageous'
Neuter – the rest are Greek letters
Atom – not a subatomic particle

DAY
9

Visual Memory

Spend 1 minute studying this path. Then cover the top half of this page and try to redraw it accurately on the empty grid below.

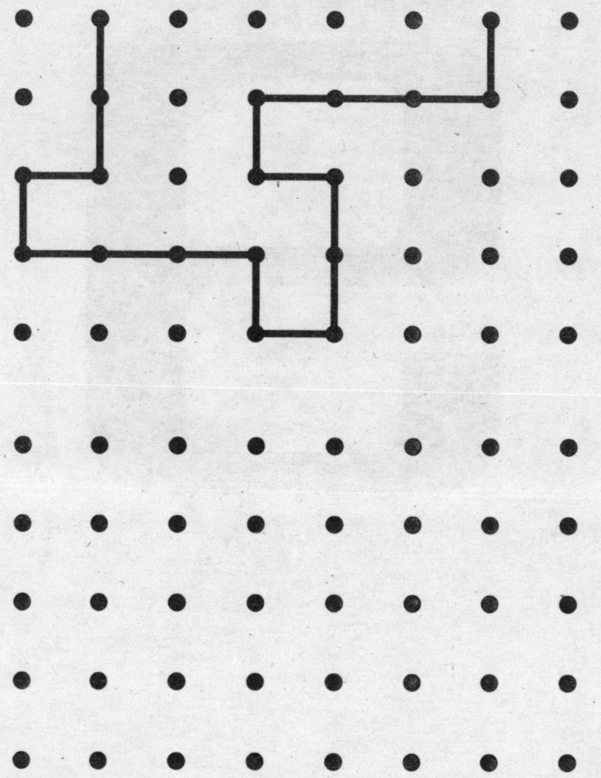

INCORRECT ANSWERS:	**TOTAL SCORE:**

Matchstick Thinking

The picture below shows 8 matchsticks arranged in the shape of a fish.

Can you move 2 matchsticks only in order to make the fish point in a different direction?

TIME TAKEN:	INCORRECT ANSWERS:
TIME POINTS:	**TOTAL SCORE:**

Missing Signs

Insert the missing sign into each of these arithmetic expressions in order to make the equation true. You will need to add, subtract, multiply, or divide.

5	☐	2	=	10	41	☐	22	=	19	30	☐	11	=	19
65	☐	16	=	49	7	☐	5	=	35	8	☐	95	=	103
101	☐	11	=	90	121	☐	11	=	11	2	☐	8	=	16
6	☐	3	=	18	75	☐	8	=	67	36	☐	4	=	9
10	☐	32	=	42	5	☐	110	=	115	5	☐	12	=	60
43	☐	28	=	71	54	☐	6	=	9	65	☐	7	=	72
11	☐	7	=	77	9	☐	6	=	54	59	☐	3	=	56
48	☐	8	=	6	41	☐	17	=	58	6	☐	10	=	60
62	☐	33	=	29	8	☐	5	=	40	5	☐	5	=	25
117	☐	9	=	13	28	☐	5	=	33	26	☐	38	=	64
6	☐	7	=	42	14	☐	2	=	7	40	☐	26	=	66
130	☐	10	=	13	137	☐	15	=	152	57	☐	14	=	43
33	☐	3	=	11	38	☐	133	=	171	19	☐	52	=	71

TIME TAKEN:	INCORRECT ANSWERS:
TIME POINTS:	**TOTAL SCORE:**

Counting and Perception

Spend no more than 10 seconds looking at each group of symbols in each turn, then try to sort them into order of increasing frequency. Write "1" in the "Order" column for the shape that occurs least often, and so on.

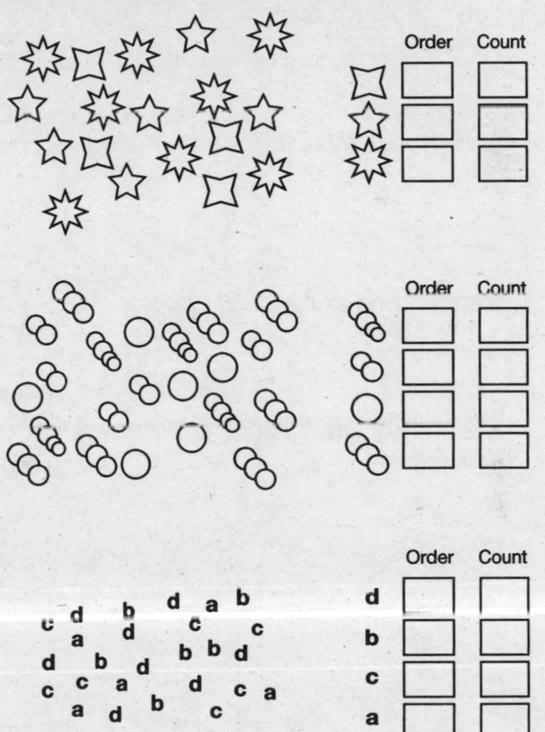

Now take as long as you think you need to write in the second column the precise count of each symbol.

TIME TAKEN:	INCORRECT ANSWERS:
TIME POINTS:	**TOTAL SCORE:**

Cryptogram

Decode each of these quotations by replacing A with Y, B with Z, C with A, and so on, through to replacing Y with W and Z with X.

Dygjgle rm njyl gq njyllgle rm dygj.

Cddgc Hmlcq

Dpgclbq ypc rfmqc pypc ncmnjc ufm yqi fmu uc ypc ylb rfcl uygr rm fcyp rfc ylqucp.

Cb Asllglefyk

G lctcp qyu y ncqqgkgqrga eclcpyj ugl y zyrrjc.

C C Askkgleq

Kmqr ncmnjc egtc sn hsqr ufcl rfcw'pc yzmsr rm yafgctc qsaacqq.

Pmqq Ncpmr

TIME TAKEN:	INCORRECT ANSWERS:
TIME POINTS:	**TOTAL SCORE:**

Ordered List

Can you memorize the order of these 24 volcanoes?

Spend 2 minutes studying the top list, then cover the table and look at the second list. Use the alphabetical labels to help recall the precise order of the words in the covered table.

Buleng	Hekla	Atitlan	Momotombo
Kilauea	Slamat	Tacana	Dukono
Izalco	Agung	Gede	Taal
Kaba	Bulusan	Pavlof	Osorno
Krakatoa	Vesuvius	Galeras	Trident
Vulcano	Llaima	Lascar	Bogoslof

Now try to recall the correct order below, by writing in the corresponding letters:

A Izalco	**B** Krakatoa	**C** Slamat	**D** Kaba
E Vulcano	**F** Momotombo	**G** Taal	**H** Vesuvius
I Hekla	**J** Osorno	**K** Atitlan	**L** Agung
M Dukono	**N** Trident	**O** Gede	**P** Bogoslof
Q Lascar	**R** Kilauea	**S** Pavlof	**T** Galeras
U Bulusan	**V** Tacana	**W** Llaima	**X** Buleng

INCORRECT ANSWERS:	TOTAL SCORE:

Creative Thinking

See if you can solve each of the following conundrums. If you get stuck then try thinking laterally – they all have logical solutions, but the logic might not be what you expect!

Time starts with a "t" and stops with an "s". Is this true? Are you sure?

There are four delicious-looking cakes in a cake box. How can you give one cake each to four different people whilst still keeping one cake in the box?

TIME TAKEN:	INCORRECT ANSWERS:
TIME POINTS:	**TOTAL SCORE:**

Observation and Counting

Look at these shapes and see how long it takes you to answer the observation questions below.

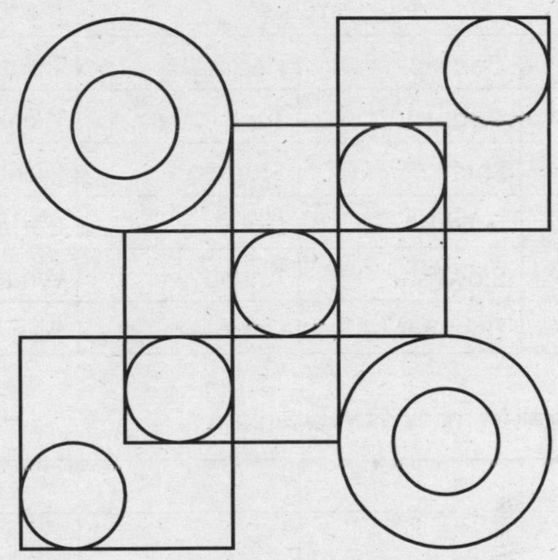

How many circles can you count?

How many squares can you count?

How many separate areas are there between the lines of the shapes?

TIME TAKEN:	INCORRECT ANSWERS:
TIME POINTS:	**TOTAL SCORE:**

Word List

Try to memorize these 24 types of fish.

After 2 minutes cover the table and write as many as you can in the boxes below. You do not need to remember the correct order.

Salmon	Cod	Herring	Trout
Perch	Turbot	Tuna	Weakfish
Skate	Sprat	Sturgeon	Pilchard
Guppy	Goldfish	Goby	Catfish
Dogfish	Blowfish	Anchovy	Whiting
Minnow	Flounder	Carp	Sole

Now try to recall as many as you can:

INCORRECT ANSWERS:	**TOTAL SCORE:**

Shape Folding

If you were to cut out this shape and fold it into a cube, which of the three pictures below would be the result?

a

b

c

TIME TAKEN:	INCORRECT ANSWERS:
TIME POINTS:	**TOTAL SCORE:**

Logical Puzzlers

Try to solve these problems – each requires only simple logic to solve, but you might find that making notes with a pencil will help!

In central France it is sunny every third day. If this is true, how many sunny days would there be in a leap year?

I use 50% of the remaining ink in my pen every day. How much ink will I have used after three days?

Katherine completes a cross-country race in precisely 2 hours, running at a constant speed. What distance of the 8 mile race will she have run half an hour after starting?

TIME TAKEN:	INCORRECT ANSWERS:
TIME POINTS:	**TOTAL SCORE:**

Missing Numbers

Insert the missing number into each of these arithmetic expressions in order to make the equations true. You should not need a calculator to do this!

□ − 17 = **5**	□ + 18 = **64**	73 − □ = **61**
46 − □ = **32**	□ + 15 = **102**	□ × 9 = **36**
□ − 7 = **42**	5 + □ = **9**	53 + □ = **69**
□ × 8 = **32**	18 + □ = **20**	□ + 10 = **87**
□ − 8 = **48**	□ + 34 = **38**	77 − □ = **64**
6 + □ = **36**	9 × □ = **81**	□ + 5 = **23**
□ + 57 = **75**	□ − 20 = **55**	□ − 1 = **37**
□ − 14 = **83**	3 + □ = **95**	81 − □ = **71**
□ + 8 = **68**	□ + 14 = **93**	89 − □ = **88**
2 × □ = **16**	14 + □ = **43**	3 × □ = **21**
62 − □ = **55**	□ − 20 = **10**	108 − □ = **92**
3 × □ = **27**	□ − 18 = **54**	□ − 9 = **47**
9 × □ = **108**	4 × □ = **20**	□ + 15 = **27**

TIME TAKEN:	INCORRECT ANSWERS:
TIME POINTS:	**TOTAL SCORE:**

Number Sequences

Look at each of these number sequences and see if you can deduce which number comes next in the series.

3	15	75	375	1875	
243	27	9	3	3	
3	9	27	81	243	
9	13	22	35	57	
174	108	66	42	24	
408	392	376	360	344	
178	149	124	103	86	
207	128	79	49	30	

TIME TAKEN:	INCORRECT ANSWERS:
TIME POINTS:	**TOTAL SCORE:**

Solutions

2: Matchstick Thinking

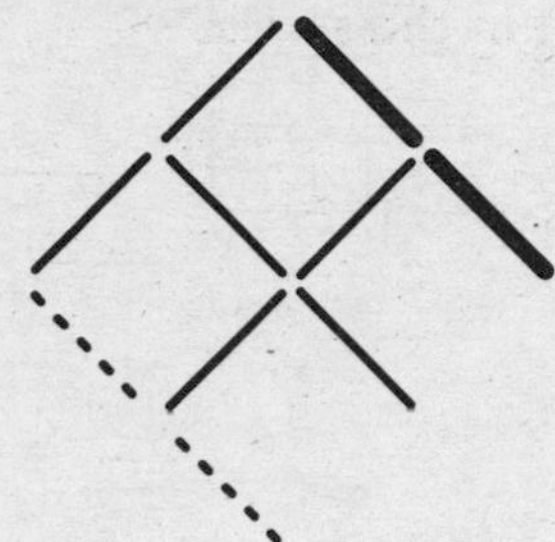

3: Missing Signs

5	×	2	=	10	41	−	22	=	19	30	−	11	=	19
65	−	16	=	49	7	×	5	=	35	8	+	95	=	103
101	−	11	=	90	121	÷	11	=	11	2	×	8	=	16
6	×	3	=	18	75	−	8	=	67	36	÷	4	=	9
10	+	32	=	42	5	+	110	=	115	5	×	12	=	60
43	+	28	=	71	54	÷	6	=	9	65	+	7	=	72
11	×	7	=	77	9	×	6	=	54	60	[illegible]	3	=	56
48	÷	8	=	6	41	+	17	=	58	6	×	10	=	60
62	−	33	=	29	8	×	5	=	40	5	×	5	=	25
117	÷	9	=	13	28	+	5	=	33	26	+	38	=	64
6	×	7	=	42	14	÷	2	=	7	40	+	26	=	66
130	÷	10	=	13	137	+	15	=	152	57	−	14	=	43
33	÷	3	=	11	38	+	133	=	171	19	+	52	=	71

4: Counting and Perception

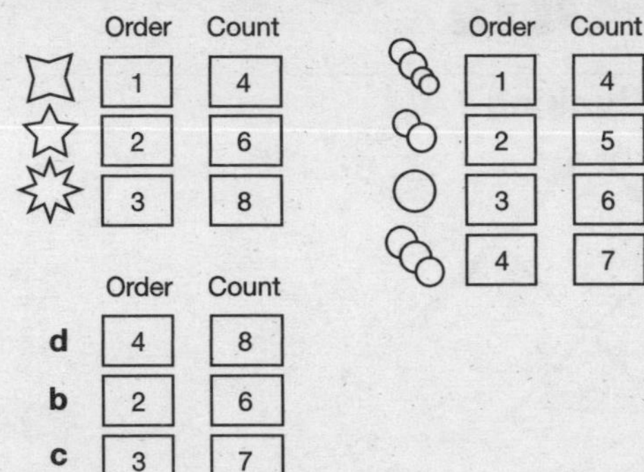

5: Cryptogram

Failing to plan is planning to fail. *Effie Jones*

Friends are those rare people who ask how we are and then wait to hear the answer. *Ed Cunningham*

I never saw a pessimistic general win a battle *E E Cummings*

Most people give up just when they're about to achieve success.

Ross Perot

6: Ordered List

X	I	K	F
R	C	V	M
A	L	O	G
D	U	S	J
B	H	T	N
E	W	Q	P

7: Creative Thinking

It is true, because stops does indeed start with an "s".

Just leave one of the cakes in the box, and hand over the cake in the box.

8: Observation and Counting

9 circles in total.

11 squares.

31 separate areas.

10: Shape Folding

c

11: Logical Puzzlers

122 days.

87.5% of the initial ink.

2 miles.

12: Missing Numbers

[22] − 17 = **5**	[46] + 18 = **64**	73 − [12] = **61**
46 − [14] = **32**	[87] + 15 = **102**	[4] × 9 = **36**
[49] − 7 = **42**	5 + [4] = **9**	53 + [16] = **69**
[4] × 8 = **32**	18 + [2] = **20**	[77] + 10 = **87**
[56] − 8 = **48**	[4] + 34 = **38**	77 − [13] = **64**
6 + [30] = **36**	9 × [9] = **81**	[18] + 5 = **23**
[18] + 57 = **75**	[75] − 20 = **55**	[38] − 1 = **37**
[97] − 14 = **83**	3 + [92] = **95**	81 − [10] = **71**
[60] + 8 = **68**	[79] + 14 = **93**	89 − [1] = **88**
2 × [8] = **16**	14 + [29] = **43**	3 × [7] = **21**
62 − [7] = **55**	[30] − 20 = **10**	108 − [16] = **92**
3 × [9] = **27**	[72] − 18 = **54**	[56] − 9 = **47**
9 × [12] = **108**	4 × [5] = **20**	[12] + 15 = **27**

13: Number Sequences
1944, 648, 216, 72, 24, **8**
Rule: divide previous number by 3

655, 651, 647, 643, 639, **635**
Rule: subtract 4 from previous number

129, 80, 49, 31, 18, **13**
Rule: subtract the previous number from the one before it

11, 41, 52, 93, 145, **238**
Rule: add the previous two numbers

410, 371, 338, 311, 290, **275**
Rule: difference between numbers decreases by 6 each time

483, 492, 511, 540, 579, **628**
Rule: difference between numbers increases by 10 each time

1115, 1031, 964, 914, 881, **865**
Rule: difference between numbers decreases by 17 each time

7, 14, 28, 56, 112, **224**
Rule: multiply previous number by 2

DAY
10

Reflective Power

Look at the three figures above the horizontal "mirror". Which of the figures below the line corresponds to the figure reflected in the mirror line?

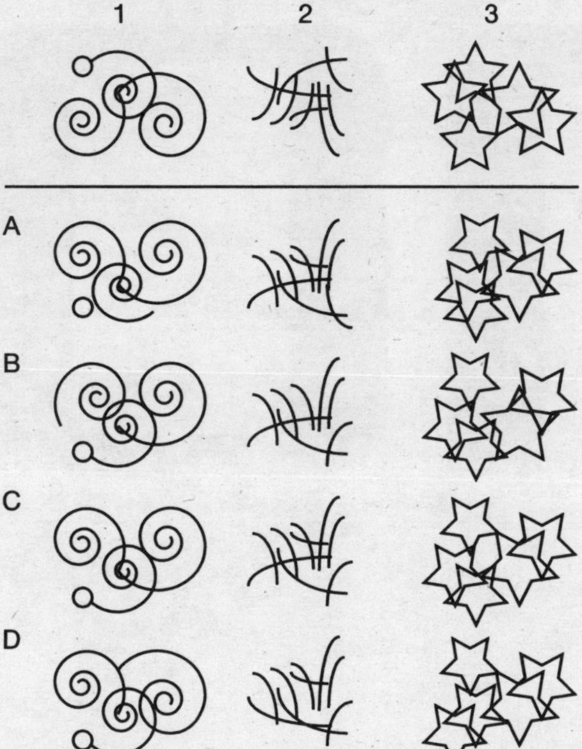

1 2 3

A

B

C

D

TIME TAKEN:	INCORRECT ANSWERS:
TIME POINTS:	**TOTAL SCORE:**

Odd One Out

Look at each of these sets of words. Can you work out which word is the odd one out in each case?

Malices Claimed
Medical
Decimal Maliced

Breeze Buzzer
Choose
Aardvark Radii

Serve Seers
Verse
Sever Veers

Crimson Scarlet
Ruby
Claret Sherry

TIME TAKEN:	INCORRECT ANSWERS:
TIME POINTS:	**TOTAL SCORE:**

Creative Thinking

See if you can solve each of the following conundrums. If you get stuck then try thinking laterally – they all have logical solutions, but the logic might not be what you expect!

If a group of penguins at the South Pole is dancing all July long, for approximately how many hours of daylight will the penguins dance in total?

How can I tie a knot in a handkerchief without letting go of it with either hand?

TIME TAKEN:	INCORRECT ANSWERS:
TIME POINTS:	**TOTAL SCORE:**

Visual Memory

Spend 1 minute studying this path. Then cover the top half of this page and try to redraw it accurately on the empty grid below.

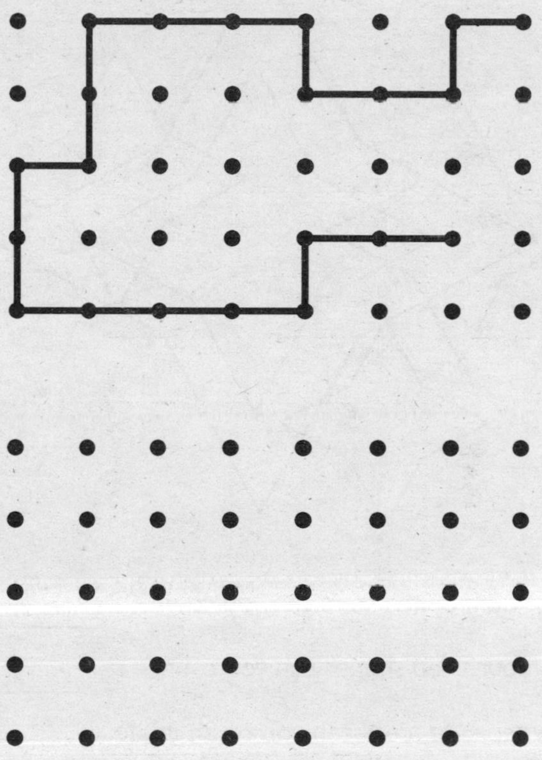

INCORRECT ANSWERS:	TOTAL SCORE:

Observation and Counting

Look at these overlapping stars and see how long it takes you to answer the observation questions below.

How many four-pointed stars can you count?

How many four-sided shapes can you count?

How many separate areas can you count inside the lines?

TIME TAKEN:	INCORRECT ANSWERS:
TIME POINTS:	**TOTAL SCORE:**

Time Elapsed

Work out how many hours and minutes have passed between each of these pairs of times.

3:10am to 4:15am =	:	5:20am to 7:40am =	:
3:20am to 7:05pm =	:	10:50am to 9:05pm =	:
1:30am to 2:05pm =	:	7:05pm to 10:55pm =	:
5:05am to 10:20am =	:	11:00am to 6:20pm =	:
4:25am to 1:10pm =	:	3:15am to 8:15pm =	:
9:50am to 8:05pm =	:	11:05am to 8:05pm =	:
10:20pm to 11:05pm =	:	9:55am to 10:30pm =	:
4:15pm to 4:20pm =	:	10:35am to 1:55pm =	:
2:55am to 7:20pm =	:	6:30am to 6:35pm =	:
5:35am to 8:35am =	:	12:35am to 10:50pm =	:
10:40am to 5:30pm =	:	12:40am to 12:10pm =	:
10:50am to 5:35pm =	:	12:45pm to 0:00pm =	:
11:55am to 2:45pm =	:	1:45am to 11:05pm =	:
12:55pm to 3:35pm =	:	7:10am to 11:40am =	:
9:40pm to 11:50pm =	:	4:35pm to 10:45pm =	:

TIME TAKEN:	INCORRECT ANSWERS:
TIME POINTS:	**TOTAL SCORE:**

Balancing

Looking at these two weighing scales. Can you say which of these three objects is the heaviest?

And which of these three objects is the heaviest?

TIME TAKEN:	INCORRECT ANSWERS:
TIME POINTS:	**TOTAL SCORE:**

Missing Words

Study each of these 3 lists of words for 2 minutes. Then cover the top half of the page and see if you can identify which word is missing from each list below.

Story	Tale	Fiction	Account
Report	Fact	Anecdote	Legend

Deposit	Place	Put	Stow
Jam	Stash	Store	Stack

Ash	Catkin	Birch	Cedar
Oak	Pecan	Acorn	Chestnut

Now try to spot the missing word from each list:

Anecdote, Story, Legend, Fiction, Fact, Account, Report

MISSING:

Jam, Stash, Deposit, Stack, Place, Put, Store

MISSING:

Acorn, Catkin, Birch, Chestnut, Cedar, Pecan, Oak

MISSING:

INCORRECT ANSWERS:	**TOTAL SCORE:**

Logical Puzzlers

Try to solve these problems – each requires only simple logic to solve, but you might find that making notes with a pencil will help!

It's a reasonable 70°F in London, but over in New York City it's 84°F, and tomorrow it will be 3°F warmer again. By how many degrees F will it be hotter in New York tomorrow?

Simone has just run a 3-mile circuit in half an hour. What was her average speed, in miles per hour?

The London freight train leaves Cambridge station at 3pm, travelling at an average of 60mph (miles per hour). The express train on the same route leaves at 3:15pm but travels at 100mph. Which is closer to London at 3:30pm?

TIME TAKEN:	INCORRECT ANSWERS:
TIME POINTS:	**TOTAL SCORE:**

Shape Dividing

Draw three straight lines in order to divide the shape into four separate areas. Each area must contain precisely one of each size of circle. The three lines may touch but they must not cross.

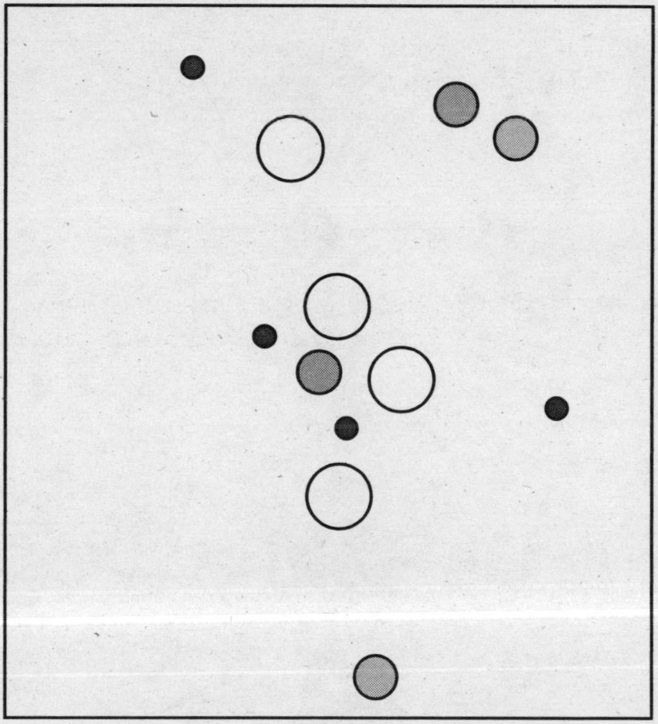

TIME TAKEN:	INCORRECT ANSWERS:
TIME POINTS:	**TOTAL SCORE:**

Rotation

If you were to rotate each of these three pictures as indicated by the arrow beneath, which of the figures below would be the result?

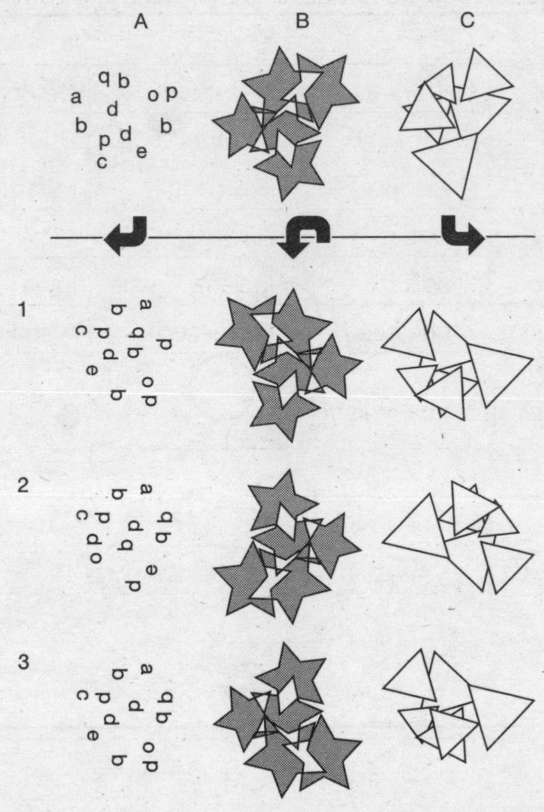

TIME TAKEN:	INCORRECT ANSWERS:
TIME POINTS:	**TOTAL SCORE:**

Word List

Try to memorize these 24 US states.

After 2 minutes, cover the table and recall as many as you can in the boxes below. You do not need to remember the correct order.

Minnesota	Delaware	New York	Oregon
Oklahoma	Texas	Arizona	Utah
California	Wisconsin	Wyoming	Missouri
New Jersey	Nevada	Hawaii	Alaska
Florida	Illinois	Indiana	Iowa
Washington	Tennessee	Connecticut	Alabama

Now try to recall as many as you can:

INCORRECT ANSWERS:	TOTAL SCORE:

Speed Arithmetic

Complete the following set of arithmetic equations as quickly as possible. You should be able to do them all in your head without using a calculator or making notes.

31 − 9 =	71 + 9 =	37 + 3 =
90 + 3 =	87 − 13 =	8 + 15 =
63 − 17 =	1 + 60 =	3 + 84 =
17 + 30 =	20 − 9 =	107 − 5 =
15 + 73 =	7 − 2 =	15 + 34 =
102 − 6 =	44 + 15 =	35 − 15 =
68 − 13 =	8 × 9 =	6 × 5 =
64 + 11 =	66 − 19 =	5 × 2 =
18 − 14 =	68 − 19 =	73 + 15 =
74 − 17 =	6 + 73 =	54 − 20 =
12 × 5 =	105 − 8 =	17 + 8 =
39 + 13 =	5 × 7 =	9 × 7 =
104 − 1 =	13 + 1 =	67 + 5 =

TIME TAKEN:	INCORRECT ANSWERS:
TIME POINTS:	**TOTAL SCORE:**

Solutions

1: Reflective Power

1C, 2C, 3C

2: Odd One Out

Malices – the rest are anagrams of each other
Buzzer – the rest have double vowels
Seers – the rest are anagrams of each other
Sherry – the rest are red in colour

3: Creative Thinking

During July at the south pole there is only night, so they dance for zero hours of daylight!

Cross your arms before grabbing hold of two corners and then uncrossing your arms.

5: Observation and Counting

5 four-pointed stars in total.

2 four-sided shapes.

14 separate areas.

6: Time Elapsed

3:10am to 4:15am =	**1:05**	5:20am to 7:40am =	**2:20**
3:20am to 7:05pm =	**15:45**	10:50am to 9:05pm =	**10:15**
1:30am to 2:05pm =	**12:35**	7:05pm to 10:55pm =	**3:50**
5:05am to 10:20am =	**5:15**	11:00am to 6:20pm =	**7:20**
4:25am to 1:10pm =	**8:45**	3:15am to 8:15pm =	**17:00**
9:50am to 8:05pm =	**10:15**	11:05am to 8:05pm =	**9:00**
10:20pm to 11:05pm =	**0:45**	9:55am to 10:30pm =	**12:35**
4:15pm to 4:20pm =	**0:05**	10:35am to 1:55pm =	**3:20**
2:55am to 7:20pm =	**16:25**	6:30am to 6:35pm =	**12:05**
5:35am to 8:35am =	**3:00**	12:35am to 10:50pm =	**22:15**
10:40am to 5:30pm =	**6:50**	12:40am to 12:10pm =	**11:30**
10:50am to 5:35pm =	**6:45**	12:45pm to 6:00pm =	**5:15**
11:55am to 2:45pm =	**2:50**	1:45am to 11:05pm =	**21:20**
12:55pm to 3:35pm =	**2:40**	7:10am to 11:40am =	**4:30**
9:40pm to 11:50pm =	**2:10**	4:35pm to 10:45pm =	**6:10**

7: Balancing

The heaviest items are:

9: Logical Puzzlers

17°F.

6mph.

The goods train, which has travelled 30 miles compared to the express train's 25 miles.

10: Shape Dividing

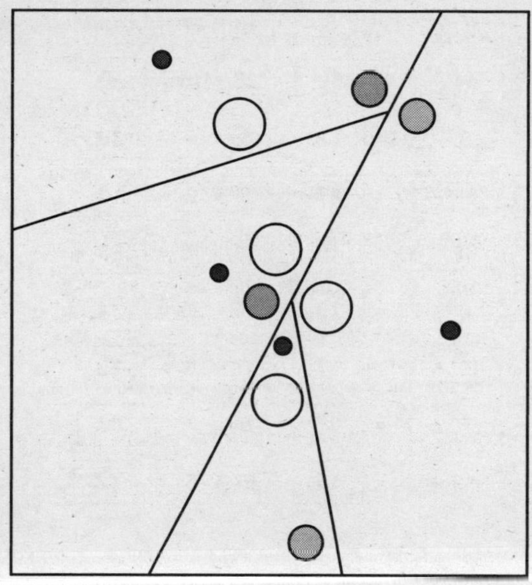

11: Rotation

A3, B2, C1

13: Speed Arithmetic

31 − 9 = **22**	71 + 9 = **80**	37 + 3 = **40**
90 + 3 = **93**	87 − 13 = **74**	8 + 15 = **23**
63 − 17 = **46**	1 + 60 = **61**	3 + 84 = **87**
17 + 30 = **47**	20 − 9 = **11**	107 − 5 = **102**
15 + 73 = **88**	7 − 2 = **5**	15 + 34 = **49**
102 − 6 = **96**	44 + 15 = **59**	35 − 15 = **20**
68 − 13 = **55**	8 × 9 = **72**	6 × 5 = **30**
64 + 11 = **75**	66 − 19 = **47**	5 × 2 = **10**
18 − 14 = **4**	68 − 19 = **49**	73 + 15 = **88**
74 − 17 = **57**	6 + 73 = **79**	54 − 20 = **34**
12 × 5 = **60**	105 − 8 = **97**	17 + 8 = **25**
39 + 13 = **52**	5 × 7 = **35**	9 × 7 = **63**
104 − 1 = **103**	13 + 1 = **14**	67 + 5 = **72**

DAY
11

Counting and Perception

Spend no more than 10 seconds looking at each group of symbols in each turn, then try to sort them into order of increasing frequency. Write "1" in the "Order" column for the shape that occurs least often, and so on.

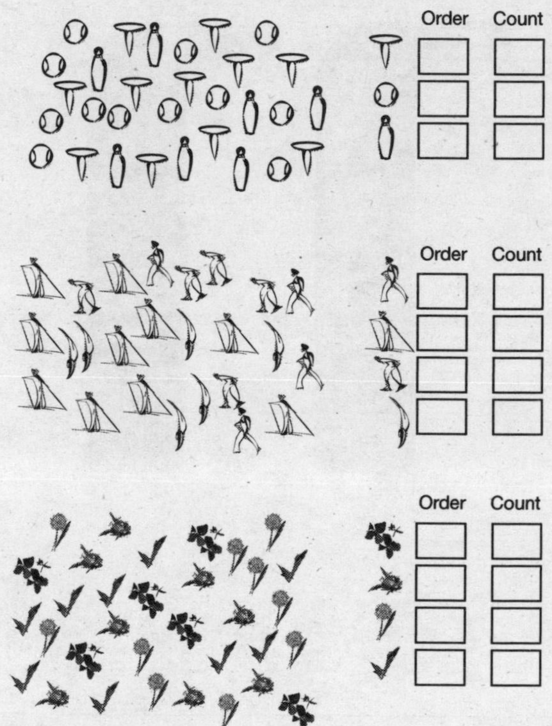

Now take as long as you think you need to write in the second column the precise count of each symbol.

TIME TAKEN:	INCORRECT ANSWERS:
TIME POINTS:	**TOTAL SCORE:**

Missing Words

Study each of these 3 lists of words for 2 minutes. Then cover the top half of the page and see if you can identify which word is missing from each list below.

Aeroplane	Car	Bus	Train
Boat	Tram	Monorail	Coach

Happy	Sad	Smiley	Frowning
Glad	Unhappy	Laughing	Crying

Now	Immediately	Later	Soon
Tomorrow	Yesterday	Slowly	Directly

Now try to spot the missing word from each list:

Tram, Car, Monorail, Coach, Bus, Train, Aeroplane

MISSING:

Frowning, Sad, Crying, Laughing, Happy, Smiley, Unhappy

MISSING:

Yesterday, Now, Directly, Tomorrow, Immediately, Later, Slowly

MISSING:

INCORRECT ANSWERS:	TOTAL SCORE:

Missing Numbers

Insert the missing number into each of these arithmetic expressions in order to make the equations true. You should not need a calculator to do this!

9 × ☐ = **81**	108 − ☐ = **90**	12 × ☐ = **144**
☐ + 23 = **27**	☐ + 13 = **76**	9 + ☐ = **43**
☐ − 5 = **18**	9 × ☐ = **72**	☐ × 4 = **36**
☐ − 11 = **22**	3 × ☐ = **15**	89 − ☐ = **70**
☐ + 16 = **105**	12 + ☐ = **24**	☐ × 7 = **77**
24 + ☐ = **28**	74 + ☐ = **85**	☐ + 4 = **22**
☐ × 5 = **55**	☐ + 66 = **75**	☐ − 4 = **30**
70 − ☐ = **50**	☐ − 19 = **78**	11 × ☐ = **44**
51 − ☐ = **37**	☐ + 87 = **101**	7 × ☐ = **14**
3 × ☐ = **36**	☐ + 79 = **87**	96 − ☐ = **76**
45 + ☐ = **47**	10 − ☐ = **1**	☐ − 1 = **51**
☐ − 17 = **84**	62 − ☐ = **42**	8 + ☐ = **51**
12 + ☐ = **50**	68 + ☐ = **80**	69 − ☐ = **65**

TIME TAKEN:	INCORRECT ANSWERS:
TIME POINTS:	**TOTAL SCORE:**

Logical Puzzlers

Try to solve these problems – each requires only simple logic to solve, but you might find that making notes with a pencil will help!

If you add up each of the digits in the number 13,579 what is the result?

San Diego Zoo has six Galapagos Island turtles. Assuming no outside intervention, if a female turtle is capable of laying no more than 3 eggs per year, what is the maximum number of eggs that the turtles can lay in total in a single year?

If a tomato has a 75% chance of ripening, and a seed has a 50% chance of growing, how many ripe tomatoes can I expect from 100 seeds, assuming there are 60 tomatoes per plant?

TIME TAKEN:	INCORRECT ANSWERS:
TIME POINTS:	**TOTAL SCORE:**

Observation and Counting

Look at these overlapping circles and see how long it takes you to answer the observation questions below.

How many circles make up this illustration?

Can you draw the entire figure without taking your pen off the paper or going over any line twice? You may cross over an existing line, however.

How many separate areas are formed by thes shapes?

TIME TAKEN:	INCORRECT ANSWERS:
TIME POINTS:	**TOTAL SCORE:**

Number Sequences

Look at each of these number sequences and see if you can deduce which number comes next in the series.

993	966	944	927	915	
379	229	150	79	71	
348	311	279	252	230	
194	176	158	140	122	
789	694	599	504	409	
725	693	667	647	633	
329	198	131	67	64	
447	434	421	408	395	

TIME TAKEN:	INCORRECT ANSWERS:
TIME POINTS:	**TOTAL SCORE:**

Reflective Power

Look at the three figures above the horizontal "mirror". Which of the figures below the line corresponds to the figure reflected in the mirror line?

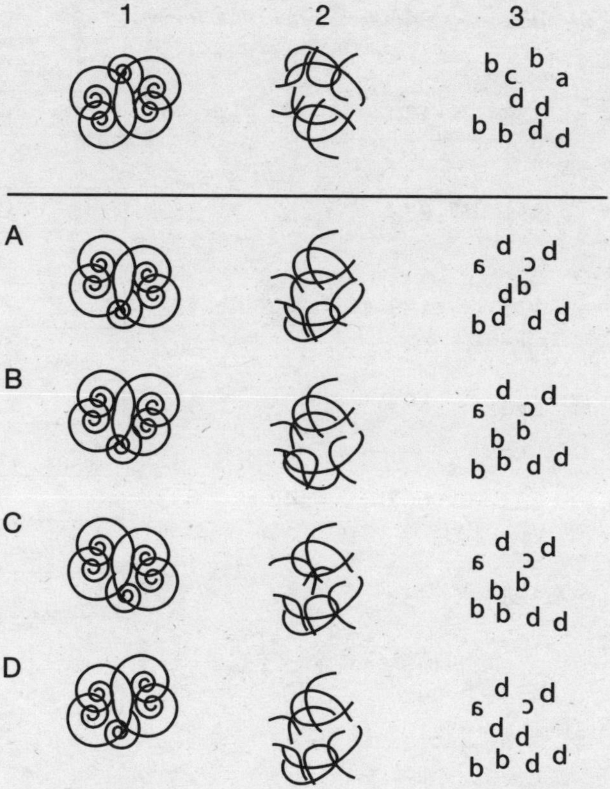

1 2 3

A

B

C

D

TIME TAKEN:	INCORRECT ANSWERS:
TIME POINTS:	**TOTAL SCORE:**

Visual Memory

Spend 1 minute studying this path. Then cover the top half of the page and try to redraw it accurately on the empty grid below.

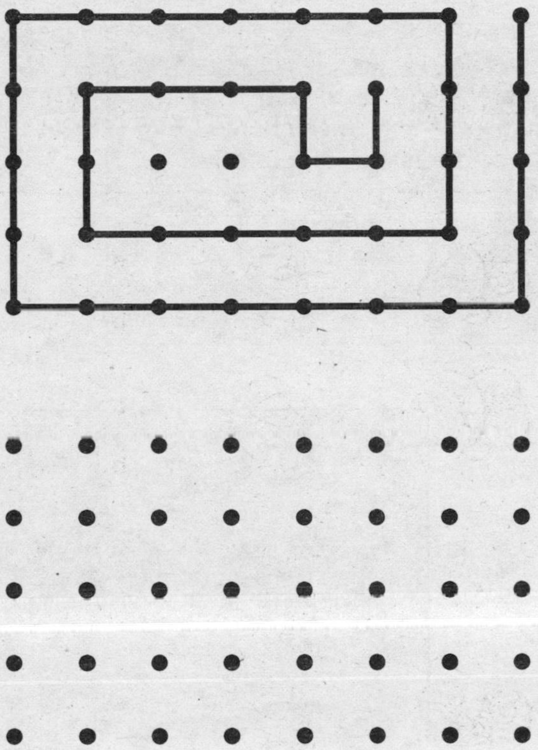

INCORRECT ANSWERS:	**TOTAL SCORE:**

Creative Thinking

See if you can solve each of the following conundrums. If you get stuck then try thinking laterally – they all have logical solutions, but the logic might not be what you expect!

A proud father gave his son a pair of engraved pens, and a different proud father gave his son a set of four pens. Yet there were only four pens in total between both sons – how can this be true?

In coin collecting, why are 1996 British pound coins worth more than 1987 British pound coins?

TIME TAKEN:	INCORRECT ANSWERS:
TIME POINTS:	**TOTAL SCORE:**

DAY: 11	WORKOUT: 10	CONCENTRATION

Time Elapsed

Work out how many hours and minutes have passed between each of these pairs of times.

3:05am to 7:40am =	:	1:20am to 2:15am =	:
10:20pm to 10:40pm =	:	1:15pm to 2:55pm =	:
5:35am to 3:00pm =	:	12:25am to 4:15am =	:
10:55am to 6:00pm =	:	2:45am to 6:30pm =	:
3:25pm to 10:55pm =	:	10:55am to 10:10pm =	:
1:45pm to 11:15pm =	:	10:50pm to 11:20pm =	:
3:15pm to 8:30pm =	:	8:15am to 9:40am =	:
2:40am to 5:15am =	:	8:35am to 8:45am =	:
12:10am to 1:40pm =	:	5:45pm to 5:50pm =	:
11:05am to 12:05pm =	:	8:35am to 10:15pm =	:
4:10pm to 6:35pm =	:	6:05am to 11:10am =	:
12:05pm to 6:35pm =	:	6:20pm to 9:00pm =	:
7:15pm to 10:05pm =	:	3:05am to 9:05am =	:
12:30am to 9:25am =	:	3:55am to 3:10pm =	:
12:15am to 4:00am =	:	10:25am to 1:55pm =	:

TIME TAKEN:	INCORRECT ANSWERS:
TIME POINTS:	**TOTAL SCORE:**

Anagrammatic

Look at each of these sets of 12 words. How many pairs of anagrams can you spot in each set, and what are they?

UMPIRING	LISTENER	SKEINING
PRUDENCE	SITUATES	SILENTER
MALADIES	EMBRACES	COMEDIES
ELECTION	BOOKINGS	BLASTOFF

SUMMER	PANTED	STRAPS
FLOATS	TENTED	RULING
RULERS	PEDANT	NETTED
MONKEY	THEIST	LURING

FILLER	COALED	REFILL
DURESS	RISKED	THREES
INSERT	IRONED	DRONES
LIABLE	SNORED	INTERS

SOLOED	OODLES	GRUDGE
SIDLES	SLIDES	PHASES
PALLED	RESCUE	SECURE
RUGGED	SHAPES	NICETY

TIME TAKEN:	INCORRECT ANSWERS:
TIME POINTS:	**TOTAL SCORE:**

Matchstick Thinking

The picture below shows 12 matchsticks arranged into 1 large and 4 small squares.

Can you move 3 matchsticks only in order to leave precisely 3 squares? You must not make any extra squares, or leave any spare matches that are not part of one of the 3 squares. You may not remove any matches.

TIME TAKEN:	INCORRECT ANSWERS:
TIME POINTS:	**TOTAL SCORE:**

Word List

Try to memorize these 24 constellations.

After 2 minutes, cover the table and recall as many as you can in the boxes below. You do not need to remember the correct order.

Orion	Sagittarius	Taurus	Scorpius
Cancer	Columba	Gemini	Lyra
Pyxis	Ursa major	Virgo	Aquarius
Aries	Aquila	Andromeda	Draco
Crux	Cepheus	Perseus	Pisces
Ursa minor	Sextans	Volans	Crater

Now try to recall as many as you can:

INCORRECT ANSWERS:	**TOTAL SCORE:**

Solutions

1: Counting and Perception

Order	Count
2	11
3	12
1	7

Order	Count
1	4
4	10
2	5
3	6

Order	Count
1	6
2	8
4	10
3	9

3: Missing Numbers

9 × 9 = **81**	108 − 18 = **90**	12 × 12 = **144**
4 + 23 = **27**	63 + 13 = **76**	9 + 34 = **43**
23 − 5 = **18**	9 × 8 = **72**	9 × 4 = **36**
33 − 11 = **22**	3 × 5 = **15**	89 − 19 = **70**
89 + 16 = **105**	12 + 12 = **24**	11 × 7 = **77**
24 + 4 = **28**	74 + 11 = **85**	18 + 4 = **22**
11 × 5 = **55**	9 + 66 = **75**	34 − 4 = **30**
70 − 20 = **50**	97 − 19 = **78**	11 × 4 = **44**
51 − 14 = **37**	14 + 87 = **101**	7 × 2 = **14**
3 × 12 = **36**	8 + 79 = **87**	96 − 20 = **76**
45 + 2 = **47**	10 − 9 = **1**	52 − 1 = **51**
101 − 17 = **84**	62 − 20 = **42**	8 + 43 = **51**
12 + 38 = **50**	68 + 12 = **80**	69 − 4 = **65**

4: Logical Puzzlers
25.

15 eggs, assuming 5 females and 1 male.

2,250 ripe tomatoes, based on 45 ripe tomatoes per plant and 50 plants.

5: Observation and Counting
9 circles in total.

Yes, you can draw it in a single stroke.

19 separate areas.

6: Number Sequences
110, 129, 154, 185, 222, **265**
Rule: difference between numbers increases by 6 each time

493, 505, 517, 529, 541, **553**
Rule: add 12 to previous number

17, 39, 56, 95, 151, **246**
Rule: add the previous two numbers

79, 48, 31, 17, 14, **3**
Rule: subtract the previous number from the one before it

335, 347, 369, 401, 443, **495**
Rule: difference between numbers increases by 10 each time

3, 3, 6, 18, 72, **360**
Rule: multiply by 1, 2, 3 etc – multiplier increases by 1 each time

493, 497, 513, 541, 581, **633**
Rule: difference between numbers increases by 12 each time

4, 25, 29, 54, 83, **137**
Rule: add the previous two numbers

7: Reflective Power
1A, 2D, 3B

9: Creative Thinking

One of the fathers was the son of the other father, so he just passed on the pens his own father gave him.

There are 9 more coins so they're bound to be worth more!

10: Time Elapsed

3:05am to 7:40am =	**4:35**	1:20am to 2:15am =	**0:55**
10:20pm to 10:40pm =	**0:20**	1:15pm to 2:55pm =	**1:40**
5:35am to 3:00pm =	**9:25**	12:25am to 4:15am =	**3:50**
10:55am to 6:00pm =	**7:05**	2:45am to 6:30pm =	**15:45**
3:25pm to 10:55pm =	**7:30**	10:55am to 10:10pm =	**11:15**
1:45pm to 11:15pm =	**9:30**	10:50pm to 11:20pm =	**0:30**
3:15pm to 8:30pm =	**5:15**	8:15am to 9:40am =	**1:25**
2:40am to 5:15am =	**2:35**	8:35am to 8:45am =	**0:10**
12:10am to 1:40pm =	**13:30**	5:45pm to 5:50pm =	**0:05**
11:05am to 12:05pm =	**1:00**	8:35am to 10:15pm =	**13:40**
4:10pm to 6:35pm =	**2:25**	6:05am to 11:10am =	**5:05**
12:05pm to 6:35pm =	**6:30**	6:20pm to 9:00pm =	**2:40**
7:15pm to 10:05pm =	**2:50**	3:05am to 9:05am =	**6:00**
12:30am to 9:25am =	**8:55**	3:55am to 3:10pm =	**11:15**
12:15am to 4:00am =	**3:45**	10:25am to 1:55pm =	**3:30**

11: Anagrammatic

Set 1: 3 pairs of anagrams:
PROUDEST and SPROUTED
PERTAINS and PAINTERS
LATRINES and ENTRAILS

Set 2: 4 pairs of anagrams:
DEVISE and SIEVED
LATHES and HALEST
ARIDER and RAIDER
PLIERS and PERILS

Set 3: 5 pairs of anagrams:
NAMELESS and SALESMEN
ROCKIEST and STOCKIER
CRUISERS and SCURRIES
WOODLAND and DOWNLOAD
REBUTTED and BUTTERED

Set 4: 4 pairs of anagrams:
TRADED and DARTED
CARESS and SCARES
REPAID and DIAPER
BASTES and BEASTS

12: Matchstick Thinking

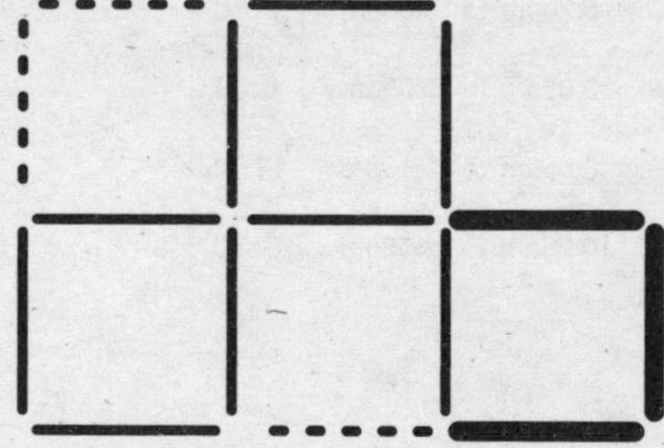

DAY
12

Missing Numbers

Insert the missing number into each of these arithmetic expressions in order to make the equations true. You should not need a calculator to do this!

3 × ☐ = **21**	☐ × 9 = **63**	70 − ☐ = **60**
99 − ☐ = **91**	11 × ☐ = **66**	☐ × 12 = **72**
☐ × 7 = **63**	88 − ☐ = **68**	6 + ☐ = **100**
☐ − 10 = **46**	☐ − 3 = **99**	☐ × 7 = **70**
☐ − 10 = **1**	☐ + 13 = **19**	16 − ☐ = **11**
☐ − 10 = **24**	☐ − 4 = **75**	☐ − 5 = **88**
☐ + 39 = **56**	12 + ☐ = **32**	☐ − 16 = **75**
☐ − 14 = **54**	107 − ☐ = **95**	79 + ☐ = **88**
31 − ☐ = **19**	74 − ☐ = **73**	☐ − 16 = **11**
☐ × 10 = **100**	☐ − 13 = **84**	☐ × 4 = **12**
12 + ☐ = **24**	3 + ☐ = **6**	☐ + 9 = **72**
3 × ☐ = **15**	☐ × 8 = **88**	☐ − 19 = **67**
9 × ☐ = **81**	☐ − 3 = **54**	☐ + 86 = **106**

TIME TAKEN:	INCORRECT ANSWERS:
TIME POINTS:	**TOTAL SCORE:**

Rotation

If you were to rotate each of these three pictures as indicated by the arrow beneath, which of the figures below would be the result?

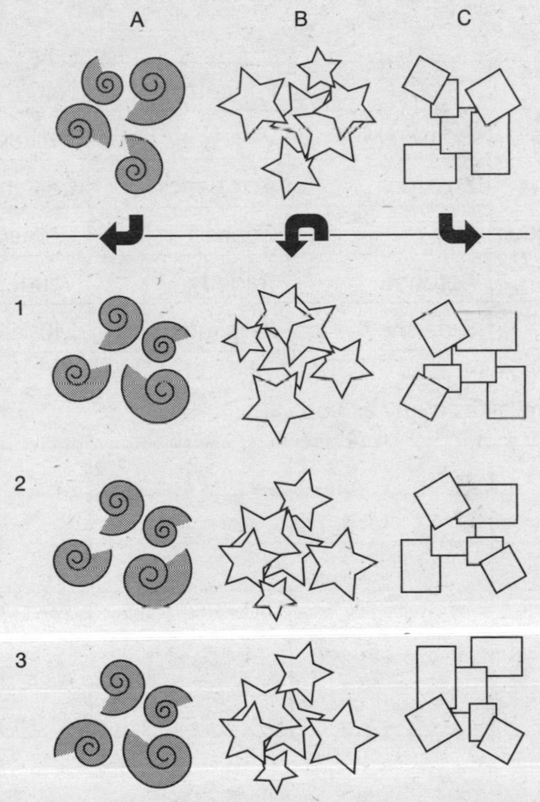

TIME TAKEN:	INCORRECT ANSWERS:
TIME POINTS:	**TOTAL SCORE:**

Word List

Try to memorize these 24 entertainment events.

After 2 minutes, cover the table and recall as many as you can in the boxes below. You do not need to remember the correct order.

Gig	Karaoke	Puppetry	Fair
Rave	Sideshow	Variety	Recital
Party	Busking	Acrobatics	Ceilidh
Fashion Show	Play	Concert	Comedy
Conjuring	Aerobatics	Tragedy	Vaudeville
Rodeo	Slide show	Juggling	Musical

Now try to recall as many as you can:

INCORRECT ANSWERS:	**TOTAL SCORE:**

Creative Thinking

See if you can solve each of the following conundrums. If you get stuck then try thinking laterally – they all have logical solutions, but the logic might not be what you expect!

My pet gerbil has got stuck in a hole in the ground, and I can't reach in to get it out. Can you think of a simple and safe way to get it out without hurting it?

If I pick up a ball and mark any three points on it at random, what is the likelihood that all three points are on the same half of the ball?

TIME TAKEN:	INCORRECT ANSWERS:
TIME POINTS:	**TOTAL SCORE:**

Logical Puzzlers

Try to solve these problems – each requires only simple logic to solve, but you might find that making notes with a pencil will help!

I buy 16 apples, but unfortunately half are insect-damaged and a quarter are bruised. Given what I have just told you, what is the maximum number of good apples I have?

On Tuesdays I work from 9am for 4 hours, then have a 1-hour break for lunch. I then work another 4 hours and drive for an hour to get home. What time do I get home?

If I walk at 2.5 mph (miles per hour) for half an hour, how far have I travelled?

TIME TAKEN:	INCORRECT ANSWERS:
TIME POINTS:	**TOTAL SCORE:**

Counting and Perception

Spend no more than 10 seconds looking at each group of symbols in each turn, then try to sort them into order of increasing frequency. Write "1" in the "Order" column for the shape that occurs least often, and so on.

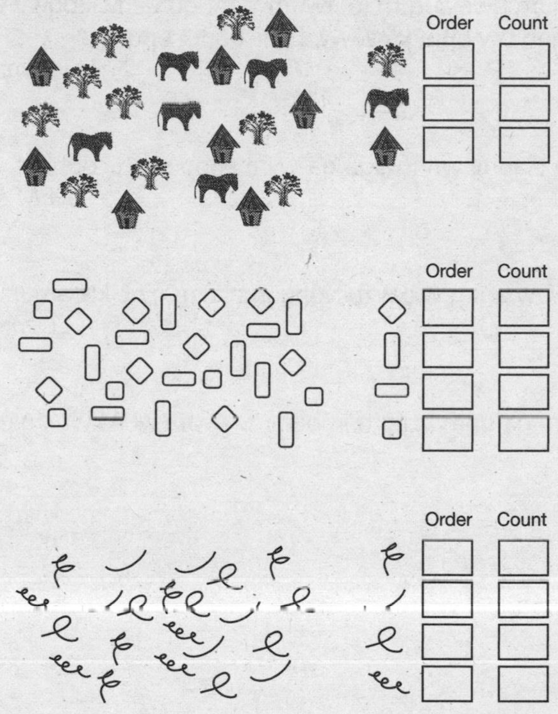

Now take as long as you think you need to write in the second column the precise count of each symbol.

TIME TAKEN:	INCORRECT ANSWERS:
TIME POINTS:	**TOTAL SCORE:**

Cryptogram

Decode each of these quotations by replacing A with I, B with J, C with K and so on, through to replacing Y with G and Z with H.

Mdmzg bqum gwc auqtm ib awumwvm, qb qa iv ikbqwv wn twdm, i oqnb bw bpib xmzawv, i jmicbqnct bpqvo.

Uwbpmz Bmzmai

Bpm uwab eiabml wn itt liga qa wvm eqbpwcb ticopbmz.

M M Kcuuqvoa

Gwc pidm bw amm wxxwzbcvqbg jmnwzm gwc kiv amqhm qb.

Ozmo Pqksuiv

Lqakqxtqvm qa bpm jzqlom jmbemmv owita ivl ikkwuxtqapumvb.

Rqu Zwpv

TIME TAKEN:	INCORRECT ANSWERS:
TIME POINTS:	**TOTAL SCORE:**

Speed Arithmetic

Complete the following set of arithmetic equations as quickly as possible. You should be able to do them all in your head without using a calculator or making notes.

11 × 2 =	4 × 6 =	57 − 16 =
70 − 14 =	9 × 7 =	73 − 16 =
6 × 4 =	10 + 65 =	44 − 9 =
46 − 20 =	50 + 12 =	17 − 16 =
10 × 10 =	2 + 95 =	21 + 4 =
71 − 16 =	32 + 13 =	41 − 6 =
47 − 3 =	84 − 18 =	77 + 3 =
3 × 8 =	3 × 9 =	27 + 11 =
6 + 93 =	6 × 3 =	12 + 4 =
46 + 11 =	8 + 30 =	106 − 1 =
3 + 81 =	67 − 17 =	12 × 9 =
100 + 12 =	29 − 5 =	95 − 16 =
27 − 3 =	11 + 4 =	108 − 9 =

TIME TAKEN:	INCORRECT ANSWERS:
TIME POINTS:	**TOTAL SCORE:**

Visual Memory

Spend 1 minute studying this path. Then cover the top half of this page and try to redraw it accurately on the empty grid below.

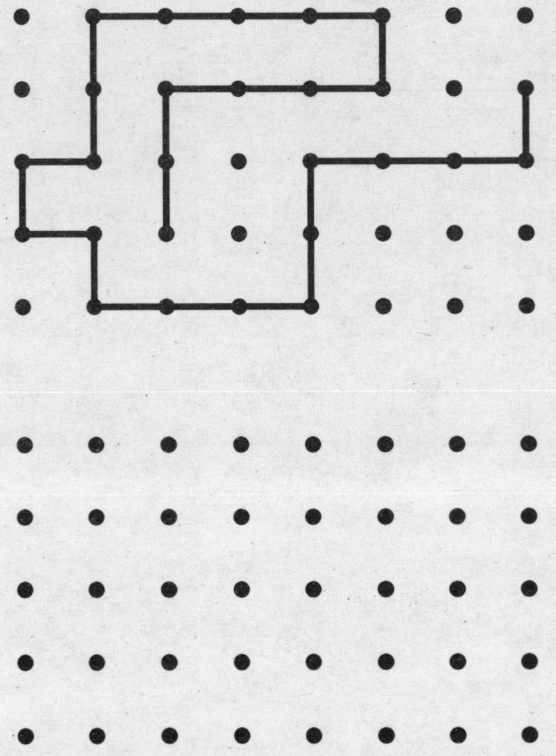

INCORRECT ANSWERS:	TOTAL SCORE:

Shape Dividing

Draw three straight lines in order to divide the shape into four separate areas. Each area must contain precisely one of each size of circle. The three lines may touch but they must not cross.

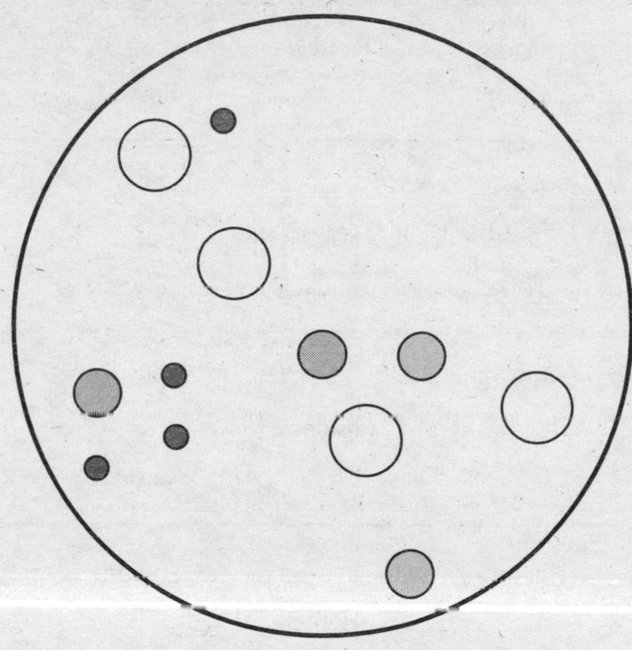

TIME TAKEN:	INCORRECT ANSWERS:
TIME POINTS:	**TOTAL SCORE:**

Odd One Out

Look at each of these sets of words. Can you work out which word is the odd one out in each case?

Reader Reread
Readier
Dearer Reared

Dazzle Glow
Polish
Flicker Blaze

Inserted Detrains
Resident
Trendies Nerdiest

Humphrey Edward
Henry
William James

TIME TAKEN:	INCORRECT ANSWERS:
TIME POINTS:	**TOTAL SCORE:**

Observation and Counting

Look at these squares and rectangles and see how long it takes you to answer these observation questions.

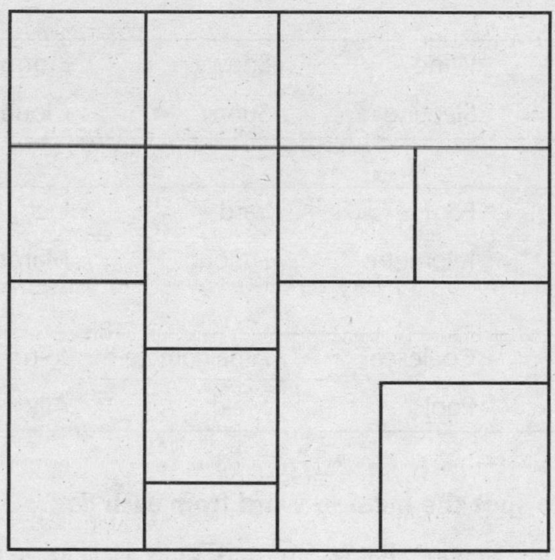

How many squares can you count?

How many rectangles, excluding squares, can you count?

TIME TAKEN:	INCORRECT ANSWERS:
TIME POINTS:	**TOTAL SCORE:**

Missing Words

Study each of these 3 lists of words for a total of 2 minutes. Then cover the top half of the page and see if you can identify which word is missing from each list below.

Rainy	Windy	Snowy	Stormy
Hailing	Sleeting	Sunny	Cloudy

Metre	Foot	Yard	Inch
Mile	Kilometre	Furlong	Marathon

Blend	Coalesce	Amalgamate	Join
Combine	Pool	Meld	Ally

Now try to spot the missing word from each list:

Sunny, Windy, Sleeting, Rainy, Stormy, Cloudy, Hailing

MISSING:

Furlong, Foot, Inch, Metre, Kilometre, Yard, Marathon

MISSING:

Ally, Combine, Pool, Coalesce, Meld, Join, Blend

MISSING:

INCORRECT ANSWERS:	TOTAL SCORE:

Solutions

1: Missing Numbers

3 × 7 = **21**	7 × 9 = **63**	70 − 10 = **60**
99 − 8 = **91**	11 × 6 = **66**	6 × 12 = **72**
9 × 7 = **63**	88 − 20 = **68**	6 + 94 = **100**
56 − 10 = **46**	102 − 3 = **99**	10 × 7 = **70**
11 − 10 = **1**	6 + 13 = **19**	16 − 5 = **11**
34 − 10 = **24**	79 − 4 = **75**	93 − 5 = **88**
17 + 39 = **56**	12 + 20 = **32**	91 − 16 = **75**
68 − 14 = **54**	107 − 12 = **95**	79 + 9 = **88**
31 − 12 = **19**	74 − 1 = **73**	27 − 16 = **11**
10 × 10 = **100**	97 − 13 = **84**	3 × 4 = **12**
12 + 12 = **24**	3 + 3 = **6**	63 + 9 = **72**
3 × 5 = **15**	11 × 8 = **88**	86 − 19 = **67**
9 × 9 = **81**	57 − 3 = **54**	20 + 86 = **106**

2: Rotation

A1, B2, C1

4: Creative Thinking

One method is to pour in sand (slowly!) until the gerbil can climb out by itself.

It's a certainty – try it if you need convincing!

5: Logical Puzzlers

8 apples, in the case where all the bruised apples are also insect-damaged.

7pm.

1¼ miles.

6: Counting and Perception

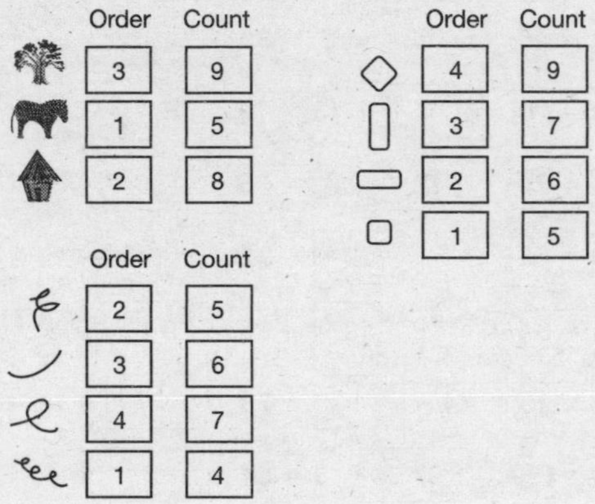

7: Cryptogram

Every time you smile at someone, it is an action of love, a gift to that person, a beautiful thing.

Mother Teresa

The most wasted of all days is one without laughter.

E E Cummings

You have to see opportunity before you can seize it.

Greg Hickman

Discipline is the bridge between goals and accomplishment.

Jim Rohn

8: Speed Arithmetic

11 × 2 = 22	4 × 6 = 24	57 – 16 = 41
70 – 14 = 56	9 × 7 = 63	73 – 16 = 57
6 × 4 = 24	10 + 65 = 75	44 – 9 = 35
46 – 20 = 26	50 + 12 = 62	17 – 16 = 1
10 × 10 = 100	2 + 95 = 97	21 + 4 = 25
71 – 16 = 55	32 + 13 = 45	41 – 6 = 35
47 – 3 = 44	84 – 18 = 66	77 + 3 = 80
3 × 8 = 24	3 × 9 = 27	27 + 11 = 38
6 + 93 = 99	6 × 3 = 18	12 + 4 = 16
46 + 11 = 57	8 + 30 = 38	106 – 1 = 105
3 + 81 = 84	67 – 17 = 50	12 × 9 = 108
100 + 12 = 112	29 – 5 = 24	95 – 16 = 79
27 – 3 = 24	11 + 4 = 15	108 – 9 = 99

10: Shape Dividing

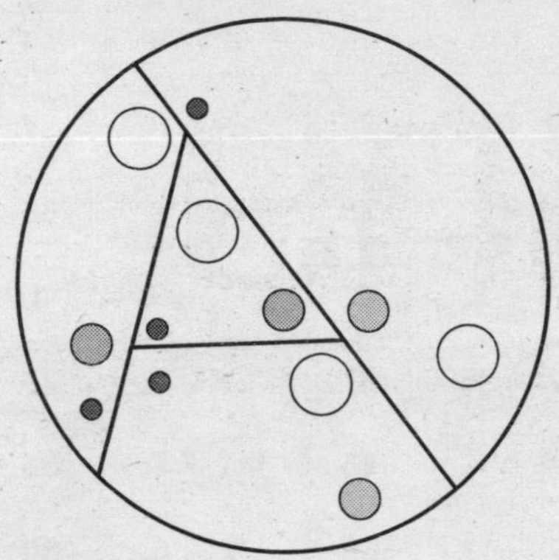

11: Odd One Out

Readier – the rest are anagrams of each other
Polish – the rest refer to light
Detrains – the rest are anagrams of each other
Humphrey – not a previous King of England

12: Observation and Counting

11 squares in total.

17 rectangles, excluding squares.

DAY
13

Missing Words

Study each of these 3 lists of words for a total of 2 minutes. Then cover the top half of the page and see if you can identify which word is missing from each list below.

Dutch	French	Norwegian	Italian
Spanish	Swedish	English	Danish

Western	Eastern	Occidental	Oriental
Northern	Southern	Central	Rural

In	Out	Away	Home
Distant	Near	Far	Long

Now try to spot the missing word from each list:

Swedish, Danish, Dutch, Spanish, French, Italian, English

MISSING:

Southern, Rural, Eastern, Occidental, Oriental, Western, Central

MISSING:

Home, Far, Distant, In, Long, Away, Out

MISSING:

INCORRECT ANSWERS:	TOTAL SCORE:

Matchstick Thinking

The picture below shows 12 matchsticks arranged into a perfect hexagon which contains 6 equilateral triangles (triangles with all sides the same length).

Can you move 4 matchsticks only in order to make precisely 3 equilateral triangles? There must be no left-over matches which do not form part of one of the three equilateral triangles.

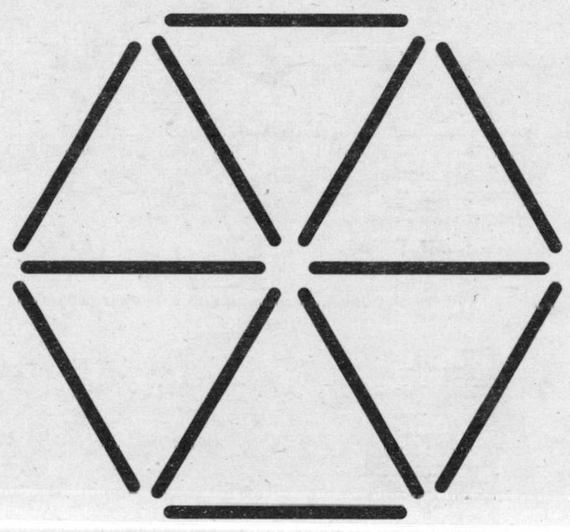

TIME TAKEN:	INCORRECT ANSWERS:
TIME POINTS:	**TOTAL SCORE:**

Rotation

If you were to rotate each of these three pictures as indicated by the arrow beneath it, which of the figures would be the result?

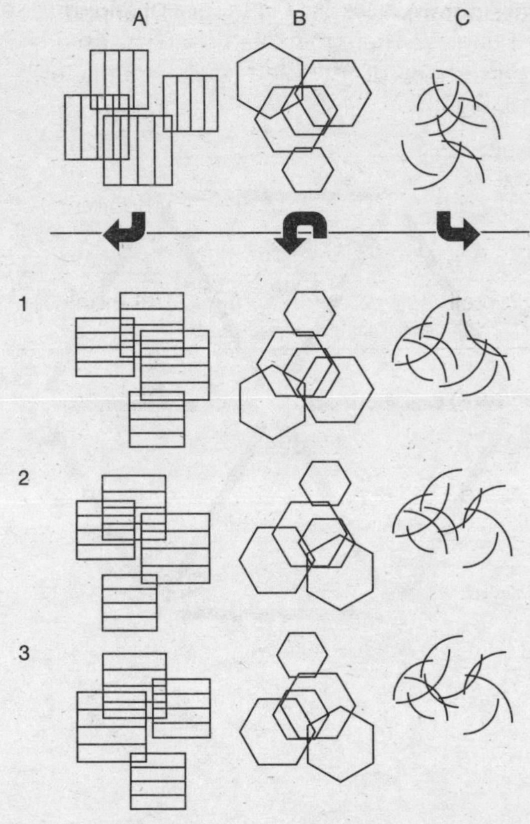

TIME TAKEN:	INCORRECT ANSWERS:
TIME POINTS:	**TOTAL SCORE:**

Odd One Out

Look at each of these sets of words. Can you work out which word is the odd one out in each case?

Parallelogram
Diamond
Rectangle
Triangle
Trapezium

Bach
Rachmaninov
Vivaldi
Purcell
Albinoni

Sitting
Dressing
Coffee
Card
Dining

Rhythm
Hymns
Gypsy
Daisy
Crypt

TIME TAKEN:	INCORRECT ANSWERS:
TIME POINTS:	**TOTAL SCORE:**

Word List

Try to memorize these 24 horseracing terms.

After 2 minutes, cover the table and write as many as you can in the boxes below. You do not need to remember the correct order.

Draw	Fence	Track	Trainer
Handicap	Apprentice	Accumulator	Length
Maiden	Turf	Unplaced	Yearling
Head	Jump	Jockey	Neck
Novice	Distance	Flat	Filly
Milepost	Weigh in	Going	Steward

Now try to recall as many as you can:

INCORRECT ANSWERS:	TOTAL SCORE:

Speed Arithmetic

Complete the following set of arithmetic equations as quickly as possible. You should be able to do them all in your head without using a calculator or making notes.

12 × 5 =	99 − 18 =	49 − 19 =
5 + 28 =	3 × 8 =	52 − 18 =
28 − 9 =	108 − 2 =	90 − 2 =
59 + 13 =	35 − 12 =	7 × 2 =
16 + 41 =	61 + 15 =	5 × 5 =
13 + 10 =	8 × 7 =	12 × 2 =
14 + 14 =	20 + 46 =	32 − 8 =
15 + 74 =	2 + 15 =	11 × 3 =
3 × 12 =	99 + 3 =	102 − 3 =
12 × 6 =	9 × 3 =	84 + 2 =
4 × 9 =	107 − 3 =	8 + 13 =
3 × 9 =	75 − 14 =	90 − 12 =
98 − 2 =	2 + 89 =	13 + 8 =

TIME TAKEN:	INCORRECT ANSWERS:
TIME POINTS:	**TOTAL SCORE:**

Observation and Counting

Look at this grid with two diagonal lines and see how long it takes you to answer the observation question below. It is fairly tricky!

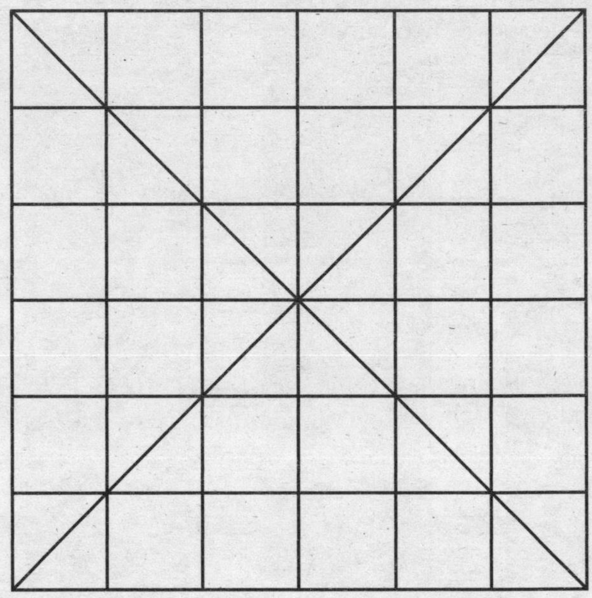

How many different triangles can you count in this figure?

TIME TAKEN:	INCORRECT ANSWERS:
TIME POINTS:	**TOTAL SCORE:**

Logical Puzzlers

Try to solve these problems – each requires only simple logic to solve, but you might find that making notes with a pencil will help!

What is ninety-nine percent of four hundred plus one percent of two hundred?

Two thirds of all supermarkets sell my favourite tea, but one third of those are out of stock. How many supermarkets out of ninety have my tea in store?

Sam drives at an average of 60mph (miles per hour) and gets home at 8pm. Given that he set off on his journey at 7:15pm, how far has he driven?

TIME TAKEN:	INCORRECT ANSWERS:
TIME POINTS:	**TOTAL SCORE:**

Time Elapsed

Work out how many hours and minutes have passed between each of these pairs of times.

11:10pm to 11:45pm =	:	4:35am to 5:20pm =	:
12:55am to 5:40pm =	:	4:35am to 7:40am =	:
7:55am to 11:30am =	:	4:50pm to 9:05pm =	:
11:40am to 11:20pm =	:	2:25am to 11:10am =	:
9:35am to 6:05pm =	:	3:30pm to 10:45pm =	:
2:20am to 9:55am =	:	6:05am to 5:10pm =	:
2:15am to 4:55am =	:	9:25am to 11:25pm =	:
12:30am to 7:30pm =	:	11:05am to 7:00pm =	:
3:00pm to 10:30pm =	:	12:50am to 5:05pm =	:
5:15pm to 8:25pm =	:	2:00am to 7:00am =	:
9:25am to 11:00am =	:	1:10pm to 2:40pm =	:
3:15pm to 11:50pm =	:	12:25am to 9:50pm =	:
2:25am to 5:35am =	:	3:05am to 1:55pm =	:
3:35am to 6:00am =	:	3:20am to 7:55am =	:
2:20am to 4:50am =	:	2:10am to 2:35am =	:

TIME TAKEN:	INCORRECT ANSWERS:
TIME POINTS:	**TOTAL SCORE:**

Shape Dividing

Draw three straight lines in order to divide the shape into four separate areas. Each area must contain precisely one of each size of circle. The three lines may touch but they must not cross.

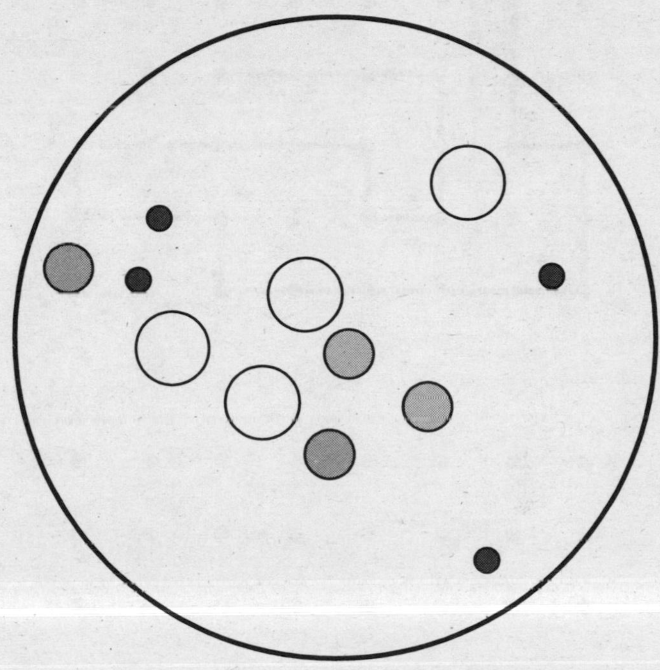

TIME TAKEN:	INCORRECT ANSWERS:
TIME POINTS:	**TOTAL SCORE:**

Visual Memory

Spend 1 minute studying this path. Then cover the top half of this page and try to redraw it accurately on the empty grid below.

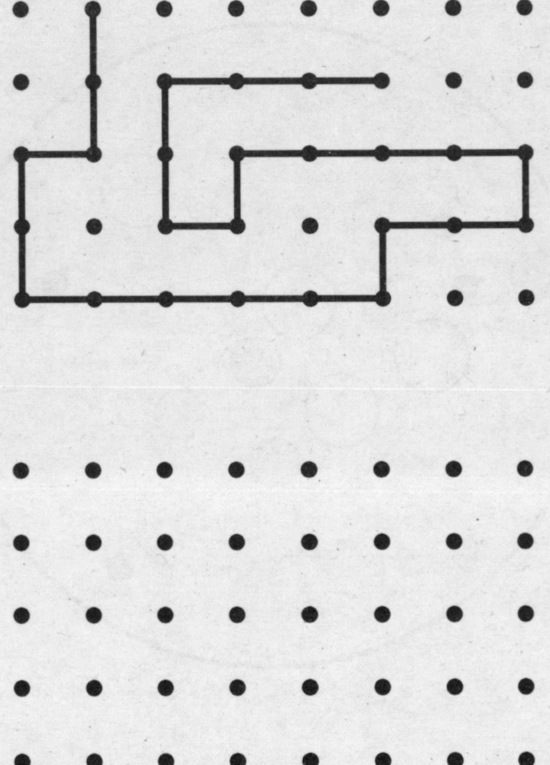

INCORRECT ANSWERS:	TOTAL SCORE:

Reflective Power

Look at the three figures above the horizontal "mirror". Which of the figures below the line corresponds to the figure when reflected in the mirror line?

1 2 3

A

B

C

D

TIME TAKEN:	INCORRECT ANSWERS:
TIME POINTS:	**TOTAL SCORE:**

Anagrammatic

Look at each of these sets of 12 words. How many pairs of anagrams can you spot in each set, and what are they?

PEEKABOO	PROUDEST	PERTAINS
COCKTAIL	ENTRAILS	LATRINES
QUIRKING	PAINTERS	REVALUED
SPROUTED	DISSECTS	ADEQUACY

PERILS	PLIERS	DEVISE
CROFTS	TWIRLS	IFFIER
SIEVED	HALEST	SURELY
LATHES	ARIDER	RAIDER

INNOCENT	REBUTTED	SALESMEN
SCURRIES	BUTTERED	WEIGHING
CRUISERS	WOODLAND	DOWNLOAD
STOCKIER	NAMELESS	ROCKIEST

DIAPER	SCARES	BEASTS
BASTES	CARESS	SHADOW
EXPERT	DARTED	REPAID
INFAMY	TRADED	HONEYS

TIME TAKEN:	INCORRECT ANSWERS:
TIME POINTS:	**TOTAL SCORE:**

Solutions

2: Matchstick Thinking

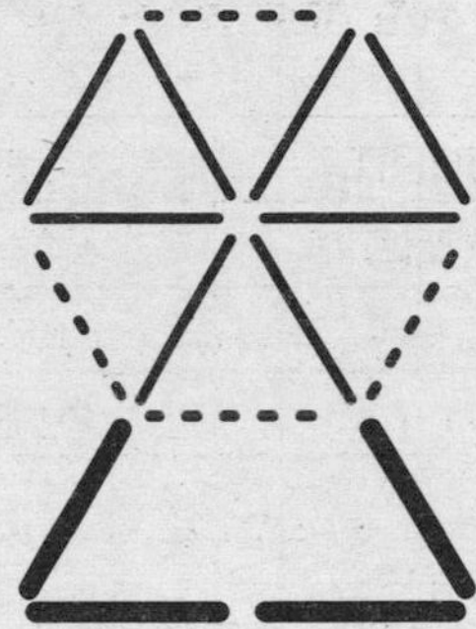

3: Rotation

A3, B3, C2

4: Odd One Out

Triangle – only shape without four sides
Rachmaninov – the rest are baroque era composers; Rachmaninov is 20th century
Sitting – the rest are common types of table
Daisy – the rest have no vowels in

6: Speed Arithmetic

12 × 5 = **60**	99 − 18 = **81**	49 − 19 = **30**
5 + 28 = **33**	3 × 8 = **24**	52 − 18 = **34**
28 − 9 = **19**	108 − 2 = **106**	90 − 2 = **88**
59 + 13 = **72**	35 − 12 = **23**	7 × 2 = **14**
16 + 41 = **57**	61 + 15 = **76**	5 × 5 = **25**
13 + 10 = **23**	8 × 7 = **56**	12 × 2 = **24**
14 + 14 = **28**	20 + 46 = **66**	32 − 8 = **24**
15 + 74 = **89**	2 + 15 = **17**	11 × 3 = **33**
3 × 12 = **36**	99 + 3 = **102**	102 − 3 = **99**
12 × 6 = **72**	9 × 3 = **27**	84 + 2 = **86**
4 × 9 = **36**	107 − 3 = **104**	8 + 13 = **21**
3 × 9 = **27**	75 − 14 = **61**	90 − 12 = **78**
98 − 2 = **96**	2 + 89 = **91**	13 + 8 = **21**

7: Observation and Counting

96 different triangles in this figure.

8: Logical Puzzlers

Three hundred and ninety eight.

40 supermarkets.

45 miles.

9: Time Elapsed

11:10pm to 11:45pm =	0:35	4:35am to 5:20pm =	12:45
12:55am to 5:40pm =	16:45	4:35am to 7:40am =	3:05
7:55am to 11:30am =	3:35	4:50pm to 9:05pm =	4:15
11:40am to 11:20pm =	11:40	2:25am to 11:10am =	8:45
9:35am to 6:05pm =	8:30	3:30pm to 10:45pm =	7:15
2:20am to 9:55am =	7:35	6:05am to 5:10pm =	11:05
2:15am to 4:55am =	2:40	9:25am to 11:25pm =	14:00
12:30am to 7:30pm =	19:00	11:05am to 7:00pm =	7:55
3:00pm to 10:30pm =	7:30	12:50am to 5:05pm =	16:15
5:15pm to 8:25pm =	3:10	2:00am to 7:00am =	5:00
9:25am to 11:00am =	1:35	1:10pm to 2:40pm =	1:30
3:15pm to 11:50pm =	8:35	12:25am to 9:50pm =	21:25
2:25am to 5:35am –	3:10	3:05am to 1:55pm =	10:50
3:35am to 6:00am =	2:25	3:20am to 7:55am =	4:35
2:20am to 4:50am =	2:30	2:10am to 2:35am =	0:25

10: Shape Dividing

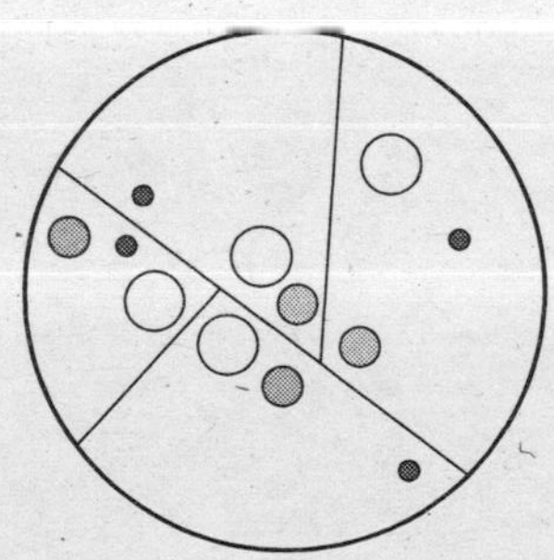

12: Reflective Power
1A, 2C, 3D

13: Anagrammatic

Set 1: 1 pair of anagrams:
ATTENTIVE and TENTATIVE

Set 2: 4 pairs of anagrams:
RESISTING and SISTERING
DECIMATED and MEDICATED
DETHRONES and SHORTENED
SHOOTINGS and SOOTHINGS

Set 3: 1 pair of anagrams:
GENERALS and ENLARGES

Set 4: 6 pairs of anagrams:
CANDIDEST and DISTANCED
DESIGNERS and REDESIGNS
GALLERIES and ALLERGIES
SUNBURNED and UNBURDENS
WANDERING and WARDENING
TEENAGERS and GENERATES

DAY
14

Visual Sequences

Can you work out which pattern comes next in each of these two visual sequences?

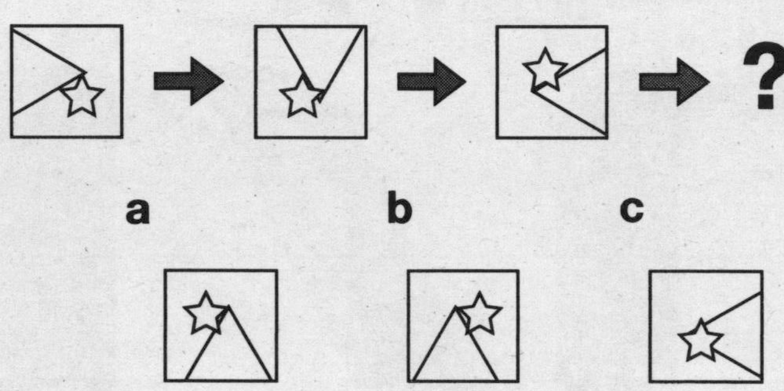

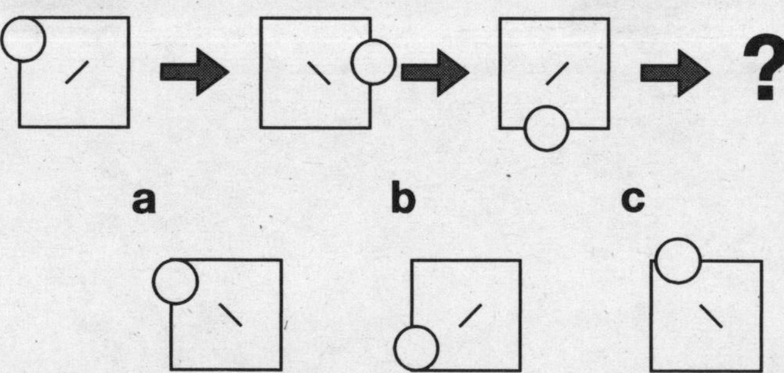

TIME TAKEN:	INCORRECT ANSWERS:
TIME POINTS:	**TOTAL SCORE:**

Reflective Power

Look at the three figures above the horizontal "mirror". Which of the figures below the line corresponds to the figure reflected in the mirror line?

1 2 3

A

B

C

D

TIME TAKEN:	INCORRECT ANSWERS:
TIME POINTS:	**TOTAL SCORE:**

Coin Conundrum

The picture below shows 4 coins in a row.

Can you rearrange the coins so that every coin is directly touching all of the other three other coins?

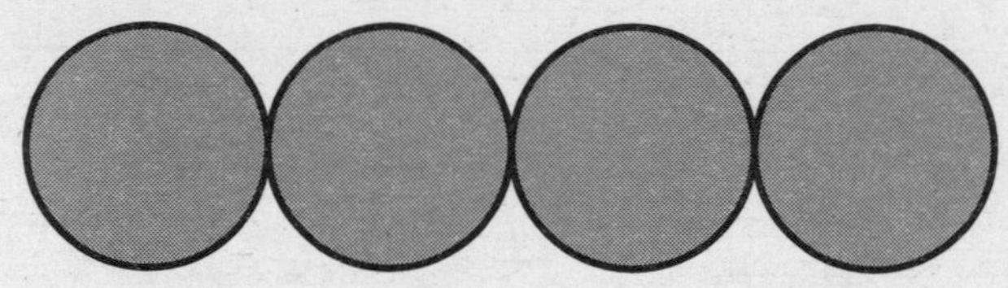

TIME TAKEN:	INCORRECT ANSWERS:
TIME POINTS:	**TOTAL SCORE:**

DAY: 14	WORKOUT: 4	CONCENTRATION

Time Elapsed

Work out how many hours and minutes have passed between each of these pairs of times.

12:45pm to 2:35pm =	:	8:35pm to 11:15pm =	:
7:50am to 11:05pm =	:	2:55am to 7:20am =	:
7:15am to 8:40am =	:	4:00pm to 8:20pm =	:
3:50am to 11:45pm =	:	6:35am to 4:50pm =	:
2:05am to 8:55pm =	:	1:00am to 8:50pm =	:
1:10am to 9:20pm =	:	3:00pm to 6:20pm =	:
3:10am to 11:55am =	:	5:55am to 8:05pm =	:
11:40am to 3:30pm =	:	2:10am to 10:00am =	:
5:35am to 6:40am =	:	12:20am to 12:45am =	:
12:35am to 10:30am =	:	8:15am to 12:15pm =	:
10:25am to 8:40pm =	:	1:25pm to 9:00pm =	:
1:30am to 6:15pm =	:	2:25pm to 3:25pm =	:
3:05am to 2:55pm =	:	1:20am to 1:55pm =	:
12:05am to 4:10pm =	:	4:35pm to 10:15pm =	:
1:05am to 5:00am =	:	4:55pm to 8:20pm =	:

TIME TAKEN:	INCORRECT ANSWERS:
TIME POINTS:	**TOTAL SCORE:**

Missing Words

Study each of these 3 lists of words for a total of 2 minutes. Then cover the top half of the page and see if you can identify which word is missing from each list below.

Easy	Facile	Simple	Straightforward
Basic	Plain	Clear	Lucid

Peach	Apple	Pear	Orange
Plum	Grape	Cherry	Banana

Cow	Sheep	Goat	Pig
Chicken	Goose	Turkey	Ostrich

Now try to spot the missing word from each list:

Simple, Lucid, Clear, Easy, Straightforward, Facile, Plain

MISSING:

Peach, Banana, Plum, Apple, Cherry, Orange, Pear

MISSING:

Ostrich, Goat, Goose, Chicken, Sheep, Pig, Turkey

MISSING:

INCORRECT ANSWERS:	TOTAL SCORE:

Visual Inference

Two symbols each with a following symbol are shown. Can you work out the rule being applied in order to deduce which of the last three symbols in each set should replace the question mark? There are two sets of puzzles on this page.

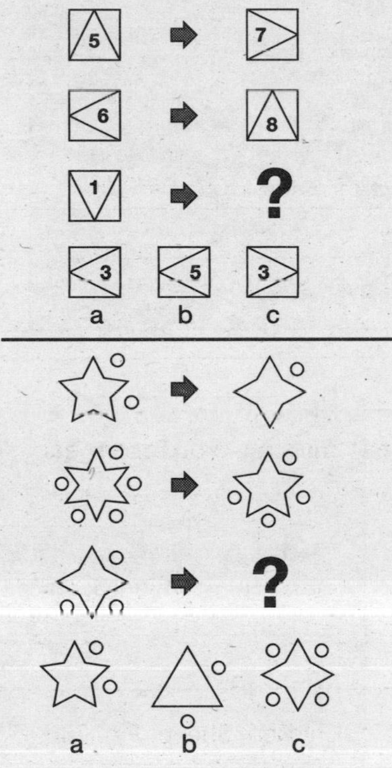

TIME TAKEN:	INCORRECT ANSWERS:
TIME POINTS:	**TOTAL SCORE:**

Creative Thinking

See if you can solve each of the following conundrums. If you get stuck then try thinking laterally – they all have logical solutions, but the logic might not be what you expect!

If I go for a walk in the countryside and come across a forest, what is the maximum distance I can walk into that forest?

Grab a pencil and quickly write down the opposite of "I'm not asleep".

TIME TAKEN:	INCORRECT ANSWERS:
TIME POINTS:	**TOTAL SCORE:**

Word List

Try to memorize these 24 snooker and billiard terms.

After 2 minutes, cover the table and write as many as you can in the boxes below. You do not need to remember the correct order.

Draw	Snooker	Spider	Cue
Frame	Triangle	Rack	Break
Pocket	Pot	Red	Blue
Ball	Foul	Cannon	Chalk
Green	Baize	Free ball	Miscue
Kiss	Rest	Safety	Stun

Now try to recall as many as you can:

INCORRECT ANSWERS:	**TOTAL SCORE:**

Counting and Perception

Spend no more than 10 seconds looking at each group of symbols in each turn, then try to sort them into order of increasing frequency. Write "1" in the "Order" column for the shape that occurs least often, and so on.

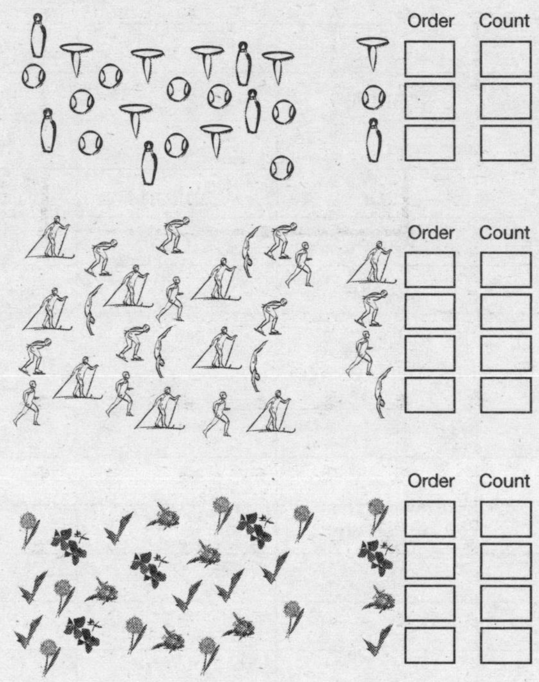

Now take as long as you think you need to write in the second column the precise count of each symbol.

TIME TAKEN:	INCORRECT ANSWERS:
TIME POINTS:	**TOTAL SCORE:**

Visual Memory

Spend 1 minute studying this path. Then cover the top half of this page and try and redraw it accurately on the empty grid below.

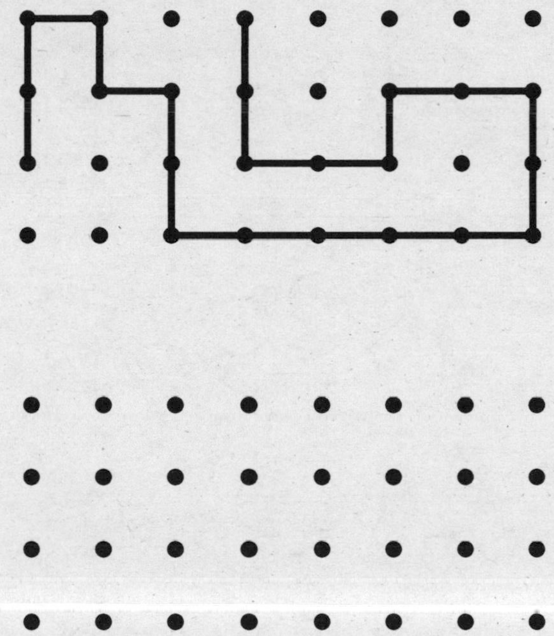

INCORRECT ANSWERS:	**TOTAL SCORE:**

Rotation

If you were to rotate each of these three pictures as indicated by the arrow beneath, which of the figures below would be the result?

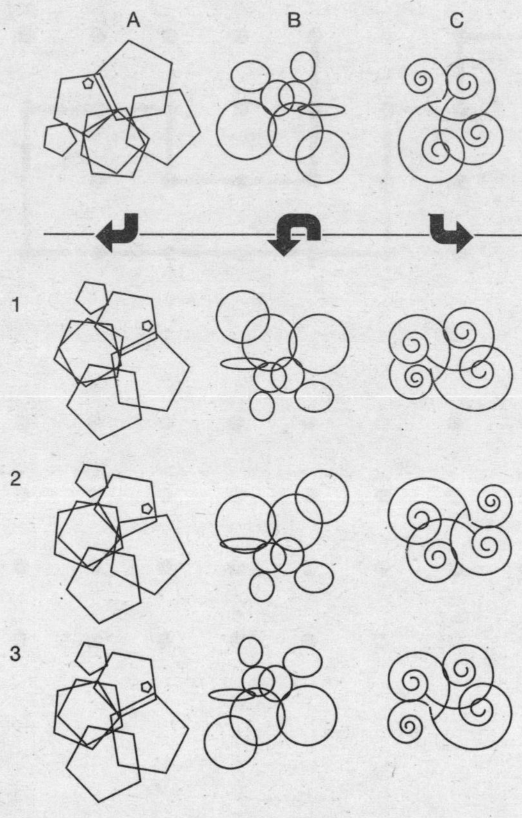

TIME TAKEN:	INCORRECT ANSWERS:
TIME POINTS:	**TOTAL SCORE:**

Missing Signs

Insert the missing sign into each of these arithmetic expressions in order to make the equation true. You will need to add, subtract, multiply, or divide.

168 ☐ 12 = 14	70 ☐ 15 = 85	26 ☐ 15 = 41
26 ☐ 62 = 88	10 ☐ 5 = 2	97 ☐ 5 = 102
8 ☐ 7 = 56	36 ☐ 9 = 4	91 ☐ 1 = 92
71 ☐ 21 = 92	25 ☐ 30 = 55	28 ☐ 82 = 110
50 ☐ 10 = 5	154 ☐ 11 = 14	4 ☐ 25 = 29
12 ☐ 10 = 120	74 ☐ 19 = 93	3 ☐ 2 = 6
18 ☐ 121 = 139	27 ☐ 3 = 9	10 ☐ 6 = 60
84 ☐ 9 = 93	22 ☐ 7 = 29	94 ☐ 33 = 127
55 ☐ 11 = 5	17 ☐ 106 = 123	5 ☐ 9 = 45
48 ☐ 4 = 12	92 ☐ 31 = 123	95 ☐ 24 = 71
32 ☐ 35 = 67	10 ☐ 4 = 40	57 ☐ 24 = 33
70 ☐ 5 = 14	63 ☐ 9 = 7	38 ☐ 27 = 65
67 ☐ 23 = 44	96 ☐ 8 = 12	100 ☐ 10 = 10

TIME TAKEN:	INCORRECT ANSWERS:
TIME POINTS:	**TOTAL SCORE:**

Logical Puzzlers

Try to solve these problems – each requires only simple logic to solve, but you might find that making notes with a pencil will help!

If Victoria runs six laps of a 1600-metre circuit, how many kilometres does she run, to the nearest whole kilometre? A kilometre is 1,000 metres.

Write the number seventeen million, nine hundred and forty six thousand and thirty seven in digits. Then add up those digits – what is the result?

I have 18 individual socks in a drawer at home. Half of them are red and half are blue. How many do I need to take out to ensure I have at least one pair of the same colour, assuming I don't look at the colours as I do so!

TIME TAKEN:	INCORRECT ANSWERS:
TIME POINTS:	**TOTAL SCORE:**

Solutions

1: Visual Sequences
b, a

2: Reflective Power
1B, 2C, 3A

3: Coins Conundrum

4: Time Elapsed

12:45pm to 2:35pm =	**1:50**	8:35pm to 11:15pm =	**2:40**
7:50am to 11:05pm =	**15:15**	2:55am to 7:20am =	**4:25**
7:15am to 8:40am =	**1:25**	4:00pm to 8:20pm =	**4:20**
3:50am to 11:45pm =	**19:55**	6:35am to 4:50pm =	**10:15**
2:05am to 8:55pm =	**18:50**	1:00am to 8:50pm =	**19:50**
1:10am to 9:20pm =	**20:10**	3:00pm to 6:20pm =	**3:20**
3:10am to 11:55am =	**8:45**	5:55am to 8:05pm =	**14:10**
11:40am to 3:30pm =	**3:50**	2:10am to 10:00am =	**7:50**
5:35am to 6:40am =	**1:05**	12:20am to 12:45am =	**0:25**
12:35am to 10:30am =	**9:55**	8:15am to 12:15pm =	**4:00**
10:25am to 8:40pm =	**10:15**	1:25pm to 9:00pm =	**7:35**
1:30am to 6:45pm =	**17:15**	2:25pm to 3:25pm =	**1:00**
3:05am to 2:55pm =	**11:50**	1:20am to 1:55pm =	**12:35**
12:05am to 4:10pm =	**16:05**	4:35pm to 10:15pm =	**5:40**
1:05am to 5:00am =	**3:55**	4:55pm to 8:20pm =	**3:25**

6: Visual Inference

a 

b 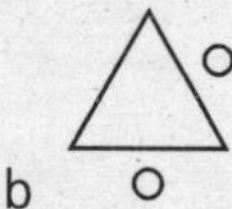

7: Creative Thinking

Half way!

It's "I'm asleep", not "I'm awake" as you might be tempted to respond!

9: Counting and Perception

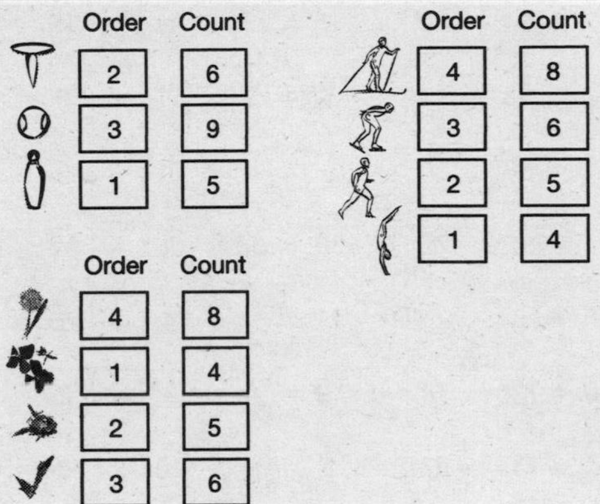

11: Rotation

A3, B1, C3

12: Missing Signs

168 ÷ 12 = 14	70 + 15 = 85	26 + 15 = 41
26 + 62 = 88	10 ÷ 5 = 2	97 + 5 = 102
8 × 7 = 56	36 ÷ 9 = 4	91 + 1 = 92
71 + 21 = 92	25 + 30 = 55	28 + 82 = 110
50 ÷ 10 = 5	154 ÷ 11 = 14	4 + 25 = 29
12 × 10 = 120	74 + 19 = 93	3 × 2 = 6
18 + 121 = 139	27 ÷ 3 = 9	10 × 6 = 60
84 + 9 = 93	22 + 7 = 29	94 + 33 = 127
55 ÷ 11 = 5	17 + 106 = 123	5 × 9 = 45
48 ÷ 4 = 12	92 + 31 = 123	95 – 24 = 71
32 + 35 = 67	10 × 4 = 40	57 – 24 = 33
70 ÷ 5 = 14	63 ÷ 9 = 7	38 + 27 = 65
67 – 23 = 44	96 ÷ 8 = 12	100 ÷ 10 = 10

13: Logical Puzzlers

10 kilometres (9,600 metres rounded up)

37, which is the sum of the digits of 17,946,037.

10 Socks.

DAY
15

Odd One Out

Look at each of these sets of words. Can you work out which word is the odd one out in each case?

Beat Throb
Dream
Broken Ache

Sooner Muddy
Sunshine
Garden Golden

Merlot Zinfandel
Rosé
Chardonnay Riesling

Hannah Malayalam
Mimic
Kayak Tenet

TIME TAKEN:	INCORRECT ANSWERS:
TIME POINTS:	**TOTAL SCORE:**

Missing Numbers

Insert the missing number into each of these arithmetic expressions in order to make the equations true. You should not need a calculator to do this!

☐ − 8 = **75**	13 − ☐ = **6**	☐ − 7 = **7**
☐ − 4 = **63**	☐ − 1 = **86**	85 − ☐ = **76**
☐ × 5 = **50**	☐ + 79 = **90**	☐ − 16 = **22**
☐ + 7 = **27**	89 − ☐ = **73**	☐ − 18 = **31**
80 + ☐ = **99**	9 + ☐ = **16**	77 − ☐ = **73**
3 + ☐ = **36**	1 + ☐ = **51**	57 + ☐ = **74**
9 × ☐ = **45**	9 × ☐ = **81**	☐ + 13 = **29**
2 × ☐ = **14**	10 + ☐ = **13**	1 + ☐ = **44**
☐ + 12 = **112**	10 × ☐ = **20**	☐ × 12 = **60**
56 + ☐ = **59**	73 − ☐ = **69**	99 + ☐ = **107**
93 + ☐ = **99**	☐ + 92 = **97**	50 − ☐ = **43**
☐ − 14 = **35**	18 + ☐ = **44**	☐ − 11 = **56**
☐ × 9 = **36**	☐ × 10 = **120**	39 − ☐ = **26**

TIME TAKEN:	INCORRECT ANSWERS:
TIME POINTS:	**TOTAL SCORE:**

Anagrammatic

Look at each of these sets of 12 words. How many pairs of anagrams can you spot in each set, and what are they?

TENTATIVE	POINTEDLY	POLLUTING
PROPELLER	CESAREANS	PLANTAINS
ATTENTIVE	REASSURED	PERVASIVE
GUACAMOLE	DYNAMICAL	PREVIEWER

RESISTING	SHOOTINGS	SOOTHINGS
SISTERING	SIXPENCES	DECIMATED
DETHRONES	MEDICATED	SHORTENED
BRAZENING	EPIDERMIS	UNEASIEST

PILLOWED	GENERALS	DEMERITS
ACRONYMS	MANDIBLE	CORRUPTS
ENLARGES	ATTENDED	DECLINED
GASOLINE	VIGOROUS	FURROWED

GALLERIES	DISTANCED	DESIGNERS
GENERATES	ALLERGIES	UNBURDENS
SUNBURNED	REDESIGNS	WARDENING
WANDERING	TEENAGERS	CANDIDEST

TIME TAKEN:	INCORRECT ANSWERS:
TIME POINTS:	**TOTAL SCORE:**

Observation and Counting

Look at these rectangles and see how long it takes you to answer the observation question below. It is fairly tricky!

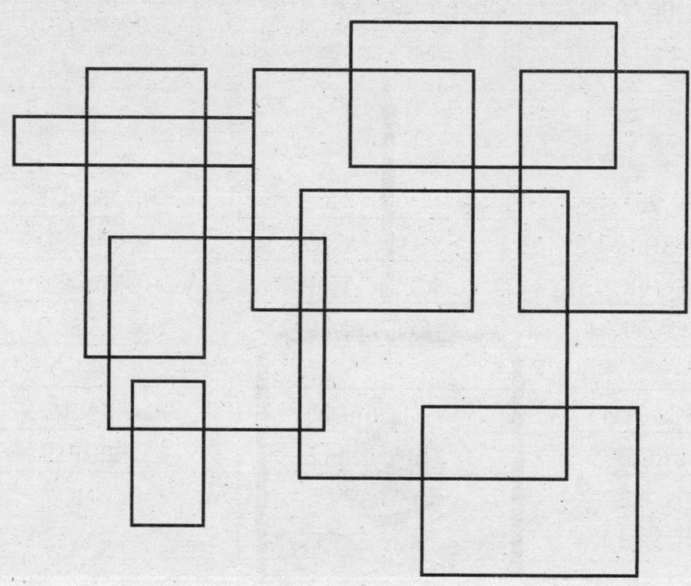

How many rectangles can you count in this picture?

TIME TAKEN:	INCORRECT ANSWERS:
TIME POINTS:	**TOTAL SCORE:**

Matchstick Thinking

The picture below shows 4 matchsticks arranged into a glass, covering a coin.

Can you move exactly 2 matchsticks in order to reshape the glass so that the coin is no longer inside it?

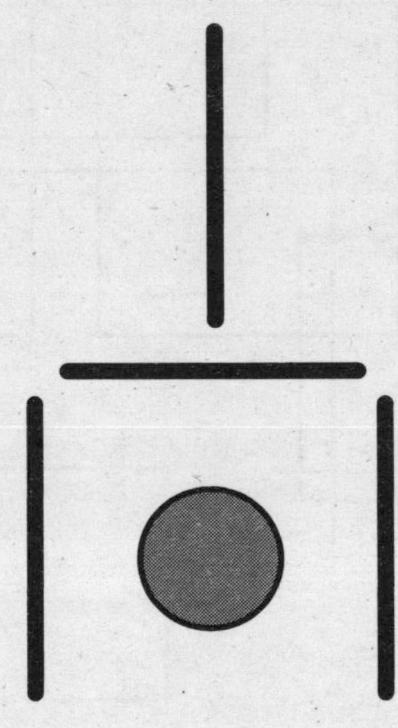

TIME TAKEN:	INCORRECT ANSWERS:
TIME POINTS:	**TOTAL SCORE:**

Logical Puzzlers

Try to solve these problems – each requires only simple logic to solve, but you might find that making notes with a pencil will help!

My neighbour has just finished installing a straight 100 metre long fence, complete with fence posts every metre. How many posts are there in the entire fence?

I use two pints of milk on Tuesday, and on Wednesday I buy another pint at the store but then drink half of all the milk I have. How much milk do I now have, given that I had five pints at the start of Tuesday?

A piece of lined writing-paper has 22 horizontal lines on it. If this is the case, how many separate regions are formed on it by the lines?

TIME TAKEN:	INCORRECT ANSWERS:
TIME POINTS:	**TOTAL SCORE:**

Shape Folding

If you were to cut out this shape and fold it into a cube, which of the three pictures below would result?

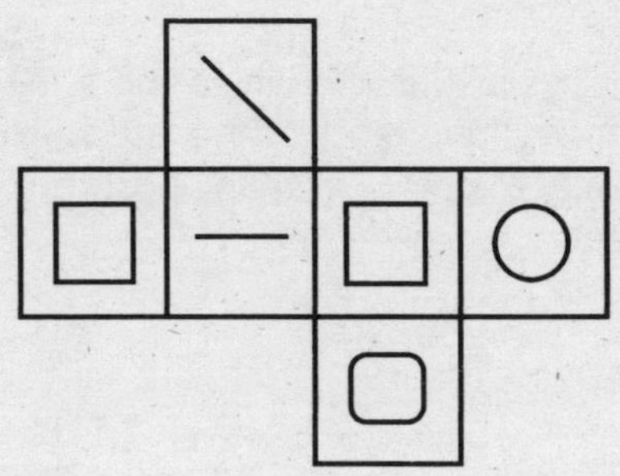

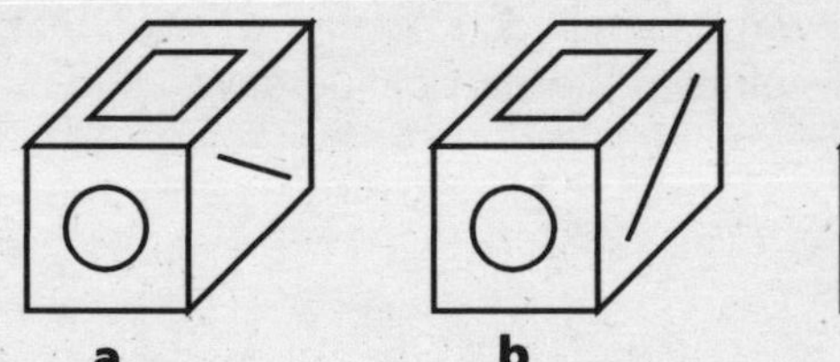

a **b** **c**

TIME TAKEN:	INCORRECT ANSWERS:
TIME POINTS:	**TOTAL SCORE:**

Speed Arithmetic

Complete the following set of arithmetic equations as quickly as possible. You should be able to do them all in your head without using a calculator or making notes.

86 − 18 =	10 × 8 =	35 + 13 =
9 + 96 =	49 − 8 =	64 + 4 =
82 − 13 =	91 + 18 =	93 − 4 =
16 + 55 =	15 − 10 =	2 × 7 =
7 × 2 =	102 − 3 =	46 − 19 =
72 + 2 =	82 + 4 =	55 + 13 =
42 − 11 =	32 − 3 =	26 − 16 =
16 + 61 =	1 + 8 =	12 × 2 =
66 − 9 =	21 − 14 =	61 − 4 =
19 + 11 =	86 − 4 =	19 + 37 =
94 + 11 =	8 + 27 =	51 − 11 =
5 × 8 =	21 + 20 =	11 × 10 =
22 + 6 =	34 − 3 =	77 + 10 =

TIME TAKEN:	INCORRECT ANSWERS:
TIME POINTS:	**TOTAL SCORE:**

Creative Thinking

See if you can solve each of the following conundrums. If you get stuck then try thinking laterally – they all have logical solutions, but the logic might not be what you expect!

If the Sea of Tranquility is on the Moon, and the Black Sea is on Earth, on which planet is the Red Sea?

If Tom the tabbycat drinks precisely half of his saucer of milk every day, and none of that milk evaporates or is removed in any other way, how long will it take him to finish a saucer containing a pint of milk?

TIME TAKEN:	INCORRECT ANSWERS:
TIME POINTS:	**TOTAL SCORE:**

Visual Memory

Spend 1 minute studying this path. Then cover the top half of this page and try to redraw it accurately on the empty grid below.

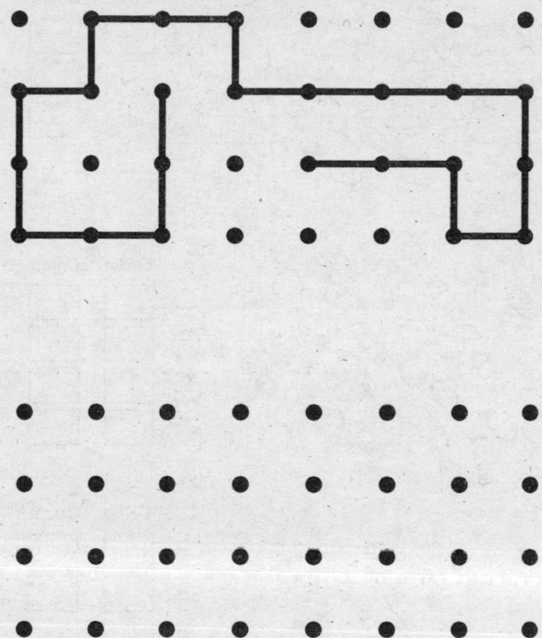

INCORRECT ANSWERS:	**TOTAL SCORE:**

Counting and Perception

Spend no more than 10 seconds looking at each group of symbols in each turn, then try to sort them into order of increasing frequency. Write "1" in the "Order" column for the shape that occurs least often, and so on.

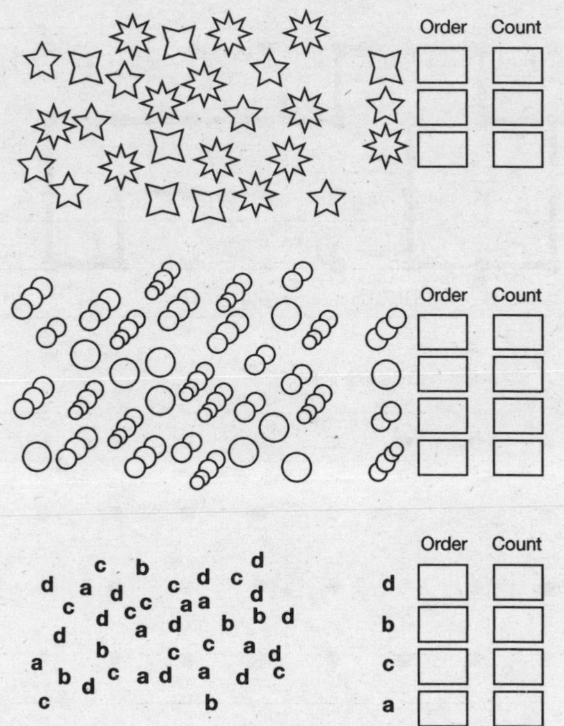

Now take as long as you think you need to write in the second column the precise count of each symbol.

TIME TAKEN:	INCORRECT ANSWERS:
TIME POINTS:	**TOTAL SCORE:**

Word List

Try to memorize these 24 golfing terms.

After 2 minutes, cover the table and write as many as you can in the boxes below. You do not need to remember the correct order.

Swing	Course	Handicap	Draw
Driver	Hole	Wedge	Iron
Pitch	Pin	Marker	Green
Rough	Fairway	Stroke	Wood
Par	Eagle	Bogey	Birdie
Albatross	Clubhouse	Fore	Links

Now try to recall as many as you can:

INCORRECT ANSWERS:	TOTAL SCORE:

Missing Words

Study each of these 3 lists of words for a total of 2 minutes. Then cover the top half of the page and see if you can identify which word is missing from each of the lists below.

Mockingbird	Starling	Skylark	Raven
Crow	Parrot	Parakeet	Chaffinch

Brake	Wheel	Dipstick	Hubcap
Headrest	Gasket	Camshaft	Bumper

Appendix	Prefix	Contents	Index
Prologue	Errata	Epilogue	Chapter

Now try and spot the missing word from each list:

Starling, Chaffinch, Mockingbird, Parakeet, Crow, Parrot, Raven

MISSING: [ ]

Brake, Headrest, Hubcap, Bumper, Gasket, Camshaft, Wheel

MISSING: [ ]

Appendix, Index, Epilogue, Prefix, Errata, Contents, Prologue

MISSING: [ ]

INCORRECT ANSWERS:	**TOTAL SCORE:**

Solutions

1: Odd One Out

Dream – the rest make new words when prefixed with "heart"
Muddy – not a US state nickname
Rosé – the rest are types of grape
Mimic – the rest are palindromes

2: Missing Numbers

[83] – 8 = **75**	13 – [7] = **6**	[14] – 7 = **7**
[67] – 4 = **63**	[87] – 1 = **86**	85 – [9] = **76**
[10] × 5 = **50**	[11] + 79 = **90**	[38] – 16 = **22**
[20] + 7 = **27**	89 – [16] = **73**	[49] – 18 = **31**
80 + [19] = **99**	9 + [7] = **16**	77 – [4] = **73**
3 + [33] = **36**	1 + [50] = **51**	57 + [17] = **74**
9 × [5] = **45**	9 × [9] = **81**	[16] + 13 = **29**
2 × [7] = **14**	10 + [3] = **13**	1 + [43] = **44**
[100] + 12 = **112**	10 × [2] = **20**	[5] × 12 = **60**
56 + [3] = **59**	73 – [4] = **69**	99 + [8] = **107**
93 + [6] = **99**	[5] + 92 = **97**	50 – [7] = **43**
[49] – 14 = **35**	18 + [26] = **44**	[67] – 11 = **56**
[4] × 9 = **36**	[12] × 10 = **120**	39 – [13] = **26**

3: Anagrammatic

Set 1: 4 pairs of anagrams:
CLOBBERS and COBBLERS

EMIRATES and STEAMIER
MEDICATE and DECIMATE
MARRIEDS and ADMIRERS

Set 2: 2 pairs of anagrams:
TRAPPINGS and STRAPPING
OVERHANGS and HANGOVERS

Set 3: 3 pairs of anagrams:
CLASPS and SCALPS
GENRES and GREENS
ANOINT and NATION

Set 4: 6 pairs of anagrams:
RECEDED and DECREED
INBREDS and REBINDS
LOOPING and POOLING
TORPEDO and TROOPED
SCHOLAR and CHORALS
DAMPEST and STAMPED

4: Observation and Counting
33 rectangles in this picture.

5: Matchsticks

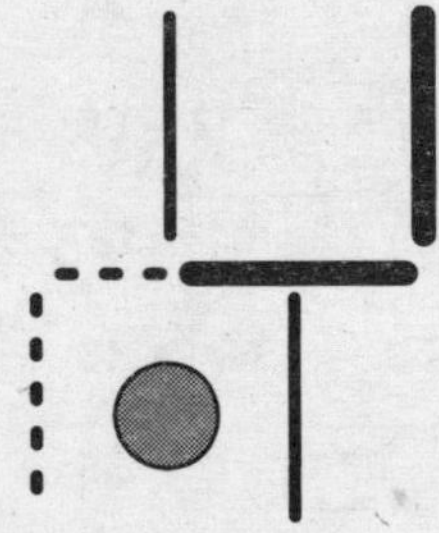

6: Logical Puzzlers
101 posts.

2 pints.

23 areas.

7: Shape Folding
b

8: Speed Arithmetic

86 − 18 = **68**	10 × 8 = **80**	35 + 13 = **48**
9 + 96 = **105**	49 − 8 = **41**	64 + 4 = **68**
82 − 13 = **69**	91 + 18 = **109**	93 − 4 = **89**
16 + 55 = **71**	15 − 10 = **5**	2 × 7 = **14**
7 × 2 = **14**	102 − 3 = **99**	46 − 19 = **27**
72 + 2 = **74**	82 + 4 = **86**	55 + 13 = **68**
42 − 11 = **31**	32 − 3 = **29**	26 − 16 = **10**
16 + 61 = **77**	1 + 8 = **9**	12 × 2 = **24**
66 − 9 = **57**	21 − 14 = **7**	61 − 4 = **57**
19 + 11 = **30**	86 − 4 = **82**	19 + 37 = **56**
94 + 11 = **105**	8 + 27 = **35**	51 − 11 = **40**
5 × 8 = **40**	21 + 20 = **41**	11 × 10 = **110**
22 + 6 = **28**	34 − 3 = **31**	77 + 10 = **87**

9: Creative Thinking
It's on Earth! Not Mars.

It will take him forever.

11: Counting and Perception

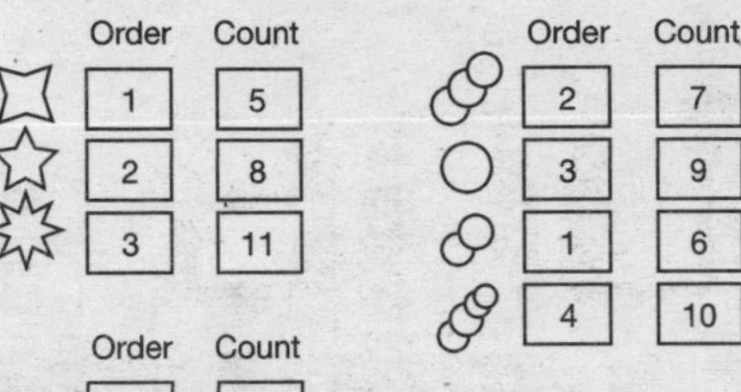

	Order	Count
d	4	13
b	1	6
c	3	11
a	2	8

DAY
16

Anagrammatic

Look at each of these sets of 12 words. How many pairs of anagrams can you spot in each set, and what are they?

DECIMATE	MEDICATE	PROVABLY
MEDIOCRE	ADMIRERS	INVITING
CLOBBERS	SNEAKERS	COBBLERS
EMIRATES	MARRIEDS	STEAMIER

SCOUNDREL	DEFORMITY	HANGOVERS
OVERDRAWS	TRAPPINGS	UNDERPAID
BILLBOARD	OVERHANGS	CONCEIVED
TEMPORARY	STRAPPING	FLATTERER

BOPPED	ORACLE	NATION
CACHES	ROTARY	CLASPS
SCALPS	ANOINT	FLUFFS
OPENED	GREENS	GENRES

DAMPEST	CHORALS	LOOPING
SCHOLAR	RECEDED	POOLING
INBREDS	STAMPED	REBINDS
TROOPED	DECREED	TORPEDO

TIME TAKEN:	INCORRECT ANSWERS:
TIME POINTS:	**TOTAL SCORE:**

Word List

Try to memorize these 24 tennis terms.

After 2 minutes, cover the table and write as many as you can in the boxes below. You do not need to remember the correct order.

Ace	Umpire	Net	Singles
Mixed	Love	Deuce	Doubles
Forehand	Court	Backhand	Clay
Chip	Drop shot	Let	Service
Sideline	Smash	Chip	Slice
Lob	Spin	Topspin	Rally

Now try to recall as many as you can:

INCORRECT ANSWERS:	TOTAL SCORE:

Missing Signs

Insert the missing sign into each of these arithmetic expressions in order to make the equation true. You will need to add, subtract, multiply, or divide.

100 ☐ 19 = 81	96 ☐ 24 = 120	21 ☐ 1 = 20
58 ☐ 15 = 43	2 ☐ 12 = 24	93 ☐ 9 = 84
7 ☐ 10 = 70	11 ☐ 47 = 58	90 ☐ 1 = 89
44 ☐ 17 = 27	10 ☐ 3 = 30	57 ☐ 37 = 20
71 ☐ 2 = 69	22 ☐ 11 = 2	9 ☐ 3 = 3
6 ☐ 2 = 12	10 ☐ 12 = 120	50 ☐ 23 = 27
1 ☐ 124 = 125	36 ☐ 3 = 12	98 ☐ 12 = 110
83 ☐ 19 = 64	107 ☐ 37 = 70	28 ☐ 30 = 58
23 ☐ 19 = 4	64 ☐ 8 = 8	8 ☐ 11 = 88
91 ☐ 7 = 13	49 ☐ 29 = 20	21 ☐ 3 = 7
30 ☐ 3 = 10	7 ☐ 9 = 63	4 ☐ 9 = 36
28 ☐ 40 = 68	86 ☐ 17 = 103	43 ☐ 32 = 75
40 ☐ 5 = 8	91 ☐ 25 = 66	32 ☐ 22 = 10

TIME TAKEN:	INCORRECT ANSWERS:
TIME POINTS:	**TOTAL SCORE:**

Creative Thinking

See if you can solve each of the following conundrums. If you get stuck then try thinking laterally – they all have logical solutions, but the logic might not be what you expect!

What is the only number which, when written out in words, has all of its letters in alphabetical order?

How many apples would you have if you took 43 out of a basket of 52 apples?

TIME TAKEN:	INCORRECT ANSWERS:
TIME POINTS:	**TOTAL SCORE:**

Cryptogram

Decode each of these quotations by replacing A with Q, B with R, C with S, and so on, through to replacing Y with O and Z with P.

Xekijed, Jhqdgkybyjo Rqiu xuhu. Jxu Uqwbu xqi bqdtut.

Rkpp Qbthyd

Y fkj kf co jxkcr qdt yj rbejjut ekj jxu fbqduj Uqhjx.

Duyb Qhcijhedw

Y sekbt xqlu wedu ed vboydw jxhekwx ifqsu vehuluh

Okhy Wqwqhyd

Ifqsu yid'j huceju qj qbb. Yj'i edbo qd xekh'i thylu qmqo yv oekh sqh sekbt we ijhqywxj kfmqhti.

Vhut Xeobu

TIME TAKEN:	INCORRECT ANSWERS:
TIME POINTS:	**TOTAL SCORE:**

Rotation

If you were to rotate each of these three pictures as indicated by the arrow beneath, which of the figures below would be the result?

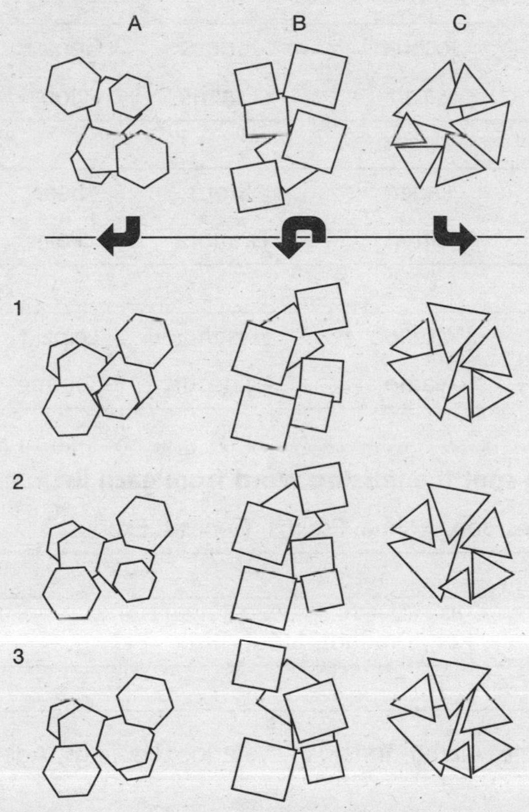

TIME TAKEN:	INCORRECT ANSWERS:
TIME POINTS:	**TOTAL SCORE:**

Missing Words

Study each of these 3 lists of words for a total of 2 minutes. Then cover the top half of the page and see if you can identify which word is missing from each of the lists below.

Ruth	Joshua	Judges	Genesis
Exodus	Isaiah	Psalms	Job

Ale	Lager	Stout	Beer
Keg	Bitter	Draught	Pale

Trafalgar	Waterloo	Hastings	Leipzig
Boyne	Alamo	Agincourt	Somme

Now try to spot the missing word from each list:

Isaiah, Judges, Job, Joshua, Psalms, Genesis, Exodus

MISSING:

Lager, Ale, Pale, Keg, Draught, Stout, Bitter

MISSING:

Leipzig, Boyne, Alamo, Trafalgar, Waterloo, Hastings, Agincourt

MISSING:

INCORRECT ANSWERS:	TOTAL SCORE:

Reflective Power

Look at each of the figures above the vertical "mirror". Work out which of the figures below the line corresponds to the same figure when reflected in the mirror line.

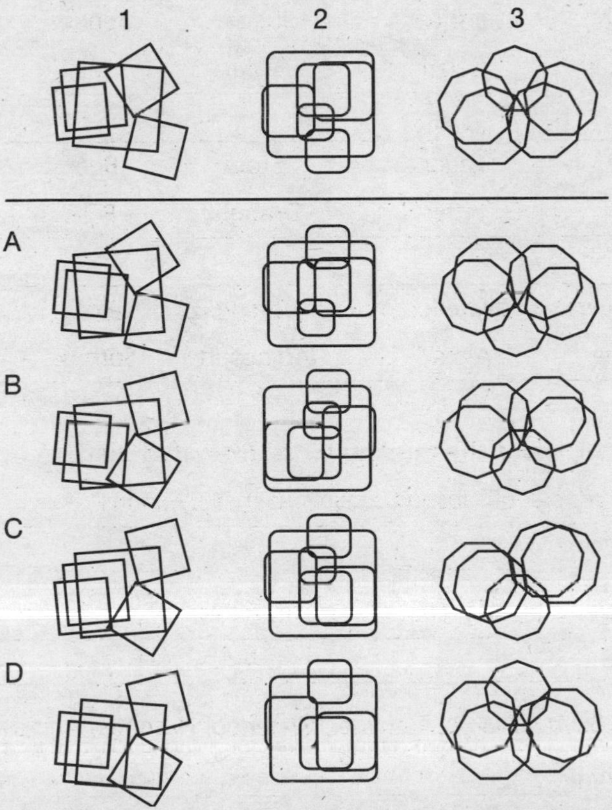

1 2 3

A

B

C

D

TIME TAKEN:	INCORRECT ANSWERS:
TIME POINTS:	**TOTAL SCORE:**

Time Elapsed

Work out how many hours and minutes have passed between each of these pairs of times.

12:30pm to 11:20pm =		1:40pm to 11:45pm =	
3:15am to 1:25pm =		12:15pm to 10:00pm =	
5:30am to 6:45am =		5:10pm to 7:55pm =	
4:15am to 10:15pm =		2:15am to 4:00am =	
7:55am to 12:30pm =		12:45pm to 3:30pm =	
5:35am to 6:20pm =		4:55am to 5:10pm =	
7:35am to 1:00pm =		1:10am to 4:20pm =	
7:10am to 6:50pm =		11:05am to 10:40pm =	
12:45am to 7:30pm =		2:40am to 7:50pm =	
12:25pm to 7:30pm =		3:25am to 8:00am =	
3:15pm to 8:55pm =		6:50am to 5:35pm =	
7:15am to 10:10am =		9:05am to 6:20pm =	
12:55pm to 3:15pm =		11:40am to 5:50pm =	
6:30pm to 7:35pm =		12:55pm to 6:30pm =	
6:35pm to 7:05pm =		5:45pm to 7:35pm =	

TIME TAKEN:	INCORRECT ANSWERS:
TIME POINTS:	**TOTAL SCORE:**

Shape Dividing

Draw three straight lines in order to divide the shape into four separate areas. Each area must contain precisely one of each size of circle. The three lines may touch but they must not cross.

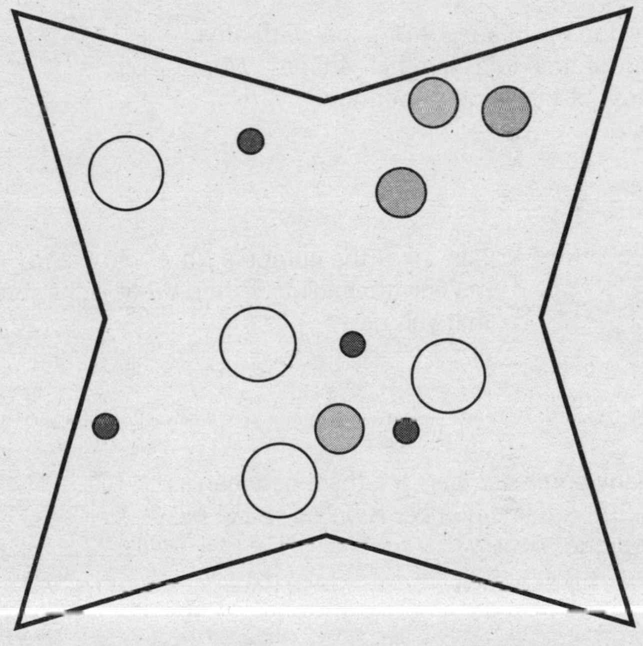

TIME TAKEN:	INCORRECT ANSWERS:
TIME POINTS:	**TOTAL SCORE:**

Logical Puzzlers

Try to solve these problems – each requires only simple logic to solve, but you might find that making notes with a pencil will help!

Simeon starts with a piece of paper with area 200cm². He then folds it in half 4 times. What is the area of the visible paper now?

Take all of the numbers from 1 to 6 and multiply them all together. What is the result that you get?

How many prime numbers are there between 10 and 30? A prime number is only divisible by itself and one.

TIME TAKEN:	INCORRECT ANSWERS:
TIME POINTS:	**TOTAL SCORE:**

Observation and Counting

Look at these stars and see how long it takes you to answer these observation questions.

How many stars can you count?

How many areas are formed between the lines?

How many diamonds can you find?

TIME TAKEN:	INCORRECT ANSWERS:
TIME POINTS:	**TOTAL SCORE:**

Visual Memory

Spend 1 minute studying this path. Then cover the top half of this page and try to redraw it accurately on the empty grid below.

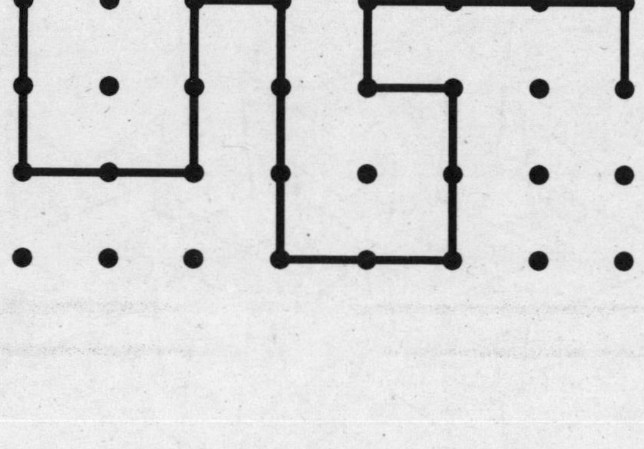

INCORRECT ANSWERS:	**TOTAL SCORE:**

Solutions

1: Anagrammatic

Set 1: 1 pair of anagrams:
DEFILING and FIELDING

Set 2: 6 pairs of anagrams:
TASTES and STATES
PLUSES and PULSES
TUTORS and TROUTS
RESIDE and DESIRE
INROAD and ORDAIN
RESIGN and SIGNER

Set 3: 2 pairs of anagrams:
RASPIER and REPAIRS
SCANTER and CANTERS

Set 4: 6 pairs of anagrams:
ALGORITHM and LOGARITHM
CERTIFIED and RECTIFIED
BOULDERED and REDOUBLED
COUNTERED and RECOUNTED
RAGGEDEST and STAGGERED
EDUCATION and CAUTIONED

3: Missing Signs

100	–	19 = 81	96	+	24 = 120	21	–	1 = 20
58	–	15 = 43	2	×	12 = 24	93	–	9 = 84
7	×	10 = 70	11	+	47 = 58	90	–	1 = 89
44	–	17 = 27	10	×	3 = 30	57	–	37 = 20
71	–	2 = 69	22	÷	11 = 2	9	÷	3 = 3
6	×	2 = 12	10	×	12 = 120	50	–	23 = 27
1	+	124 = 125	36	÷	3 = 12	98	+	12 = 110
83	–	19 = 64	107	–	37 = 70	28	+	30 = 58
23	–	19 = 4	64	÷	8 = 8	8	×	11 = 88
91	÷	7 = 13	49	–	29 = 20	21	÷	3 = 7
30	÷	3 = 10	7	×	9 = 63	4	×	9 = 36
28	+	40 = 68	86	+	17 = 103	43	+	32 = 75
40	÷	5 = 8	91	–	25 = 66	32	–	22 = 10

4: Creative Thinking

Forty.

You'd have 43, since that's how many you took!

5: Cryptograms

Houston, Tranquility Base here. The Eagle has landed.

Buzz Aldrin

I put up my thumb and it blotted out the planet Earth.

Neil Armstrong

I could have gone on flying through space forever

Yuri Gagarin

Space isn't remote at all. It's only an hour's drive away if your car could go straight upwards.

Fred Hoyle

6: Rotation

A2, B2, C2

8: Reflective Power

1B, 2C, 3A

9: Time Elapsed

12:30pm to 11:20pm =	**10:50**	1:40pm to 11:45pm =	**10:05**
3:15am to 1:25pm =	**10:10**	12:15pm to 10:00pm =	**9:45**
5:30am to 6:45am =	**1:15**	5:10pm to 7:55pm =	**2:45**
4:15am to 10:15pm =	**18:00**	2:15am to 4:00am =	**1:45**
7:55am to 12:30pm =	**4:35**	12:45pm to 3:30pm =	**2:45**
5:35am to 6:20pm =	**12:45**	4:55am to 5:10pm =	**12:15**
7:35am to 1:00pm =	**5:25**	1:10am to 4:20pm =	**15:10**
7:10am to 6:50pm –	**11:40**	11:05am to 10:40pm =	**11:35**
12:45am to 7:30pm =	**18:45**	2:40am to 7:50pm =	**17:10**
12:25pm to 7:30pm =	**7:05**	3:25am to 8:00am =	**4:35**
3:15pm to 8:55pm =	**5:40**	6:50am to 5:35pm =	**10:45**
7:15am to 10:10am =	**2:55**	9:05am to 6:20pm =	**9:15**
12:55pm to 3:15pm =	**2:20**	11:40am to 5:50pm =	**6:10**
6:30pm to 7:35pm =	**1:05**	12:55pm to 6:30pm =	**5:35**
6:35pm to 7:05pm =	**0:30**	5:45pm to 7:35pm =	**1:50**

10: Shape Dividing

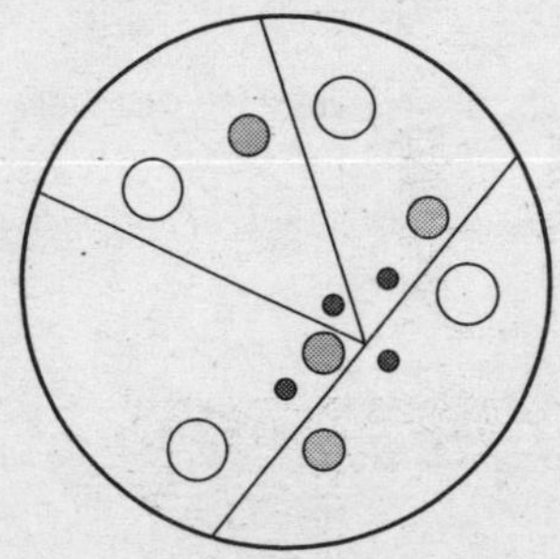

11: Logical Puzzlers

12.5cm^2.

720.

6 primes. They are 11, 13, 17, 19, 23 and 29.

12: Observation and Counting

6 stars in total.

12 areas are formed between the lines.

2 diamonds.

DAY
17

Word List

Try to memorize these 24 Native American tribes.

After 2 minutes cover the table and recall as many as you can in the boxes below. You do not need to remember the correct order.

Sioux	Ute	Yuma	Mohican
Chinook	Apache	Aguaruna	Omaha
Cherokee	Kickapoo	Maya	Wappo
Yaqui	Zuni	Mohawk	Natchez
Araucan	Biloxi	Dogrib	Chilcal
Crow	Kiowa	Lipan	Delaware

Now try to recall as many as you can:

INCORRECT ANSWERS:	**TOTAL SCORE:**

Reflective Power

Look at each of the figures above the horizontal "mirror". Work out which of the figures below the line corresponds to the figure reflected in the mirror line.

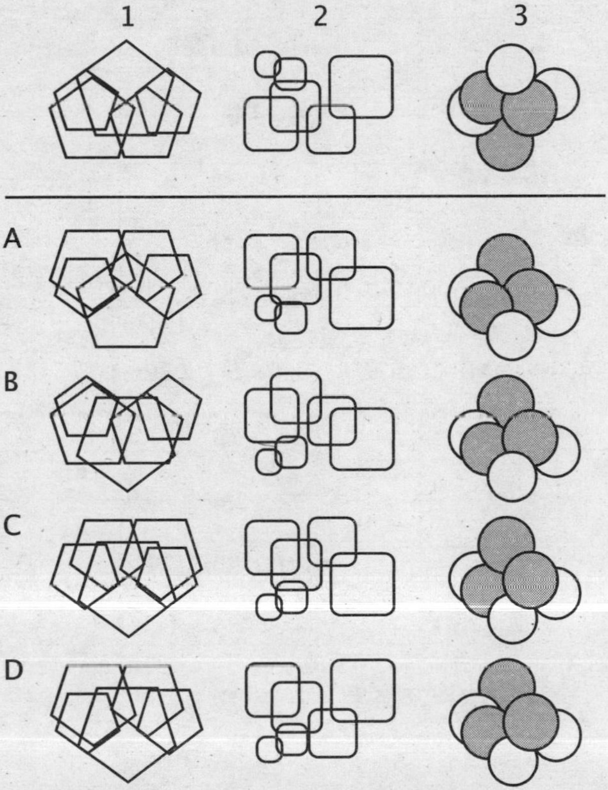

1 2 3

A

B

C

D

TIME TAKEN:	INCORRECT ANSWERS:
TIME POINTS:	**TOTAL SCORE:**

Missing Numbers

Insert the missing number into each of these arithmetic expressions in order to make the equations true. You should not need a calculator to do this!

35 − ☐ = **20**	☐ − 2 = **32**	80 − ☐ = **74**
5 − ☐ = **1**	☐ + 5 = **38**	☐ − 7 = **68**
☐ + 58 = **67**	☐ + 41 = **56**	9 + ☐ = **50**
☐ + 16 = **79**	94 + ☐ = **96**	☐ − 16 = **90**
☐ + 5 = **102**	☐ × 3 = **33**	16 + ☐ = **55**
103 − ☐ = **98**	☐ + 2 = **12**	35 − ☐ = **27**
☐ + 9 = **18**	9 × ☐ = **54**	65 − ☐ = **62**
☐ − 8 = **40**	☐ − 11 = **19**	91 + ☐ = **100**
☐ + 49 = **60**	☐ × 12 = **24**	88 + ☐ = **92**
99 − ☐ = **80**	☐ − 13 = **59**	17 − ☐ = **10**
15 + ☐ = **110**	☐ − 15 = **60**	☐ − 20 = **52**
☐ − 16 = **18**	8 × ☐ = **16**	☐ + 6 = **76**
☐ − 19 = **74**	66 − ☐ = **59**	1 + ☐ = **6**

TIME TAKEN:	INCORRECT ANSWERS:
TIME POINTS:	**TOTAL SCORE:**

Odd One Out

Look at each of these sets of words. Can you work out which word is the odd one out in each case?

Potomac Mississippi
Hudson
Amazon Missouri

Chips Book
Soda
Pants Cookie

Dictionary Diary
Thesaurus
Almanac Encyclopaedia

Vermont Washington
Hoover
Lincoln Garfield

TIME TAKEN:	INCORRECT ANSWERS:
TIME POINTS:	**TOTAL SCORE:**

Missing Words

Study each of these 3 lists of words for 2 minutes. Then cover the top half of the page and see if you can identify which word is missing from each list below.

Backpack	Briefcase	Rucksack	Suitcase
Valise	Knapsack	Carrier	Satchel

Acrylic	Oil	Watercolour	Crayon
Chalk	Pastel	Charcoal	Ink

Cosine	Tangent	Division	Sum
Radius	Sine	Obtuse	Scalar

Now try to spot the missing word from each list:

Suitcase, Satchel, Valise, Rucksack, Briefcase, Knapsack, Backpack

MISSING:

Ink, Charcoal, Watercolour, Crayon, Pastel, Chalk, Oil

MISSING:

Sine, Division, Cosine, Tangent, Radius, Obtuse, Sum

MISSING:

INCORRECT ANSWERS:	TOTAL SCORE:

Creative Thinking

See if you can solve each of the following conundrums. If you get stuck then try thinking laterally – they all have logical solutions, but the logic might not be what you expect!

In a question of morality, may a man legally marry his widow's sister?

I'm holding a horse-race but I want there to be a twist on the usual proceedings: the horse that comes in last will win. However I don't want the race to last forever, so what can I do to persuade the jockeys to ride normally?

TIME TAKEN:	INCORRECT ANSWERS:
TIME POINTS:	**TOTAL SCORE:**

Logical Puzzlers

Try to solve these problems – each requires only simple logic to solve, but you might find that making notes with a pencil will help!

Danielle's garden has three trees in it, each of which spreads enough seeds to cause three more trees to grow each year. Unfortunately, half of all the trees in her garden die each year due to a fungal disease. Assuming the trees reproduce at a consistent rate even from the first year of growth, how many trees will she have after two full years?

If a ship that departs Galveston at 3:00pm and normally takes 15 hours to cross to Mexico is delayed by bad weather and so takes half as long again as usual to make the crossing, at what time will it end its crossing?

If daylight today lasts for 7 hours, how many hours of the day are night-time?

TIME TAKEN:	INCORRECT ANSWERS:
TIME POINTS:	**TOTAL SCORE:**

Visual Memory

Spend 1 minute studying this path. Then cover the top half of this page and try to redraw it accurately on the empty grid below.

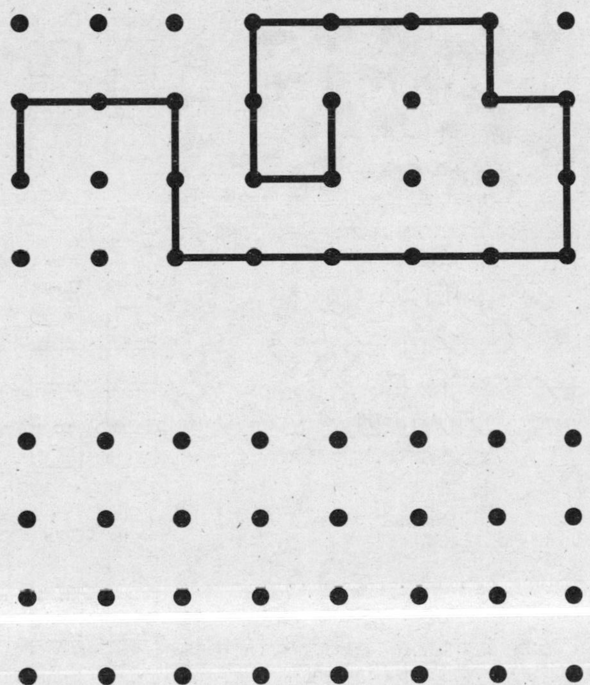

INCORRECT ANSWERS:	TOTAL SCORE:

Counting and Perception

Spend no more than 10 seconds looking at each group of symbols in each turn, then try to sort them into order of increasing frequency. Write "1" in the "Order" column for the shape that occurs least often, and so on.

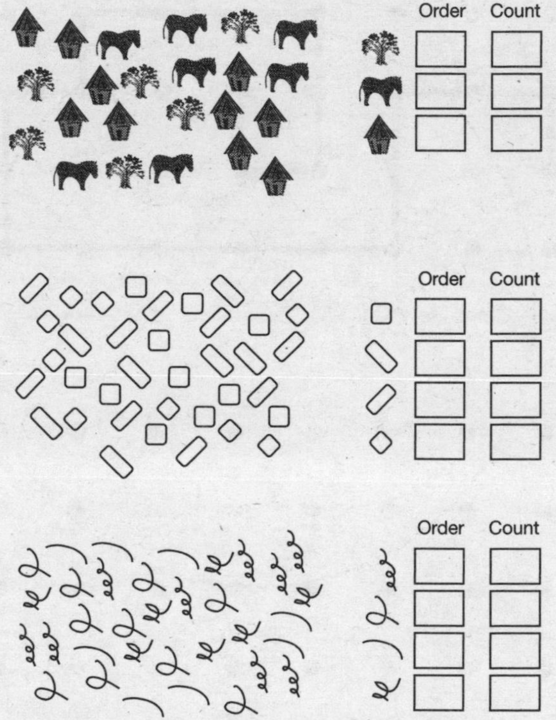

Now take as long as you think you need to write in the second column the precise count of each symbol.

TIME TAKEN:	INCORRECT ANSWERS:
TIME POINTS:	**TOTAL SCORE:**

Shape Dividing

Draw three straight lines in order to divide the shape into four separate areas. Each area must contain precisely one of each size of circle. The three lines may touch but they must not cross.

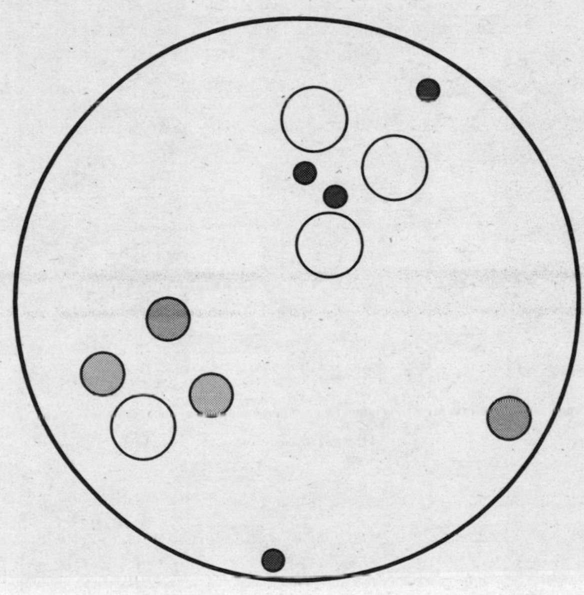

TIME TAKEN:	INCORRECT ANSWERS:
TIME POINTS:	**TOTAL SCORE:**

Speed Arithmetic

Complete the following set of arithmetic equations as quickly as possible. You should be able to do them all in your head without using a calculator or making notes.

1 + 64 =	25 − 19 =	89 − 4 =
66 − 4 =	106 − 5 =	32 − 6 =
9 + 87 =	100 − 7 =	6 × 6 =
77 + 12 =	74 − 16 =	41 − 9 =
91 − 13 =	93 − 6 =	5 + 98 =
7 × 8 =	20 + 98 =	86 − 17 =
2 + 84 =	17 + 79 =	16 + 96 =
18 + 67 =	40 − 13 =	74 − 14 =
65 + 18 =	55 − 19 =	51 − 10 =
42 − 5 =	65 + 19 =	17 + 64 =
25 − 5 =	8 × 5 =	43 + 6 =
16 + 72 =	47 − 11 =	12 + 76 =
51 − 15 =	9 × 4 =	2 × 12 =

TIME TAKEN:	INCORRECT ANSWERS:
TIME POINTS:	**TOTAL SCORE:**

Shape Folding

If you were to cut out this shape and fold it into a cube, which of the three pictures below would result?

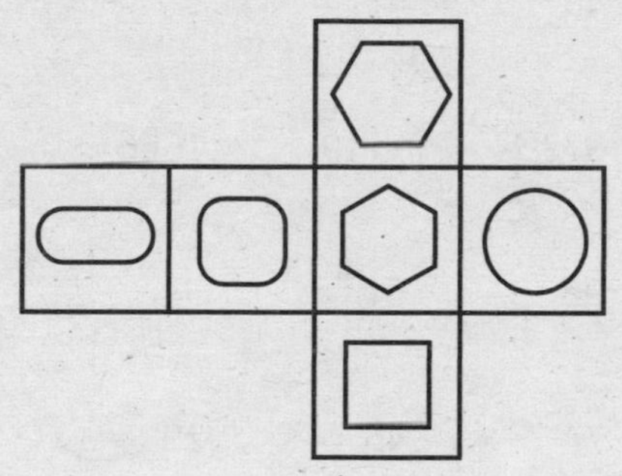

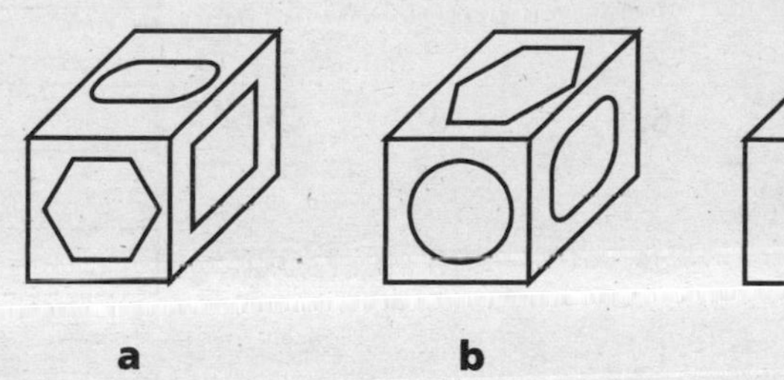

a **b** **c**

TIME TAKEN:	INCORRECT ANSWERS:
TIME POINTS:	**TOTAL SCORE:**

Number Sequences

Look at each of these number sequences and see if you can deduce which number comes next in the series.

1	40	41	81	122	
25	572	1119	1666	2213	
139	96	61	34	15	
119	74	45	29	16	
4	12	36	108	324	
668	1167	1666	2165	2664	
366	356	346	336	326	
2048	512	128	32	8	

TIME TAKEN:	INCORRECT ANSWERS:
TIME POINTS:	**TOTAL SCORE:**

Solutions

2: Reflective Power

1B, 2D, 3A

3: Missing Numbers

35 − [15] = **20**	[34] − 2 = **32**	80 − [6] = **74**
5 − [4] = **1**	[33] + 5 = **38**	[75] − 7 = **68**
[9] + 58 = **67**	[15] + 41 = **56**	9 + [41] = **50**
[63] + 16 = **79**	94 + [2] = **96**	[106] − 16 = **90**
[97] + 5 = **102**	[11] × 3 = **33**	16 + [39] = **55**
103 − [5] = **98**	[10] + 2 = **12**	35 − [8] = **27**
[9] + 9 = **18**	9 × [6] = **54**	65 − [3] = **62**
[48] − 8 = **40**	[30] − 11 = **19**	91 + [9] = **100**
[11] + 49 = **60**	[2] × 12 = **24**	88 + [4] = **92**
99 − [19] = **80**	[72] − 13 = **59**	17 − [7] = **10**
15 + [95] = **110**	[75] − 15 = **60**	[72] − 20 = **52**
[34] − 16 = **18**	8 × [2] = **16**	[70] + 6 = **76**
[93] − 19 = **74**	66 − [7] = **59**	1 + [5] = **6**

4: Odd One Out

Amazon – the rest are rivers in the USA
Book – the rest have different meanings in British and American English
Diary – the rest are pre-printed reference books; a diary you write yourself
Vermont – not a president of the USA

6: Creative Thinking

No, because the man is already dead!

You get each jockey to swap horses with another, so they naturally want to beat the horse they are no longer riding and thus they all try to win.

7: Logical Puzzlers

12 trees. Plant 3, have 9 offspring. Half die, giving 6. These then have 18 offspring, but half of the total die, leaving 12.

1:30pm tomorrow.

17 hours.

9: Counting and Perception

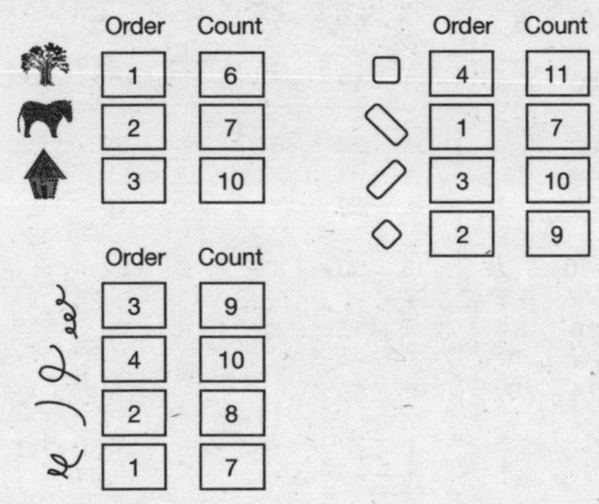

10: Shape Dividing

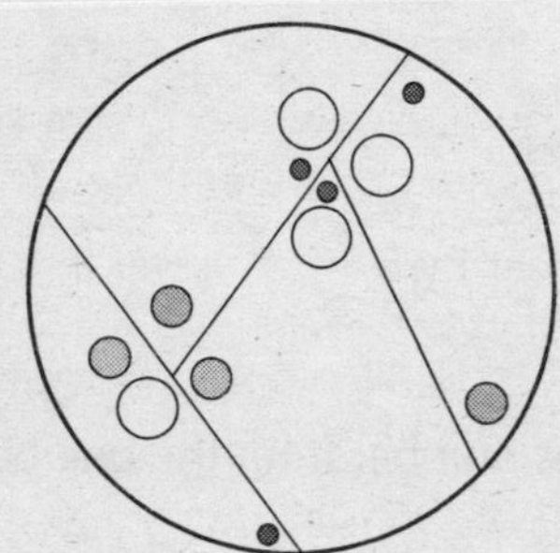

11: Speed Arithmetic

1 + 64 = **65**	25 − 19 = **6**	89 − 4 = **85**
66 − 4 = **62**	106 − 5 = **101**	32 − 6 = **26**
9 + 87 = **96**	100 − 7 = **93**	6 × 6 = **36**
77 + 12 = **89**	74 − 16 = **58**	41 − 9 = **32**
91 − 13 = **78**	93 − 6 = **87**	5 + 98 = **103**
7 × 8 = **56**	20 + 98 = **118**	86 − 17 = **69**
2 + 84 = **86**	17 + 79 = **96**	16 + 96 = **112**
18 + 67 = **85**	40 − 13 = **27**	74 − 14 = **60**
65 + 18 = **83**	55 − 19 = **36**	51 − 10 = **41**
42 − 5 = **37**	65 + 19 = **84**	17 + 64 = **81**
25 − 5 = **20**	8 × 5 = **40**	43 + 6 = **49**
16 + 72 = **88**	47 − 11 = **36**	12 + 76 = **88**
51 − 15 = **36**	9 × 4 = **36**	2 × 12 = **24**

12: Shape Folding

C

13: Number Sequences

15552, 2592, 432, 72, 12, **2**
Rule: divide previous number by 6

285, 173, 112, 61, 51, **10**
Rule: subtract the previous number from the one before it

13, 93, 106, 199, 305, **504**
Rule: add the previous two numbers

256, 157, 99, 58, 41, **17**
Rule: subtract the previous number from the one before it

605, 562, 526, 497, 475, **460**
Rule: difference between numbers decreases by 7 each time

1, 8, 9, 17, 26, **43**
Rule: add the previous two numbers

3, 6, 9, 15, 24, **39**
Rule: add the previous two numbers

655, 648, 641, 634, 627, **620**
Rule: subtract 7 from previous number

DAY
18

Visual Memory

Spend 1 minute studying this path. Then cover the top half of this page and try to redraw it accurately on the empty grid below.

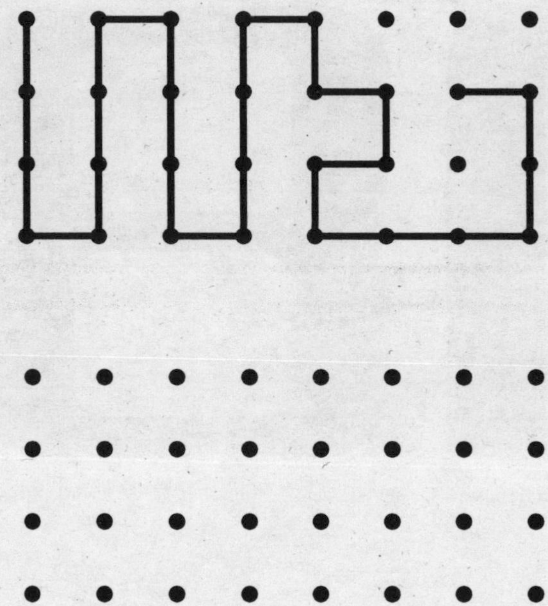

INCORRECT ANSWERS:	**TOTAL SCORE:**

Rotation

If you were to rotate each of the three pictures as indicated by the arrow beneath, which of the figures below would be the result?

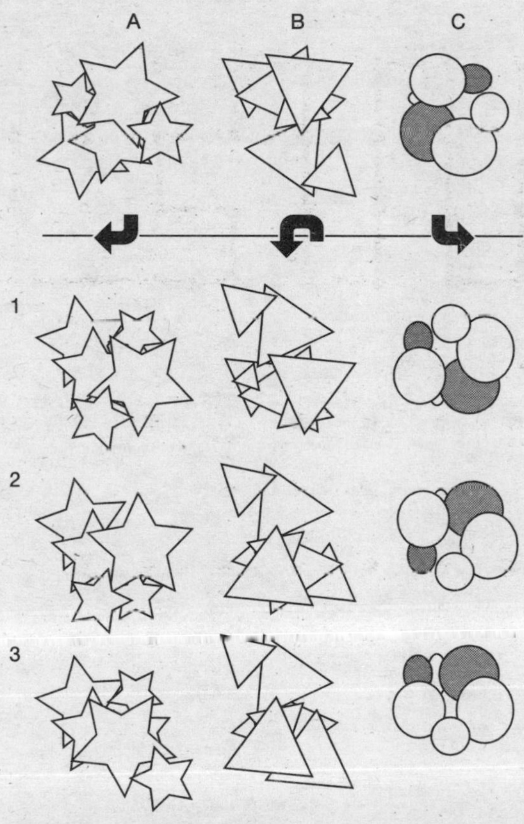

TIME TAKEN:	INCORRECT ANSWERS:
TIME POINTS:	**TOTAL SCORE:**

Time Elapsed

Work out how many hours and minutes have passed between each of these pairs of times.

3:10am to 2:50pm =		5:35am to 9:00am =	
1:10am to 9:55am =		1:55am to 8:50pm =	
11:25am to 5:35pm =		1:45pm to 4:35pm =	
9:30am to 11:20am =		8:05am to 9:00pm =	
6:10pm to 8:55pm =		7:45am to 11:05pm =	
7:20am to 8:55am =		11:45am to 8:30pm =	
2:55am to 10:40am =		7:35am to 7:45am =	
10:10am to 7:00pm =		3:50am to 5:45am =	
12:25am to 5:40am =		12:35pm to 10:35pm =	
12:40am to 7:25pm =		3:55pm to 10:20pm =	
5:00am to 11:05pm =		12:30am to 3:25pm =	
1:30pm to 4:50pm =		10:45am to 11:25am =	
1:45pm to 10:40pm =		2:10am to 2:45am =	
6:30am to 7:10pm =		6:40am to 4:35pm =	
3:50pm to 10:15pm =		11:50am to 4:35pm =	

TIME TAKEN:	INCORRECT ANSWERS:
TIME POINTS:	**TOTAL SCORE:**

Observation and Counting

Look at these overlapping images and see how long it takes you to answer the observation questions below.

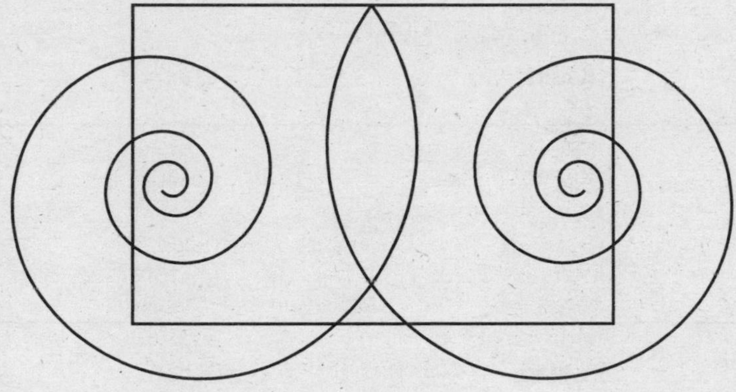

How many areas are there between these lines?

Can you draw the entire figure in a single pen stroke, without going over a line more than once? You may cross over an existing line.

If you were to colour in each area so that no two areas of the same colour touched on any side, how many colours would you need?

TIME TAKEN:	INCORRECT ANSWERS:
TIME POINTS:	**TOTAL SCORE:**

Odd One Out

Look at each of these sets of words. Can you work out which word is the odd one out in each case?

Grape
Fig
Elderberry
Raisin
Cherry

Moment
Instant
Point
Interval
Juncture

Instead
Detains
Trained
Satined
Stained

Man
Fence
Mark
Script
Box

TIME TAKEN:	INCORRECT ANSWERS:
TIME POINTS:	**TOTAL SCORE:**

Matchstick Thinking

The picture below shows 4 matchsticks arranged into a cross shape.

Can you move 1 matchstick only in order to create a perfect square?

TIME TAKEN:	INCORRECT ANSWERS:
TIME POINTS:	**TOTAL SCORE:**

Word List

Try to memorize these 24 European races.

After 2 minutes, cover the table and write as many as you can in the boxes below. You do not need to remember the correct order.

French	Greek	Celt	Prussian
Slovak	Jute	Russian	Hellenic
Fleming	English	Aryan	Albanian
Visigoth	Saxon	Scot	Maltese
Manx	Irish	Icelandic	Iberian
Welsh	Swede	Swiss	Turk

Now try to recall as many as you can:

INCORRECT ANSWERS:	**TOTAL SCORE:**

Logical Puzzlers

Try to solve these problems – each requires only simple logic to solve, but you might find that making notes with a pencil will help!

If I eat half a cake, then a third of what's left, and finally a quarter of the remainder, how much is left of 12 original slices?

If I toss a coin into the air five times, what is the likelihood of it landing heads-down all five times?

If my three cats each have five kittens, and the kittens in turn later have five more kittens each, how many cats would I have in total?

TIME TAKEN:	INCORRECT ANSWERS:
TIME POINTS:	**TOTAL SCORE:**

Creative Thinking

See if you can solve each of the following conundrums. If you get stuck then try thinking laterally – they all have logical solutions, but the logic might not be what you expect!

If I dig a hole in the ground to a total volume of two metres cubed, how much soil is there in the hole?

Can you find a set of four letters, consisting of the letter "O" and three consonants, from which you can make six different four-letter words using all four letters each time? The words are all fairly common.

TIME TAKEN:	INCORRECT ANSWERS:
TIME POINTS:	**TOTAL SCORE:**

Missing Words

Study each of these 3 lists of words for a total of 2 minutes. Then cover the top half of the page and see if you can identify which word is missing from each list below.

Dinner	Brunch	Lunch	Breakfast
Supper	Tea	Snack	Feast

Geriatrics	Cardiology	Psychology	Neurology
Pathology	Virology	Dermatology	Chiropody

Quartz	Graphite	Agate	Dolomite
Mica	Zircon	Opal	Malachite

Now try to spot the missing word from each list:

Brunch, Snack, Dinner, Lunch, Supper, Breakfast, Tea

MISSING:

Dermatology, Neurology, Psychology, Virology, Pathology, Chiropody, Cardiology

MISSING:

Opal, Agate, Dolomite, Mica, Zircon, Quartz, Graphite

MISSING:

INCORRECT ANSWERS:	TOTAL SCORE:

Reflective Power

Look at each of the figures above the vertical "mirror". Work out which of the figures below the line corresponds to the figure when reflected in the mirror line.

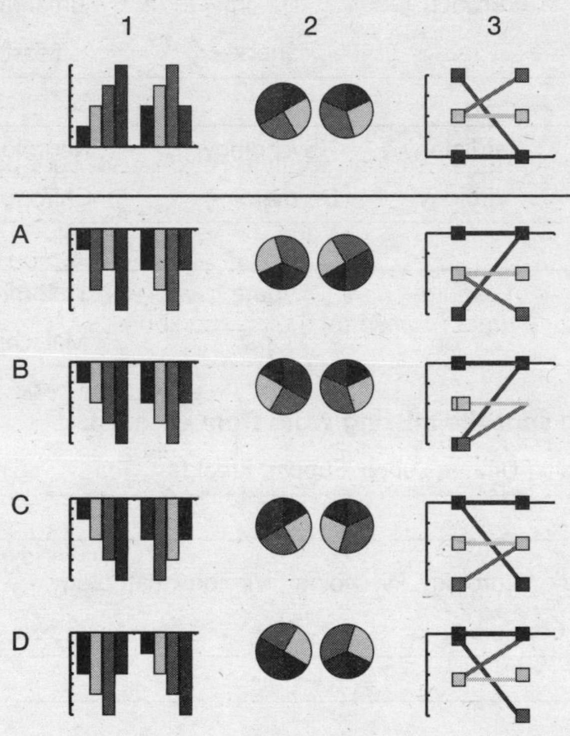

TIME TAKEN:	INCORRECT ANSWERS:
TIME POINTS:	**TOTAL SCORE:**

Cryptogram

Decode each of these quotations by replacing A with E, B with F, C with G, and so on, through to replacing Y with C and Z with D.

Npwjoh gspn Xbmft up Jubmz jt mjlf npwjoh up b ejggfsfou dpvousz

Jbo Svti

Tvsf uifsf ibwf cffo jokvsjft boe efbuit jo cpyjoh - cvu opof pg uifn tfsjpvt

Bmbo Njoufs

Zpv xbudi uif qjumbof xijmf J tupq uif tubsu xbudi...

Nvssbz Xbmlfs

Uif gjstu ojofuz njovuft pg b gppucbmm nbudi bsf uif nptu jnqpsubou.

Cpccz Spctpo.

TIME TAKEN:	INCORRECT ANSWERS:
TIME POINTS:	**TOTAL SCORE:**

Speed Arithmetic

Complete the following set of arithmetic equations as quickly as possible. You should be able to do them all in your head without using a calculator or making notes.

7 + 27 =	7 × 3 =	5 × 12 =
3 + 10 =	9 + 16 =	92 + 6 =
11 × 9 =	63 + 3 =	4 + 57 =
4 + 67 =	7 × 7 =	59 + 5 =
8 − 5 =	62 + 18 =	44 − 18 =
9 + 22 =	71 − 12 =	11 + 52 =
69 − 18 =	18 + 38 =	66 + 10 =
8 + 13 =	91 − 10 =	19 + 9 =
11 + 70 =	93 + 6 =	55 + 11 =
11 + 10 =	95 − 5 =	23 − 19 =
3 + 32 =	3 + 97 =	14 + 11 =
60 + 4 =	19 + 54 =	65 + 8 =
87 − 6 =	10 × 11 =	11 + 38 =

TIME TAKEN:	INCORRECT ANSWERS:
TIME POINTS:	**TOTAL SCORE:**

Solutions

2: Rotation

A1, B2, C1

3: Time Elapsed

3:10am to 2:50pm =	:	5:35am to 9:00am =	:
1:10am to 9:55am =	:	1:55am to 8:50pm =	:
11:25am to 5:35pm =	:	1:45pm to 4:35pm =	:
9:30am to 11:20am =	:	8:05am to 9:00pm =	:
6:10pm to 8:55pm =	:	7:45am to 11:05pm =	:
7:20am to 8:55am =	:	11:45am to 8:30pm =	:
2:55am to 10:40am =	:	7:35am to 7:45am =	:
10:10am to 7:00pm =	:	3:50am to 5:45am =	:
12:25am to 5:40am =	:	12:35pm to 10:35pm =	:
12:40am to 7:25pm =	:	3:55pm to 10:20pm =	:
5:00am to 11:05pm =	:	12:30am to 3:25pm =	:
1:30pm to 4:50pm =	:	10:45am to 11:25am =	:
1:45pm to 10:40pm =	:	2:10am to 2:45am =	:
6:30am to 7:10pm =	:	6:40am to 4:35pm =	:
3:50pm to 10:15pm =	:	11:50am to 4:35pm =	:

4: Observation and Counting

10 areas between the lines.

Yes, you can draw it in a single stroke.

3 colours are needed.

5: Odd One Out
Raisin – it is a dried, not fresh, fruit
Interval – the rest refer to a particular instant in time, as opposed to a period of time
Trained – the rest are anagrams of each other
Fence – the rest make new words when prefixed with 'post'

6: Matchstick Thinking

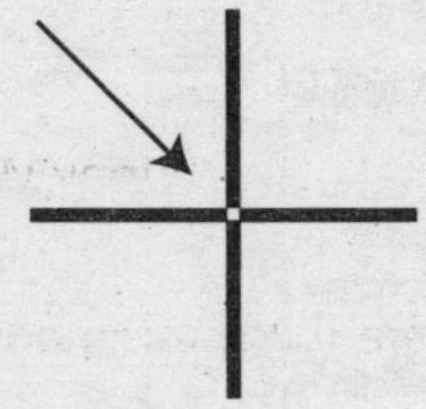

8: Logical Puzzlers
3 slices.

The likelihood is 1 in 32, or in other words a half multiplied by itself 5 times.

93 cats, which is 3 + (3 times 5) + (15 times 5).

9: Creative Thinking
There's no soil in the hole; you've already dug it out.

The letters are O, P, S and T, making post, spot, stop, opts, tops and pots.

11: Reflective Power
1B, 2A, 3C

12: Cryptogram

Moving from Wales to Italy is like moving to a different country.

Ian Rush

Sure there have been injuries and deaths in boxing – but none of them serious.

Alan Minter

You watch the pitlane while I stop the start watch...

Murray Walker

The first ninety minutes of a football match are the most important.

Bobby Robson.

12: Speed Arithmetic

7 + 27 = **34**	7 × 3 = **21**	5 × 12 = **60**
3 + 10 = **13**	9 + 16 = **25**	92 + 6 = **98**
11 × 9 = **99**	63 + 3 = **66**	4 + 57 = **61**
4 + 67 = **71**	7 × 7 = **49**	59 + 5 = **64**
8 − 5 = **3**	62 + 18 = **80**	44 − 18 = **26**
9 + 22 = **31**	71 − 12 = **59**	11 + 52 = **63**
69 − 18 = **51**	18 + 38 = **56**	66 + 10 = **76**
8 + 13 = **21**	91 − 10 = **81**	19 + 9 = **28**
11 + 70 = **81**	93 + 6 = **99**	55 + 11 = **66**
11 + 10 = **21**	95 − 5 = **90**	23 − 19 = **4**
3 + 32 = **35**	3 + 97 = **100**	14 + 11 = **25**
60 + 4 = **64**	19 + 54 = **73**	65 + 8 = **73**
87 − 6 = **81**	10 × 11 = **110**	11 + 38 = **49**

DAY
19

Word List

Try to memorize these 24 American Football terms.

After 2 minutes cover the table and write as many as you can in the boxes below. You do not need to remember the correct order.

Backfield	Safety	Tackle	Halfback
Gridiron	End zone	Turnover	Pass
Offense	Lineman	Touchback	Touchdown
Play	Blitz	Guard	Interception
Kicker	Cheerleader	Punt	Shotgun
Snap	Cornerback	Football	Overtime

Now try to recall as many as you can:

INCORRECT ANSWERS:	**TOTAL SCORE:**

Counting and Perception

Spend no more than 10 seconds looking at each group of symbols in each turn, then try to sort them into order of increasing frequency. Write "1" in the "Order" column for the shape that occurs least often, and so on.

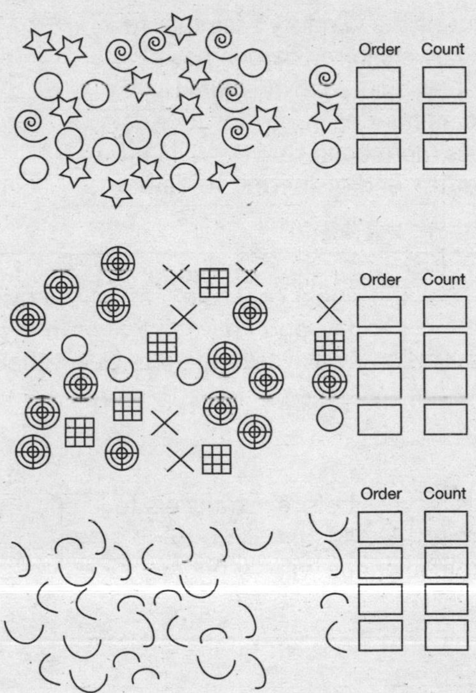

Now take as long as you think you need to write in the second column the precise count of each symbol.

TIME TAKEN:	INCORRECT ANSWERS:
TIME POINTS:	**TOTAL SCORE:**

Logical Puzzlers

Try to solve these problems – each requires only simple logic to solve, but you might find that making notes with a pencil will help!

When I look out of the window I see that four times as many flowers in my garden have opened as the previous day. If this same improvement continues each day for four days, how many times more open flowers will I have in my garden at the end of the fourth day?

If a single cow eats grass at the rate of $10m^2$ per day, and I have five cows in my field, how long will it take them to clear a field of $200m^2$?

My phone rings 8 times before it transfers to voicemail. If I miss 12 calls that all go to voicemail, how many rings will my phone have made?

TIME TAKEN:	INCORRECT ANSWERS:
TIME POINTS:	**TOTAL SCORE:**

Missing Signs

Insert the missing sign into each of these arithmetic expressions in order to make the equation true. You will need to add, subtract, multiply, or divide.

19 ☐ 108 = 127	7 ☐ 12 = 84	108 ☐ 20 = 88
12 ☐ 7 = 84	12 ☐ 25 = 37	33 ☐ 11 = 3
27 ☐ 9 = 3	114 ☐ 2 = 116	26 ☐ 23 = 3
42 ☐ 29 = 71	24 ☐ 62 = 86	11 ☐ 9 = 99
108 ☐ 9 = 12	52 ☐ 1 = 51	6 ☐ 4 = 24
44 ☐ 3 = 41	55 ☐ 11 = 5	66 ☐ 11 = 6
80 ☐ 32 = 48	1 ☐ 12 = 13	36 ☐ 3 = 12
8 ☐ 8 = 1	30 ☐ 62 = 92	31 ☐ 56 = 87
54 ☐ 6 = 9	7 ☐ 9 = 63	11 ☐ 12 = 132
12 ☐ 6 = 72	85 ☐ 1 = 84	137 ☐ 36 = 173
11 ☐ 7 = 77	45 ☐ 38 = 7	9 ☐ 9 = 1
88 ☐ 36 = 52	10 ☐ 5 = 50	7 ☐ 10 = 17
39 ☐ 28 = 67	110 ☐ 11 = 10	24 ☐ 8 = 3

TIME TAKEN:	INCORRECT ANSWERS:
TIME POINTS:	**TOTAL SCORE:**

Visual Memory

Spend 1 minute studying this path. Then cover the top half of this page and try to redraw it accurately on the empty grid below.

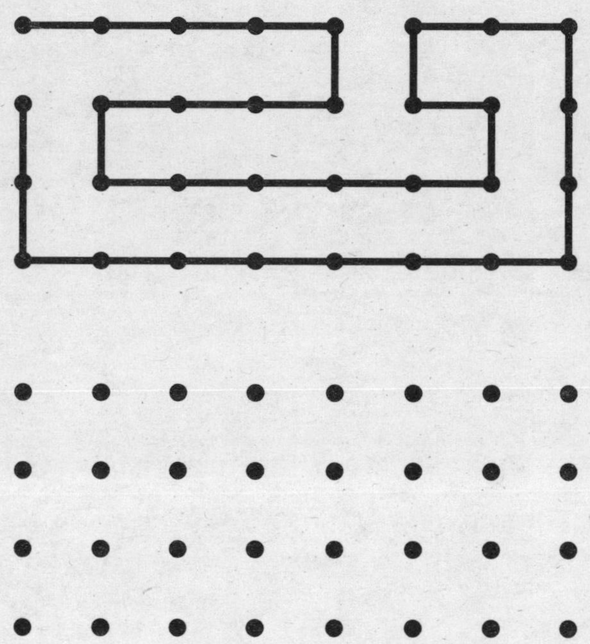

INCORRECT ANSWERS:	TOTAL SCORE:

Cryptogram

Decode each of these quotations by replacing A with D, B with E, C with F, and so on, through to replacing Y with B and Z with C.

E zivfep gsrxvegx mwr'x asvxl xli tetiv mx'w avmxxir sr

Weqyip Ksphacr

M lezi rsxlmrk xs higpevi ibgitx qc kirmyw.

Swgev Amphi

M eq jvii sj epp tvinyhmgiw. M lexi izivcsri iuyeppc.

AG Jmiphw

Mj ex jmvwx csy hsr'x wyggiih... Ws qygl jsv wochmzmrk.

Lirvc Csyrkqer.

TIME TAKEN:	INCORRECT ANSWERS:
TIME POINTS:	**TOTAL SCORE:**

Creative Thinking

See if you can solve each of the following conundrums. If you get stuck then try thinking laterally – they all have logical solutions, but the logic might not be what you expect!

If you stand over a bare concrete floor how can you drop a raw egg from a distance of one metre without it breaking? You may not modify the egg in any way.

Giving it your "best shot", what is the maximum number of sandwiches that you can eat on an empty stomach?

TIME TAKEN:	INCORRECT ANSWERS:
TIME POINTS:	**TOTAL SCORE:**

Reflective Power

Look at the three figures on the left-hand side. If each of these was reflected in the diagonal "mirror" adjacent to it, which of the three figures on the right would be the result?

A B C

1

2

3

TIME TAKEN:	INCORRECT ANSWERS:
TIME POINTS:	**TOTAL SCORE:**

Time Elapsed

Work out how many hours and minutes have passed between each of these pairs of times.

8:45am to 6:25pm =		9:10am to 5:45pm =	
1:35am to 11:35am =		10:25am to 12:35pm =	
5:45am to 6:55pm =		2:05pm to 10:10pm =	
1:50pm to 8:40pm =		10:50am to 11:40am =	
8:30am to 4:35pm =		7:45am to 3:30pm =	
12:30am to 6:15pm =		7:55pm to 10:45pm =	
10:10am to 4:10pm =		4:55am to 11:10am =	
6:20am to 8:20am =		10:10am to 11:35pm =	
12:45am to 7:20am =		2:15am to 4:05am =	
6:55am to 10:10am =		1:20pm to 7:15pm =	
11:45am to 7:30pm =		3:45pm to 3:55pm =	
9:05am to 10:30am =		3:45pm to 5:40pm =	
3:15pm to 4:55pm =		3:40am to 9:20am =	
8:20pm to 10:50pm =		9:25pm to 9:35pm =	
5:00am to 10:05pm =		11:40pm to 11:55pm =	

TIME TAKEN:	INCORRECT ANSWERS:
TIME POINTS:	**TOTAL SCORE:**

Anagrammatic

Look at each of these sets of 12 words. How many pairs of anagrams can you spot in each set, and what are they?

MAMMOTHS	TACTICAL	SQUALLED
GROUPING	REGIMENS	FIELDING
BRUSQUER	MENTIONS	VANQUISH
DEFILING	PURVEYOR	NOBODIES

SIGNER	PLUSES	DESIRE
INROAD	TUTORS	RESIDE
STATES	ORDAIN	TASTES
RESIGN	PULSES	TROUTS

RETAKES	SCANTER	GROCERS
RASPIER	ROOKIES	GIFTING
JABBING	ESTUARY	TURNING
DEDUCTS	CANTERS	REPAIRS

CAUTIONED	EDUCATION	COUNTERED
ALGORITHM	RAGGEDEST	CERTIFIED
LOGARITHM	REDOUBLED	STAGGERED
RECOUNTED	BOULDERED	RECTIFIED

TIME TAKEN:	INCORRECT ANSWERS:
TIME POINTS:	**TOTAL SCORE:**

Observation and Counting

Look at these triangles and see how long it takes you to answer the observation questions below.

How many triangles can you count?

How many separate areas are formed by these shapes?

If you were to colour in each area so that no two areas of the same colour touched on any side, how many colours would you need?

TIME TAKEN:	INCORRECT ANSWERS:
TIME POINTS:	**TOTAL SCORE:**

Shape Dividing

Draw three straight lines in order to divide the shape into four separate areas. Each area must contain precisely one of each size of circle. The three lines may touch but they must not cross.

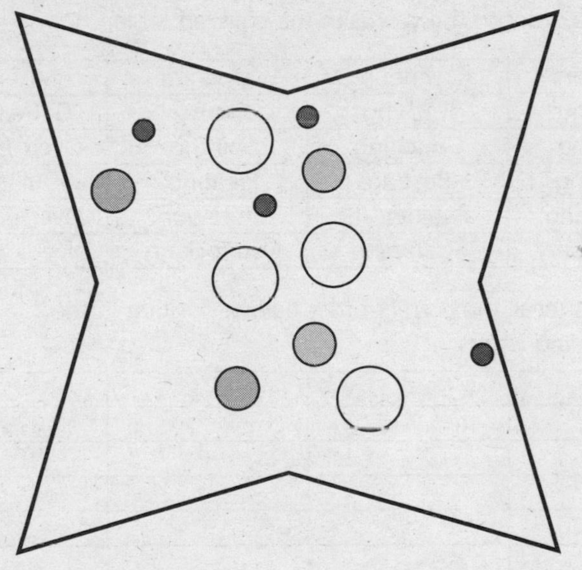

TIME TAKEN:	INCORRECT ANSWERS:
TIME POINTS:	**TOTAL SCORE:**

Ordered List

Can you memorize the order of these 24 sewing techniques?

Spend 2 minutes studying the top list, then cover the table and look at the second list below. Use the alphabetical labels to recall the precise order of the words in the covered table.

Cutwork	Crocheting	Applique	Mitring
Tucking	Ruching	Facing	Gathering
Binding	Couching	Shirring	Overcasting
Darning	Basting	Pleating	Quilting
Smocking	Patchwork	Whitework	Oversewing
Embroidery	Scalloping	Overlocking	Needlepoint

Now try to recall the correct order below, writing in the corresponding letters:

A Whitework	**B** Scalloping	**C** Pleating	**D** Applique
E Crocheting	**F** Shirring	**G** Overcasting	**H** Embroidery
I Darning	**J** Couching	**K** Binding	**L** Patchwork
M Basting	**N** Tucking	**O** Gathering	**P** Needlepoint
QSmocking	**R** Overlocking	**S** Quilting	**T** Ruching
U Oversewing	**V** Facing	**W** Mitring	**X** Cutwork

INCORRECT ANSWERS:	**TOTAL SCORE:**

Solutions

2: Counting and Perception

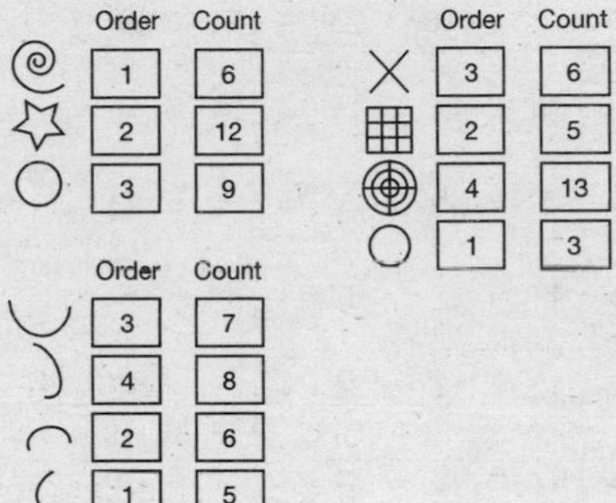

3: Logical Puzzlers

256 times as many flowers. (4 x 4 x 4 x 4)

4 days.

96 times.

4: Missing Signs

19	+	108	=	127	7	×	12	=	84	108	–	20	=	88
12	×	7	=	84	12	+	25	=	37	33	÷	11	=	3
27	÷	9	=	3	114	+	2	=	116	26	–	23	=	3
42	+	29	=	71	24	+	62	=	86	11	×	9	=	99
108	÷	9	=	12	52	–	1	=	51	6	×	4	=	24
44	–	3	=	41	55	÷	11	=	5	66	÷	11	=	6
80	–	32	=	48	1	+	12	=	13	36	÷	3	=	12
8	÷	8	=	1	30	+	62	=	92	31	+	56	=	87
54	÷	6	=	9	7	×	9	=	63	11	×	12	=	132
12	×	6	=	72	85	–	1	=	84	137	+	36	=	173
11	×	7	=	77	45	–	38	=	7	9	÷	9	=	1
88	–	36	=	52	10	×	5	=	50	7	+	10	=	17
39	+	28	=	67	110	÷	11	=	10	24	÷	8	=	3

6: Cryptogram

A verbal contract isn't worth the paper it's written on.

Samuel Goldwyn

I have nothing to declare except my genius.

Oscar Wilde

I am free of all prejudices. I hate everyone equally.

WC Fields

If at first you don't succeed ... So much for skydiving.

Henny Youngman

7: Creative Thinking

You simply catch the egg after dropping it.

You can only eat one; after that you no longer have an empty stomach!

8: Reflective Power

1B, 2A, 3C

9: Time Elapsed

8:45am to 6:25pm =	9:40	9:10am to 5:45pm =	8:35
1:35am to 11:35am =	10:00	10:25am to 12:35pm =	2:10
5:45am to 6:55pm =	13:10	2:05pm to 10:10pm =	8:05
1:50pm to 8:40pm =	6:50	10:50am to 11:40am =	0:50
8:30am to 4:35pm =	8:05	7:45am to 3:30pm =	7:45
12:30am to 6:15pm =	17:45	7:55pm to 10:45pm =	2:50
10:10am to 4:10pm =	6:00	4:55am to 11:10am =	6:15
6:20am to 8:20am =	2:00	10:10am to 11:35pm =	13:25
12:45am to 7:20am =	6:35	2:15am to 4:05am =	1:50
6:55am to 10:10am =	3:15	1:20pm to 7:15pm =	5:55
11:45am to 7:30pm =	7:45	3:45pm to 3:55pm =	0:10
9:05am to 10:30am =	1:25	3:45pm to 5:40pm =	1:55
3:15pm to 4:55pm =	1:40	3:40am to 9:20am =	5:40
8:20pm to 10:50pm =	2:30	9:25pm to 9:35pm =	0:10
5:00am to 10:05pm =	17:05	11:40pm to 11:55pm =	0:15

10: Anagrammatic

Set 1: 4 pairs of anagrams:
MARINE and REMAIN
LATHER and HALTER
GIRTHS and RIGHTS
BROTHS and THROBS

Set 2: 4 pairs of anagrams:
CLEANERS and CLEANSER
CRASHING and CHAGRINS
KEYNOTES and KEYSTONE

SNOOPING and SPOONING
PRAISING and ASPIRING
Set 3: 2 pairs of anagrams:
SERIALS and AIRLESS
RETIRED and TIREDER
Set 4: 3 pairs of anagrams:
SUBTLE and SUBLET
HORDES and SHORED
CANOES and OCEANS

11: Observation and Counting
17 triangles in total.

18 separate areas are formed by these shapes.

2 colours.

12: Shape Dividing

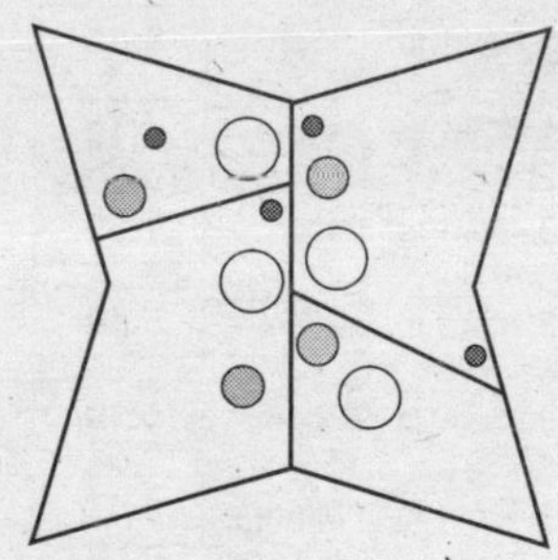

13: Ordered List

F	A	V	K
B	S	L	U
I	O	N	X
M	T	W	G
D	C	P	H
R	E	Q	J

DAY
20

Counting and Perception

Spend no more than 10 seconds looking at each group of symbols in each turn, then try to sort them into order of increasing frequency. Write "1" in the "Order" column for the shape that occurs least often, and so on.

	Order	Count
□		
○		
☆		

	Order	Count
◇		
△		
⬡		
heptagon		

	Order	Count
large circle		
small circle		
vertical oval		
horizontal oval		

Now take as long as you think you need to write in the second column the precise count of each symbol.

TIME TAKEN:	INCORRECT ANSWERS:
TIME POINTS:	**TOTAL SCORE:**

Matchstick Thinking

The picture below shows 7 matchsticks arranged in a row.

Can you move only 2 matchsticks and take away only 1 in order to create nothing?

TIME TAKEN:	INCORRECT ANSWERS:
TIME POINTS:	**TOTAL SCORE:**

Word List

Try to memorize these 24 mythological creatures.

After 2 minutes, cover the table and write as many as you can in the boxes below. You do not need to remember the correct order.

Fairy	Pixie	Dwarf	Hippogriff
Gremlin	Faun	Elf	Centaur
Griffin	Banshee	Hobbit	Salamander
Sylph	Mermaid	Nymph	Hydra
Goblin	Troll	Unicorn	Dragon
Phoenix	Satyr	Roc	Cyclops

Now try to recall as many as you can:

INCORRECT ANSWERS:	**TOTAL SCORE:**

Odd One Out

Look at each of these sets of words. Can you work out which word is the odd one out in each case?

Ladder
Children
Son
Tone
Father

Stable
Blasts
Tables
Ablest
Bleats

Slides
Ladies
Ideals
Sailed
Aisled

William
Anne
Edward
Charles
Andrew

TIME TAKEN:	INCORRECT ANSWERS:
TIME POINTS:	**TOTAL SCORE:**

Time Elapsed

Work out how many hours and minutes have passed between each of these pairs of times.

10:20am to 6:35pm =		1:45pm to 3:15pm =	
11:40am to 7:45pm =		6:50am to 9:55pm =	
2:05am to 2:25am =		6:35am to 3:30pm =	
12:05pm to 10:30pm =		5:50am to 7:35am =	
1:10pm to 3:05pm =		5:00pm to 7:15pm =	
12:50am to 8:00pm =		11:50am to 9:20pm =	
11:10am to 11:45pm =		9:30am to 1:25pm =	
1:10am to 8:55am =		11:55am to 12:40pm =	
11:10am to 2:55pm =		2:05pm to 5:10pm =	
3:35am to 11:55pm =		2:55pm to 7:00pm =	
9:50am to 8:35pm =		6:00am to 3:05pm =	
9:40am to 11:25am =		3:30am to 11:50pm =	
5:35pm to 10:40pm =		2:35am to 8:45pm =	
3:10am to 11:40am =		12:45pm to 7:25pm =	
3:25am to 3:35pm =		7:00am to 12:20pm =	

TIME TAKEN:	INCORRECT ANSWERS:
TIME POINTS:	**TOTAL SCORE:**

Missing Words

Study each of these 3 lists of words for a total of 2 minutes. Then cover the top half of the page and see if you can identify which word is missing from each of the lists below.

Giraffe	Elephant	Lion	Tiger
Monkey	Chimpanzee	Panther	Leopard

Myth	Comedy	Motif	Discourse
Fantasy	Fable	Polemic	Metaphor

Liberty	Liberation	Release	Autonomy
Freedom	Emancipation	Permission	Immunity

Now try to spot the missing word from each list:

Giraffe, Tiger, Panther, Lion, Elephant, Leopard, Chimpanzee

MISSING:

Myth, Fantasy, Fable, Polemic, Discourse, Metaphor, Motif

MISSING:

Freedom, Release, Immunity, Permission, Liberty, Autonomy, Emancipation

MISSING:

INCORRECT ANSWERS:	TOTAL SCORE:

Rotation

If you were to rotate each of these three pictures as indicated by the arrow beneath, which of the figures below would be the result?

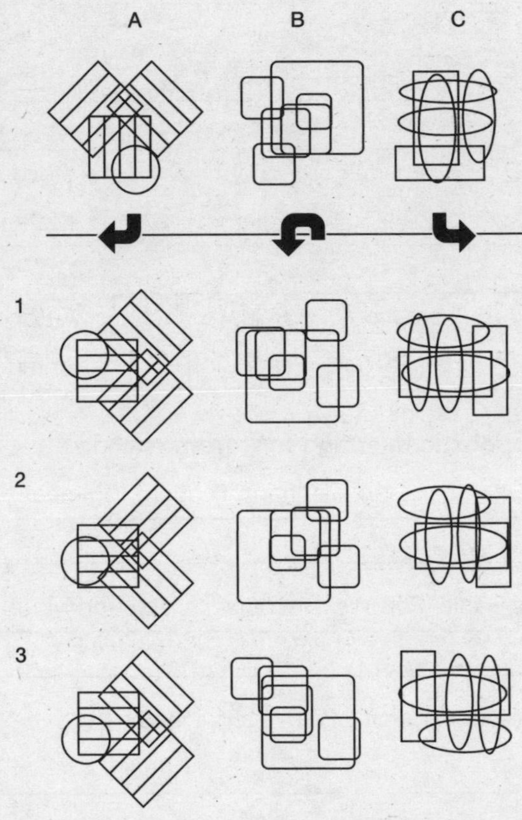

TIME TAKEN:	INCORRECT ANSWERS:
TIME POINTS:	**TOTAL SCORE:**

Logical Puzzlers

Try to solve these problems – each requires only simple logic to solve, but you might find that making notes with a pencil will help!

If a tree has 2 branches on it, and each of those branches has 4 more branches sprouting from them, and then if those branches each have a further 5 more branches; how many leaves will the tree have, assuming there are 10 leaves per branch?

David hangs up 40 T-shirts on the washing line to dry, but the wind blows 5 of them off the line every day. David isn't paying much attention, but when he next looks at the line he sees there are only 15 T-shirts left. How many days have passed since he hung them up?

If a = 1, b = 2, c = 3 and so on, then baa = 2+1+1 = 4 and cab = 3+1+2 = 6. What then is the value of one?

TIME TAKEN:	INCORRECT ANSWERS:
TIME POINTS:	**TOTAL SCORE:**

Shape Dividing

Draw three straight lines in order to divide the shape into four separate areas. Each area must contain precisely one of each size of circle. The three lines may touch but they must not cross.

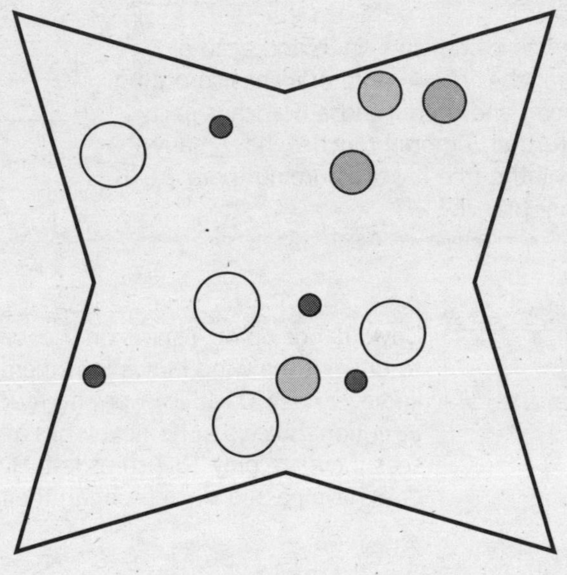

TIME TAKEN:	INCORRECT ANSWERS:
TIME POINTS:	**TOTAL SCORE:**

Visual Memory

Spend 1 minute studying this path. Then cover the top half of this page and try to redraw it accurately on the empty grid below.

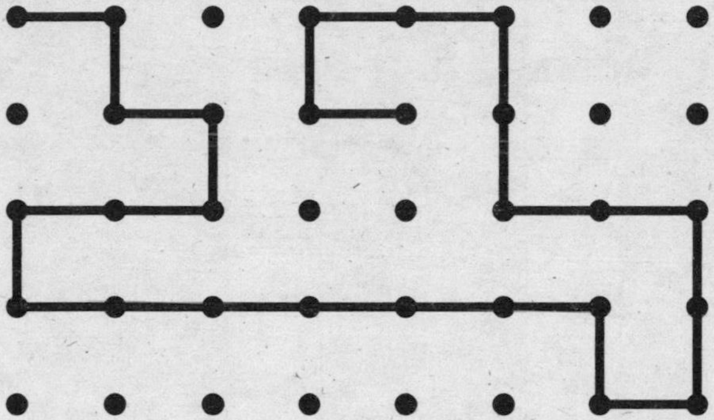

INCORRECT ANSWERS:	TOTAL SCORE:

Speed Arithmetic

Complete the following set of arithmetic equations as quickly as possible. You should be able to do them all in your head without using a calculator or making notes.

87 + 4 =	13 + 3 =	11 + 19 =
1 + 4 =	18 − 4 =	52 − 8 =
99 + 3 =	75 − 6 =	53 + 15 =
89 − 6 =	78 − 1 =	54 − 8 =
5 + 87 =	30 − 15 =	43 + 13 =
70 − 5 =	59 + 1 =	47 + 20 =
55 − 1 =	103 − 14 =	1 + 20 =
13 + 1 =	59 + 5 =	58 + 11 =
37 − 18 =	17 + 76 =	35 − 13 =
10 × 4 =	24 + 14 =	31 + 10 =
44 − 9 =	3 × 9 =	4 × 2 =
2 × 9 =	9 + 56 =	10 × 2 =
2 + 20 =	53 − 6 =	31 − 14 =

TIME TAKEN:	INCORRECT ANSWERS:
TIME POINTS:	**TOTAL SCORE:**

Reflective Power

Look at the three figures on the left-hand side. If each of these was reflected in the diagonal "mirror" adjacent to it, which of the three figures on the right would be the result?.

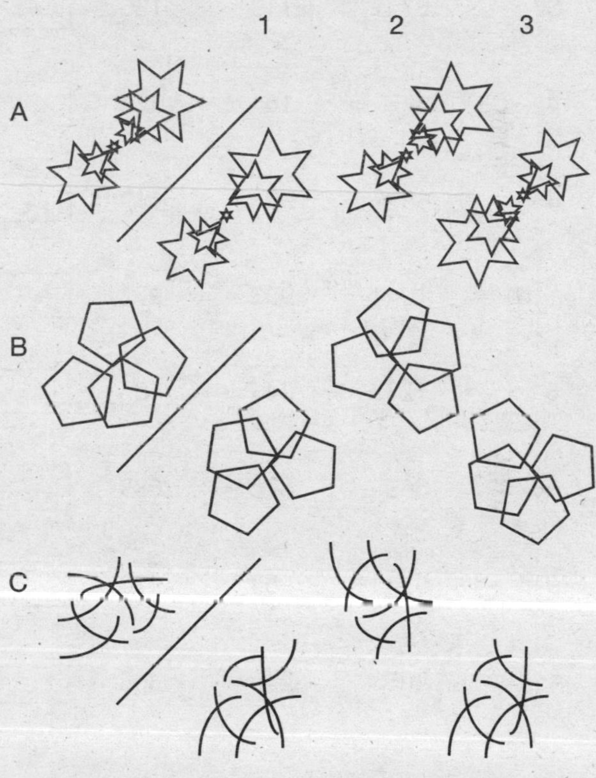

TIME TAKEN:	INCORRECT ANSWERS:
TIME POINTS:	**TOTAL SCORE:**

Number Sequences

Look at each of these number sequences and see if you can deduce which number comes next in the series.

15	52	67	119	186	
2	4	8	16	32	
33	46	68	99	139	
1178	1101	1041	998	972	
3	6	12	24	48	
655	662	669	676	683	
898	916	934	952	970	
155	174	205	248	303	

TIME TAKEN:	INCORRECT ANSWERS:
TIME POINTS:	**TOTAL SCORE:**

Solutions

1: Counting and Perception

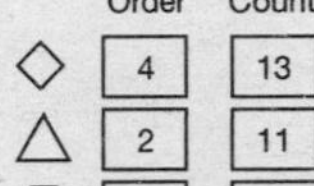

	Order	Count
◇	4	13
△	2	11
⬡	1	6
⬡	3	12

	Order	Count
◇	4	13
△	2	11
⬡	1	6
⬡	3	12

	Order	Count
○	1	6
o	4	18
0	3	12
⬭	2	10

2: Matchstick Thinking

4: Odd One Out

Tone – the rest make new words when prefixed with "step"
Blasts – the rest are anagrams of each other
Slides – the rest are anagrams of each other

5: Time Elapsed

10:20am to 6:35pm =	**8:15**	1:45pm to 3:15pm =	**1:30**
11:40am to 7:45pm =	**8:05**	6:50am to 9:55pm =	**15:05**
2:05am to 2:25am =	**0:20**	6:35am to 3:30pm =	**8:55**
12:05pm to 10:30pm =	**10:25**	5:50am to 7:35am =	**1:45**
1:10pm to 3:05pm =	**1:55**	5:00pm to 7:15pm =	**2:15**
12:50am to 8:00pm =	**19:10**	11:50am to 9:20pm =	**9:30**
11:10am to 11:45pm =	**12:35**	9:30am to 1:25pm =	**3:55**
1:10am to 8:55am =	**7:45**	11:55am to 12:40pm =	**0:45**
11:10am to 2:55pm =	**3:45**	2:05pm to 5:10pm =	**3:05**
3:35am to 11:55pm =	**20:20**	2:55pm to 7:00pm =	**4:05**
9:50am to 8:35pm =	**10:45**	6:00am to 3:05pm =	**9:05**
9:40am to 11:25am =	**1:45**	3:30am to 11:50pm =	**20:20**
5:35pm to 10:40pm =	**5:05**	2:35am to 8:45pm =	**18:10**
3:10am to 11:40am =	**8:30**	12:45pm to 7:25pm =	**6:40**
3:25am to 3:35pm =	**12:10**	7:00am to 12:20pm =	**5:20**

6: Missing words

The missing words are as follows: Monkey, Comedy and Liberation

7: Rotation

A3, B2, C1

8: Logical Puzzlers

500 leaves, which is 2 + (2x4) + (8x5) all multiplied by 10.

5 days.

34. This is 15 (o) + 14 (n) + 5 (e).

9: Shape Dividing

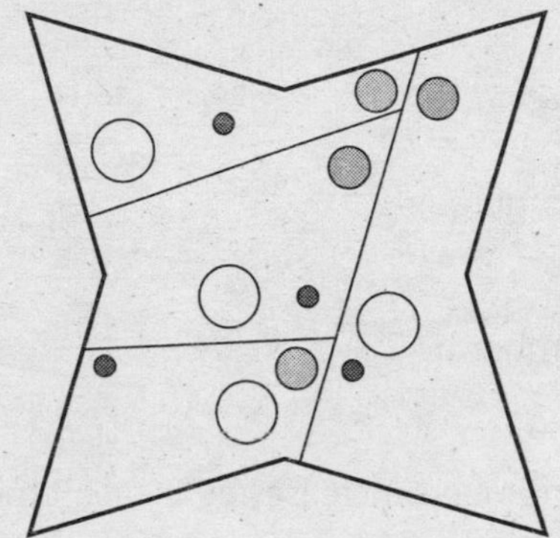

11: Speed Arithmetic

87 + 4 = **91**	13 + 3 = **16**	11 + 19 = **30**
1 + 4 = **5**	18 − 4 = **14**	52 − 8 = **44**
99 + 3 = **102**	75 − 6 = **69**	53 + 15 = **68**
89 − 6 = **83**	78 − 1 = **77**	54 − 8 = **46**
5 + 87 = **92**	30 − 15 = **15**	43 + 13 = **56**
70 − 5 = **65**	59 + 1 = **60**	47 + 20 = **67**
55 − 1 = **54**	103 − 14 = **89**	1 + 20 = **21**
13 + 1 = **14**	59 + 5 = **64**	58 + 11 = **69**
37 − 18 = **19**	17 + 76 = **93**	35 − 13 = **22**
10 × 4 = **40**	24 + 14 = **38**	31 + 10 = **41**
44 − 9 = **35**	3 × 9 = **27**	4 × 2 = **8**
2 × 9 = **18**	9 + 56 = **65**	10 × 2 = **20**
2 + 20 = **22**	53 − 6 = **47**	31 − 14 = **17**

12: Reflective Power
1C, 2B, 3B

13: Number Sequences
15, 52, 67, 119, 186, **305**
Rule: add the previous two numbers

2, 4, 8, 16, 32, **64**
Rule: multiply previous number by 2

33, 46, 68, 99, 139, **188**
Rule: difference between numbers increases by 9 each time

963, 972, 998, 1041, 1101, **1178**
Rule: difference between numbers increases by 17 each time

96, 48, 24, 12, 6, **3**
Rule: divide previous number by 2

655, 662, 669, 676, 683, **690**
Rule: add 7 to previous number

898, 916, 934, 952, 970, **988**
Rule: add 18 to previous number

370, 303, 248, 205, 174, **155**
Rule: difference between numbers decreases by 12 each time

DAY
21

Missing Words

Study each of these 3 lists of words for a total of 2 minutes. Then cover the top half of the page and see if you can identify which word is missing from each list below.

Albino	Bay	Black	Cream
Dapple	Dapplegrey	Palomino	Piebald

Quaternary	Tertiary	Cretaceous	Jurassic
Triassic	Permian	Carboniferous	Devonian

Eneolithic	Gravettian	Helladic	Mycenaean
Neobabylonian	Neolithic	Palaeolithic	Magdalenian

Now try to spot the missing word from each list:

Black, Cream, Albino, Dapplegrey, Bay, Dapple, Palomino

MISSING:

Tertiary, Devonian, Cretaceous, Triassic, Quaternary, Permian, Carboniferous

MISSING:

Eneolithic, Neobabylonian, Palaeolithic, Gravettian, Magdalenian, Helladic, Neolithic

MISSING:

INCORRECT ANSWERS:	TOTAL SCORE:

DAY: 21 | WORKOUT: 2 | CONCENTRATION

Speed Arithmetic

Complete the following set of arithmetic equations as quickly as possible. You should be able to do them all in your head without using a calculator or making notes.

10 × 10 =	44 − 9 =	97 − 18 =
55 − 3 =	73 − 7 =	80 + 9 =
8 × 9 =	4 × 7 =	12 × 9 =
75 − 6 =	5 × 11 =	85 + 5 =
93 − 10 =	43 + 8 =	15 + 66 =
76 − 18 =	14 + 100 =	14 − 13 =
46 + 6 =	100 + 19 =	26 − 11 =
12 + 6 =	81 − 14 =	60 + 8 =
51 + 16 =	48 − 5 =	82 − 13 =
30 + 17 =	104 − 5 =	17 − 2 =
10 × 3 =	60 − 19 =	48 + 15 =
87 + 8 =	68 + 4 =	6 + 70 =
47 − 10 =	8 + 10 =	4 × 3 =

TIME TAKEN:	INCORRECT ANSWERS:
TIME POINTS:	**TOTAL SCORE:**

Observation and Counting

Look at these ellipses and see how long it takes you to answer the observation questions below.

How many ellipses can you count?

How many areas are formed between the lines?

What is the total number of ellipses that overlap at any one place in the figure?

TIME TAKEN:	INCORRECT ANSWERS:
TIME POINTS:	**TOTAL SCORE:**

Reflective Power

Look at the three figures on the left hand side. If each of these was reflected in the diagonal "mirror" adjacent to it, which of the figures on the right would be the result?

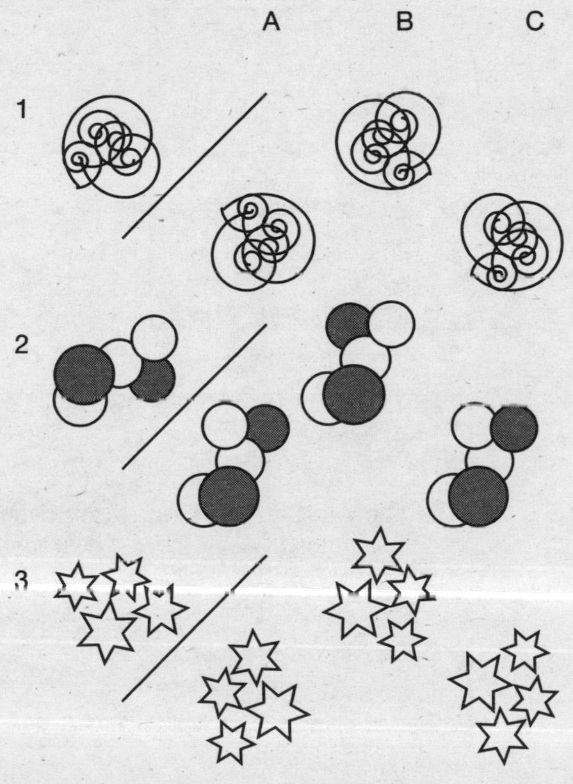

TIME TAKEN:	INCORRECT ANSWERS:
TIME POINTS:	**TOTAL SCORE:**

Creative Thinking

See if you can solve each of the following conundrums. If you get stuck then try thinking laterally – they all have logical solutions, but the logic might not be what you expect!

The Post Office refuses to send a package which is more than 20 inches wide, tall or deep. How then can I send a 30-inch-long poster tube through the post?

Multiply forty-three minutes and twenty-one seconds by sixty. If you take more than 10 seconds to solve this then you've taken too long! Why?

TIME TAKEN:	INCORRECT ANSWERS:
TIME POINTS:	**TOTAL SCORE:**

Logical Puzzlers

Try to solve these problems – each requires only simple logic to solve, but you might find that making notes with a pencil will help!

If Sean drives his car from his house to the cinema at 30mph (miles per hour) through a town centre, but his brother Dan drives the same route via a ring road at 60mph, who arrives first? Sean's route is 5 miles long and Dan's is 8 miles.

During the New York summer, Sydney's time zone is GMT+9 (meaning 9 hours ahead of GMT) whilst New York's is GMT-5. What, then, is the time in Sydney when it is 8am in New York?

If I use 2 teabags for 4 cups of tea, how many teabags will I use in a week if I have 8 cups per day?

TIME TAKEN:	INCORRECT ANSWERS:
TIME POINTS:	**TOTAL SCORE:**

Shape Folding

If you were to cut out this shape and fold it into a cube, which of the three pictures below would be the result?

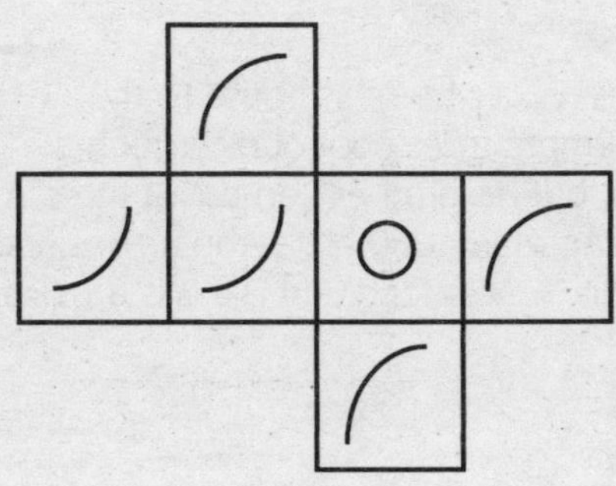

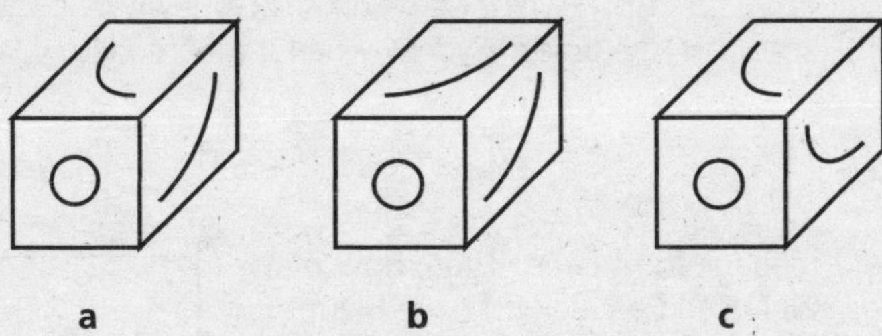

a b c

TIME TAKEN:	INCORRECT ANSWERS:
TIME POINTS:	**TOTAL SCORE:**

Visual Memory

Spend 1 minute studying this path. Then cover the top half of this page and try to redraw it accurately on the empty grid below.

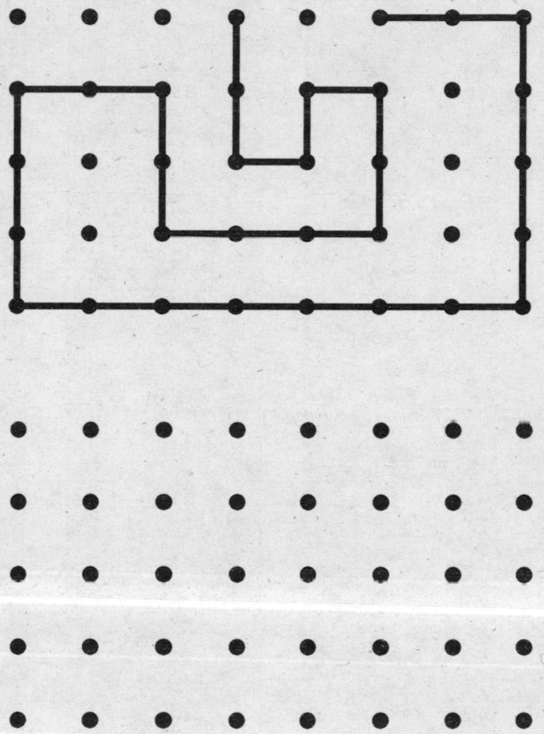

INCORRECT ANSWERS:	**TOTAL SCORE:**

Missing Signs

Insert the missing sign into each of these arithmetic expressions in order to make the equation true. You will need to add, subtract, multiply, or divide.

29 ☐ 14 = 43	16 ☐ 8 = 2	5 ☐ 14 = 19
32 ☐ 11 = 21	9 ☐ 4 = 36	84 ☐ 6 = 14
60 ☐ 12 = 5	9 ☐ 15 = 24	12 ☐ 10 = 120
30 ☐ 10 = 3	5 ☐ 19 = 24	12 ☐ 9 = 108
4 ☐ 35 = 39	8 ☐ 2 = 16	8 ☐ 38 = 46
12 ☐ 45 = 57	21 ☐ 63 = 84	51 ☐ 3 = 54
87 ☐ 21 = 66	6 ☐ 5 = 30	90 ☐ 25 = 115
4 ☐ 8 = 32	109 ☐ 25 = 134	26 ☐ 80 = 106
33 ☐ 88 = 121	56 ☐ 26 = 30	50 ☐ 5 = 10
2 ☐ 32 = 34	98 ☐ 3 = 95	50 ☐ 13 = 63
5 ☐ 10 = 50	22 ☐ 11 = 11	32 ☐ 23 = 55
104 ☐ 38 = 66	91 ☐ 10 = 101	42 ☐ 7 = 6
9 ☐ 2 = 18	7 ☐ 7 = 49	22 ☐ 37 = 59

TIME TAKEN:	INCORRECT ANSWERS:
TIME POINTS:	**TOTAL SCORE:**

Anagrammatic

Look at each of these sets of 12 words. How many pairs of anagrams can you spot in each set, and what are they?

RIGHTS	BROTHS	WARMLY
REMAIN	HALTER	MARINE
PIRATE	LOANED	LATHER
THROBS	RECOIL	GIRTHS

SNOOPING	FAMISHES	KEYNOTES
ASPIRING	CLEANSER	KEYSTONE
PRAISING	CLEANERS	CHAGRINS
DAZZLING	SPOONING	CRASHING

PEBBLED	PUNCHED	FAWNING
RETIRED	IMPURER	EMBLEMS
TIREDER	AIRLESS	STIMULI
CAPSIZE	QUANTUM	SERIALS

THIGHS	HORDES	SUBTLE
FAINTS	CANOES	BROOMS
UPPITY	OCEANS	UPTOWN
SUBLET	SHORED	FUNGUS

TIME TAKEN:	INCORRECT ANSWERS:
TIME POINTS:	**TOTAL SCORE:**

Word List

Try to memorize these 24 musical terms.

After 2 minutes, cover the table and recall as many as you can in the boxes below. You do not need to remember the correct order.

Legato	Piano	Largo	Animato
Allegro	Staccato	Vivace	Sotto voce
Pizzicato	Grave	Animato	Andante
Accelerando	Energico	Espressivo	Molto
Moderate	Sostenuto	Sforzando	Rubato
Presto	Pomposo	Volante	Mezzo

Now try to recall as many as you can:

INCORRECT ANSWERS:	**TOTAL SCORE:**

Visual Inference

Two symbols each with a following symbol are shown. Can you work out the rule being applied in order to deduce which of the last three symbols should replace each question mark?

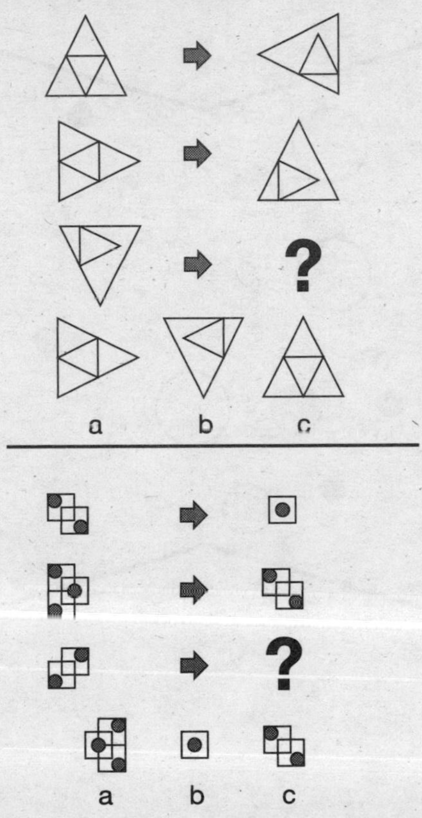

TIME TAKEN:	INCORRECT ANSWERS:
TIME POINTS:	**TOTAL SCORE:**

Shape Dividing

Draw three straight lines in order to divide the shape into four separate areas. Each area must contain precisely one of each size of circle. The three lines may touch but they must not cross.

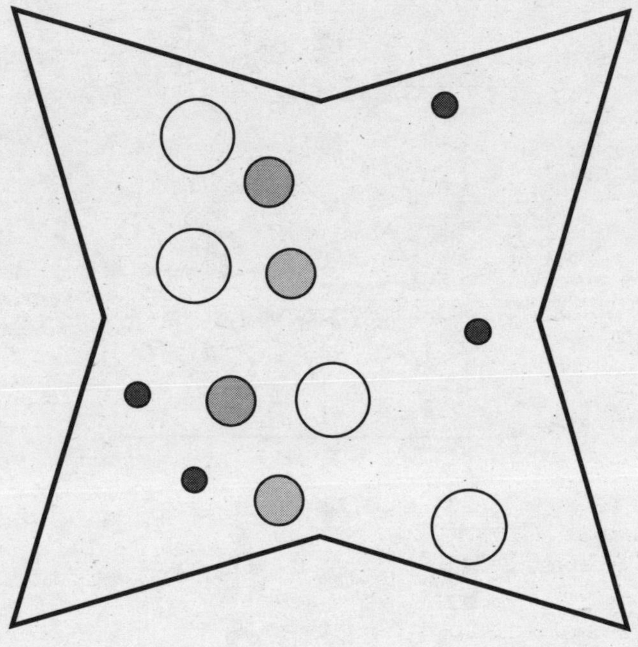

TIME TAKEN:	INCORRECT ANSWERS:
TIME POINTS:	**TOTAL SCORE:**

Solutions

2: Speed Arithmetic

10 × 10 = **100**	44 − 9 = **35**	97 − 18 = **79**
55 − 3 = **52**	73 − 7 = **66**	80 + 9 = **89**
8 × 9 = **72**	4 × 7 = **28**	12 × 9 = **108**
75 − 6 = **69**	5 × 11 = **55**	85 + 5 = **90**
93 − 10 = **83**	43 + 8 = **51**	15 + 66 = **81**
76 − 18 = **58**	14 +100 = **114**	14 − 13 = **1**
46 + 6 = **52**	100+ 19 = **119**	26 − 11 = **15**
12 + 6 = **18**	81 − 14 = **67**	60 + 8 = **68**
51 + 16 = **67**	48 − 5 = **43**	82 − 13 = **69**
30 + 17 = **47**	104− 5 = **99**	17 − 2 = **15**
10 × 3 = **30**	60 − 19 = **41**	48 + 15 = **63**
87 + 8 = **95**	68 + 4 = **72**	6 + 70 = **76**
47 − 10 = **37**	8 + 10 = **18**	4 × 3 = **12**

3: Observation and Counting

7 ellipses in total.

19 areas are formed between the lines.

3 is the maximum number of ellipses that overlap at any place in the figure.

4: Reflective Power

1C, 2A, 3A

5: Creative Thinking
Place it in a box with all three dimensions of 20 inches and it will fit comfortably at a diagonal. (The longest diagonal is then over 34 inches long).

The answer is 43 hours and 21 minutes, since multiplying seconds by 60 gives an equivalent number of minutes, and similarly for minutes into hours. Simply changing the units should not take more than 10 seconds!

6: Logical Puzzlers
Dan arrives first.

10pm.

28 teabags.

7: Shape Folding
a

9: Missing Signs

29 + 14 = 43			16 ÷ 8 = 2			5 + 14 = 19		
32 – 11 = 21			9 × 4 = 36			84 ÷ 6 = 14		
60 ÷ 12 = 5			9 + 15 = 24			12 × 10 = 120		
30 ÷ 10 = 3			5 + 19 = 24			12 × 9 = 108		
4 + 35 = 39			8 × 2 = 16			8 + 38 = 46		
12 + 45 = 57			21 + 63 = 84			51 + 3 = 54		
87 – 21 = 66			6 × 5 = 30			90 + 25 = 115		
4 × 8 = 32			109 + 25 = 134			26 + 80 = 106		
33 + 88 = 121			56 – 26 = 30			50 ÷ 5 = 10		
2 + 32 = 34			98 – 3 = 95			50 + 13 = 63		
5 × 10 = 50			22 – 11 = 11			32 + 23 = 55		
104 – 38 = 66			91 + 10 = 101			42 ÷ 7 = 6		
9 × 2 = 18			7 × 7 = 49			22 + 37 = 59		

10: Anagrammatic

Set 1: 5 pairs of anagrams:
CROONERS and CORONERS
SLIGHTER and LIGHTERS
HEISTING and NIGHTIES
REVILING and RELIVING
THICKEST and THICKETS

Set 2: 2 pairs of anagrams:
SLEETED and STEELED
DEAFEST and FEASTED

Set 3: 4 pairs of anagrams:
SLEETS and STEELS
ASSORT and ROASTS
PASTES and SPATES
MOUSES and MOUSSE

Set 4: 4 pairs of anagrams:
SALLOW and ALLOWS
ROOSTS and TORSOS
DIETED and EDITED
SANEST and ASSENT

12: Visual Inference

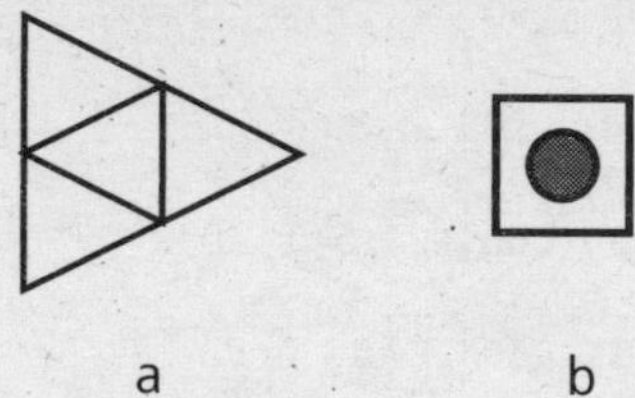

a b

13: Shape Dividing

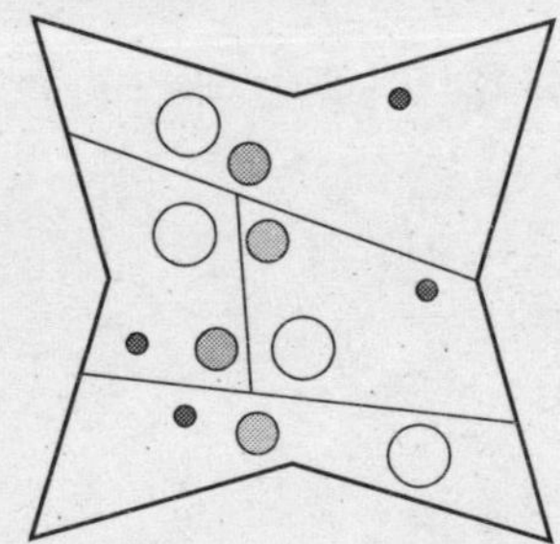

DAY
22

Logical Puzzlers

Try to solve these problems – each requires only simple logic to solve, but you might find that making notes with a pencil will help!

My calculator has an 8-digit display. If I type in the largest standard 8-digit number it can display, and then write this down rounded to the nearest million, what is the final written number?

A particular blackbird in a tree nearby sings for half an hour every morning and evening. How many hours in total does it sing for during the month of July?

If a bottle of wine takes five years to mature, how many years will it take for 10 bottles to mature?

TIME TAKEN:	INCORRECT ANSWERS:
TIME POINTS:	**TOTAL SCORE:**

Counting and Perception

Spend no more than 10 seconds looking at each group of symbols in each turn, then try to sort them into order of increasing frequency. Write "1" in the "Order" column for the shape that occurs least often, and so on.

Now take as long as you think you need to write in the second column the precise count of each symbol.

TIME TAKEN:	INCORRECT ANSWERS:
TIME POINTS:	**TOTAL SCORE:**

Visual Memory

Spend 1 minute studying this path. Then cover the top half of this page and try to redraw it accurately on the empty grid below.

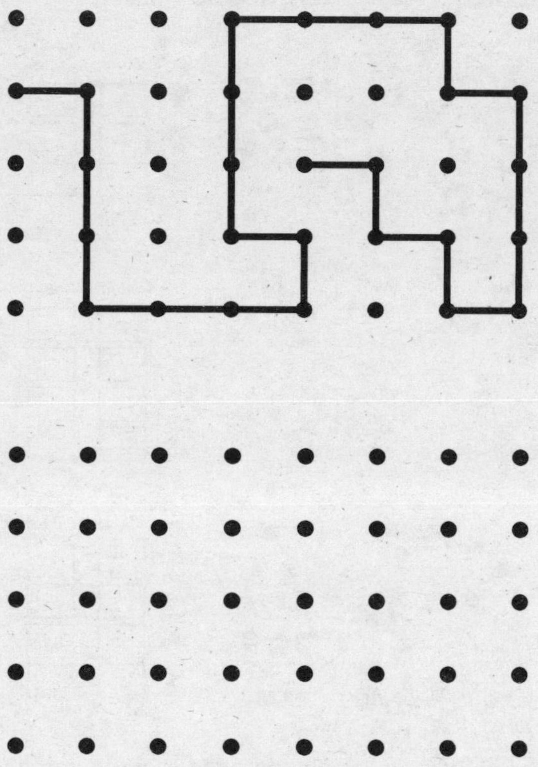

INCORRECT ANSWERS:	**TOTAL SCORE:**

Number Sequences

Look at each of these number sequences and see if you can deduce which number comes next in the series.

239	145	94	51	43	
5	20	80	320	1280	
307	185	122	63	59	
208	127	81	46	35	
867	875	896	930	977	
1211	1113	1015	917	819	
10	97	107	204	311	
436	448	460	472	484	

TIME TAKEN:	INCORRECT ANSWERS:
TIME POINTS:	**TOTAL SCORE:**

Time Elapsed

Work out how many hours and minutes have passed between each of these pairs of times.

12:55am to 7:35pm =	:	6:00am to 11:35am =	:
12:05pm to 5:45pm =	:	8:05am to 10:40am =	:
11:05am to 7:10pm =	:	2:45pm to 9:15pm =	:
3:15pm to 4:35pm =	:	6:25am to 2:15pm =	:
10:30am to 6:50pm =	:	4:50am to 6:15pm =	:
10:25am to 7:15pm =	:	12:05am to 8:50pm =	:
2:05pm to 8:15pm =	:	12:25am to 11:45pm =	:
6:40am to 8:55pm =	:	6:20pm to 11:05pm =	:
10:35am to 2:15pm =	:	4:10pm to 5:50pm =	:
6:25pm to 7:05pm =	:	6:55am to 3:25pm =	:
6:10am to 1:40pm =	:	9:05am to 7:15pm =	:
2:35am to 9:20am =	:	3:00am to 10:05am =	:
12:30pm to 2:45pm =	:	4:55pm to 6:05pm =	:
2:45pm to 4:20pm =	:	12:10pm to 7:45pm =	:
5:50pm to 8:10pm =	:	1:55am to 12:35pm =	:

TIME TAKEN:	INCORRECT ANSWERS:
TIME POINTS:	**TOTAL SCORE:**

Creative Thinking

See if you can solve each of the following conundrums. If you get stuck then try thinking laterally – they all have logical solutions, but the logic might not be what you expect!

Can you tell me what is in the centre of the universe?

I have a bottle of lemonade which I have started drinking. There's more than half left but it isn't full. I've promised to leave exactly half a bottle for my brother. How can I be sure to do this, without making use of any other item to help measure it?

TIME TAKEN:	INCORRECT ANSWERS:
TIME POINTS:	**TOTAL SCORE:**

Observation and Counting

Look at these rectangles and see how long it takes you to answer the observation question below. It is a little bit tricky, so take care!

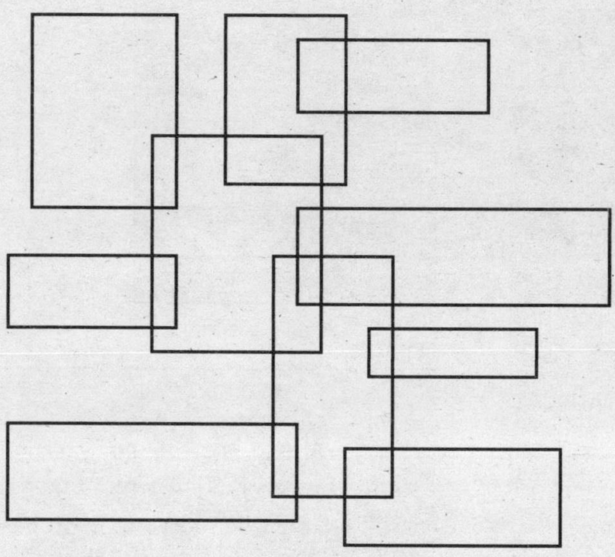

How many rectangles in total can you count?

TIME TAKEN:	INCORRECT ANSWERS:
TIME POINTS:	**TOTAL SCORE:**

Speed Arithmetic

Complete the following set of arithmetic equations as quickly as possible. You should be able to do them all in your head without using a calculator or making notes.

80 − 13 =	19 + 89 =	71 + 12 =
10 × 6 =	8 × 5 =	36 + 18 =
3 × 7 =	5 × 9 =	3 + 68 =
20 + 12 =	65 + 4 =	59 − 18 =
9 × 4 =	28 − 18 =	19 + 16 =
11 × 5 =	65 + 3 =	3 × 5 =
18 − 17 =	9 × 11 =	2 × 10 =
32 + 17 =	93 + 9 =	9 + 4 =
66 − 10 =	2 + 17 =	2 × 9 =
63 + 9 =	5 + 30 =	72 − 18 =
88 + 2 =	69 − 2 =	74 − 8 =
106 − 17 =	93 − 11 =	26 + 4 =
10 × 2 =	99 − 14 =	11 × 8 =

TIME TAKEN:	INCORRECT ANSWERS:
TIME POINTS:	**TOTAL SCORE:**

Matchstick Thinking

The picture below shows 12 matchsticks arranged to read '4 – 3 ='.

Can you move 3 matchsticks only in order to turn this into a valid equation, to give the same result on both sides of the equals sign?

TIME TAKEN:	INCORRECT ANSWERS:
TIME POINTS:	**TOTAL SCORE:**

Cryptogram

Decode each of these quotations by replacing A with Y, B with Z, C with A and so on, through to replacing Y with W and Z with X.

L xvhg wr vhoo ixuqlwxuh iru d olylqj. Wkh wurxeoh zdv, lw zdv pb rzq.

Ohv Gdzvrq

L fdq uhvlvw hyhubwklqj hafhsw whpswdwlrq.

Rvfdu Zlogh

D edujdlq lv vrphwklqj brx fdq'w xvh dw d sulfh brx fdq'w uhvlvw.

Iudqnolq Mrqhv

Doo L dvn lv wkh fkdqfh wr suryh wkdw prqhb fdq'w pdnh ph kdssb.

Vslnh Plooljdq

TIME TAKEN:	INCORRECT ANSWERS:
TIME POINTS:	**TOTAL SCORE:**

Missing Words

Study each of these 3 lists of words for a total of 2 minutes. Then cover the top half of the page and see if you can identify which word is missing from each list below.

Australorp	Bantam	Brahma	Houdan
Leghorn	Minorca	Sussex	Wyandotte

Boron	Magnesium	Calcium	Titanium
Chromium	Iron	Nickel	Zinc

Erie	Eyre	Rudolf	Superior
Victoria	Volta	Windermere	Lomond

Now try to spot the missing word from each list:

Sussex, Bantam, Leghorn, Australorp, Houdan, Minorca, Brahma

MISSING:

Zinc, Iron, Nickel, Boron, Titanium, Chromium, Calcium

MISSING:

Erie, Rudolf, Volta, Superior, Eyre, Victoria, Windermere

MISSING:

INCORRECT ANSWERS:	TOTAL SCORE:

Ordered List

Can you memorize the order of these 24 desserts?

Spend 2 minutes studying the top list, then cover the table and look at the second list below. Use the alphabetical labels to help recall the precise order of the words in the covered table.

Jelly	Tapioca	Apfelstrudel	Zabaglione
Parfait	Pavlova	Souffle	Crumble
Whip	Trifle	Yogurt	Custard
Granita	Fool	Spumoni	Bavaroise
Entremets	Semolina	Cobbler	Baklava
Sorbet	Mousse	Cajeta	Junket

Now try to recall the correct order below, by writing in the corresponding letters:

A Tapioca	**B** Parfait	**C** Semolina	**D** Entremets
E Mousse	**F** Jelly	**G** Bavaroise	**H** Baklava
I Whip	**J** Junket	**K** Zabaglione	**L** Souffle
M Granita	**N** Yogurt	**O** Trifle	**P** Cobbler
Q Cajeta	**R** Sorbet	**S** Pavlova	**T** Fool
U Crumble	**V** Apfelstrudel	**W** Spumoni	**X** Custard

INCORRECT ANSWERS:	**TOTAL SCORE:**

Rotation

If you were to rotate each of these three pictures as indicated by the arrow beneath, which of the figures below would be the result?

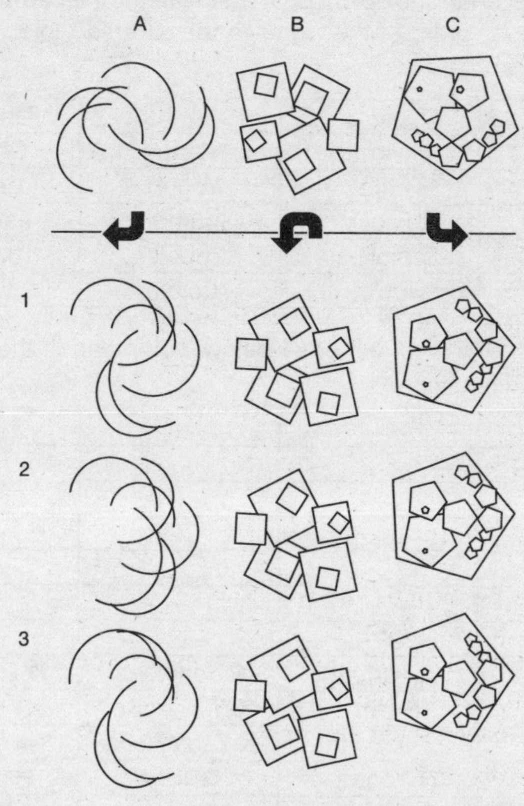

TIME TAKEN:	INCORRECT ANSWERS:
TIME POINTS:	**TOTAL SCORE:**

Solutions

1: Logical Puzzlers

100 million, since the display can show up to 99,999,999.

31 hours in total.

5 years – they can all mature simultaneously!

2: Counting and Perception

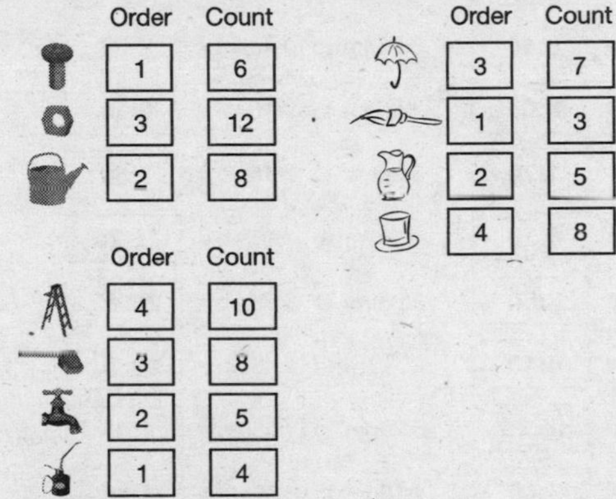

4: Number Sequences

239, 145, 94, 51, 43, **8**
Rule: subtract the previous number from the one before

5, 20, 80, 320, 1280, **5120**
Rule: multiply previous number by 4

59, 63, 122, 185, **307**
Rule: add the previous two numbers

11, 35, 46, 81, 127, **208**
Rule: add the previous two numbers

867, 875, 896, 930, 977, **1037**
Rule: difference between numbers increases by 13 each time

1211, 1113, 1015, 917, 819, **721**
Rule: subtract 98 from previous number

10, 97, 107, 204, 311, **515**
Rule: add the previous two numbers

436, 448, 460, 472, 484, **496**
Rule: add 12 to previous number

5: Time Elapsed

12:55am to 7:35pm =	**18:40**	6:00am to 11:35am =	**5:35**
12:05pm to 5:45pm =	**5:40**	8:05am to 10:40am =	**2:35**
11:05am to 7:10pm =	**8:05**	2:45pm to 9:15pm =	**6:30**
3:15pm to 4:35pm =	**1:20**	6:25am to 2:15pm =	**7:50**
10:30am to 6:50pm =	**8:20**	4:50am to 6:15pm =	**13:25**
10:25am to 7:15pm =	**8:50**	12:05am to 8:50pm =	**20:45**
2:05pm to 8:15pm =	**6:10**	12:25am to 11:45pm =	**23:20**
6:40am to 8:55pm =	**14:15**	6:20pm to 11:05pm =	**4:45**
10:35am to 2:15pm =	**3:40**	4:10pm to 5:50pm =	**1:40**
6:25pm to 7:05pm =	**0:40**	6:55am to 3:25pm =	**8:30**
6:10am to 1:40pm =	**7:30**	9:05am to 7:15pm =	**10:10**
2:35am to 9:20am =	**6:45**	3:00am to 10:05am =	**7:05**
12:30pm to 2:45pm =	**2:15**	4:55pm to 6:05pm =	**1:10**
2:45pm to 4:20pm =	**1:35**	12:10pm to 7:45pm =	**7:35**
5:50pm to 8:10pm =	**2:20**	1:55am to 12:35pm =	**10:40**

6: Creative Thinking

The letter "i" is at the centre of "the universe".

If you put the bottle flat on its side (with the lid on!) then you will be able to see clearly whether it is still more than half full. You can then keep checking in this way until the bottle is precisely half full.

7: Observation and Counting

26 rectangles in total.

8: Speed Arithmetic

80 − 13 =	**67**	19 + 89 =	**108**	71 + 12 =	**83**
10 × 6 =	**60**	8 × 5 =	**40**	36 + 18 =	**54**
3 × 7 =	**21**	5 × 9 =	**45**	3 + 68 =	**71**
20 + 12 =	**32**	65 + 4 =	**69**	59 − 18 =	**41**
9 × 4 =	**36**	28 − 18 =	**10**	19 + 16 =	**35**
11 × 5 =	**55**	65 + 3 =	**68**	3 × 5 =	**15**
18 − 17 =	**1**	9 × 11 =	**99**	2 × 10 =	**20**
32 + 17 =	**49**	93 + 9 =	**102**	9 + 4 =	**13**
66 − 10 =	**56**	2 + 17 =	**19**	2 × 9 =	**18**
63 + 9 =	**72**	5 + 30 =	**35**	72 − 18 =	**54**
88 + 2 =	**90**	69 − 2 =	**67**	74 − 8 =	**66**
106 − 17 =	**89**	93 − 11 =	**82**	26 + 4 =	**30**
10 × 2 =	**20**	99 − 14 =	**85**	11 × 8 =	**88**

9: Matchstick Thinking

10: Cryptogram

I used to sell furniture for a living. The trouble was, it was my own.
Les Dawson

I can resist everything except temptation.
Oscar Wilde

A bargain is something you can't use at a price you can't resist.
Franklin Jones

All I ask is the chance to prove that money can't make me happy.
Spike Milligan

12: Ordered List

F	A	V	K
B	S	L	U
I	O	N	X
M	T	W	G
D	C	P	H
R	E	Q	J

13: Rotation

A1, B1, C2

DAY
23

Shape Folding

If you were to cut out this shape and fold it into a cube, which of the three pictures below would be the result?

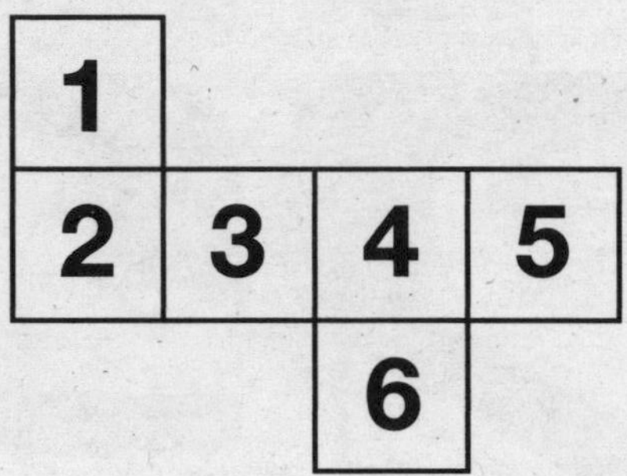

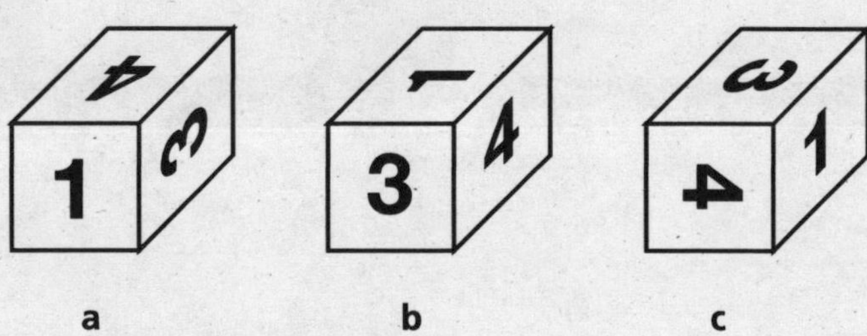

a b c

TIME TAKEN:	INCORRECT ANSWERS:
TIME POINTS:	**TOTAL SCORE:**

Matchstick Thinking

The picture below shows 9 matchsticks arranged into 3 equilateral triangles.

Can you move 3 matchsticks only in order to make 4 equilateral triangles? You may not overlap any matches or leave any unused.

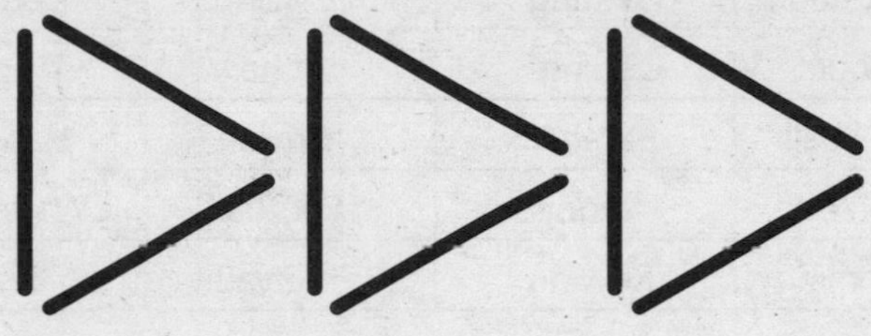

TIME TAKEN:	INCORRECT ANSWERS:
TIME POINTS:	**TOTAL SCORE:**

Word List

Try to memorize these 24 sports.

After 2 minutes, cover the table and recall as many as you can in the boxes below. You do not need to remember the correct order.

Gliding	Golf	Gymnastics	Javelin
Shooting	Skating	Cycling	Bowls
Croquet	Skiing	Archery	Angling
Volleyball	Baseball	Cricket	Handball
Hockey	Rugby	Football	Water polo
Swimming	Rowing	Pole vault	Discus

Now try to recall as many as you can:

INCORRECT ANSWERS:	TOTAL SCORE:

Anagrammatic

Look at each of these sets of 12 words. How many pairs of anagrams can you spot in each set, and what are they?

PRANCING	GIGANTIC	REVILING
CORONERS	THICKETS	SLIGHTER
LIGHTERS	HEISTING	RELIVING
CROONERS	THICKEST	NIGHTIES

FEASTED	BARROOM	STEELED
SLEETED	CRACKER	ARSENIC
BEELINE	REPLIES	CARRION
DOUBTED	DEAFEST	IMPALES

VERIER	PASTES	MENTOR
MOUSES	TOXINS	MOUSSE
ASSORT	SLEETS	SPATES
SNORTS	STEELS	ROASTS

ASSENT	FAGGED	SPENDS
ALLOWS	PEARLS	ROOSTS
EDITED	SALLOW	TORSOS
AROMAS	SANEST	DIETED

TIME TAKEN:	INCORRECT ANSWERS:
TIME POINTS:	**TOTAL SCORE:**

Reflective Power

Look at the three figures on the left-hand side . If each of these was reflected in the diagonal "mirror" adjacent to it, which of the figures on the right would be the result?

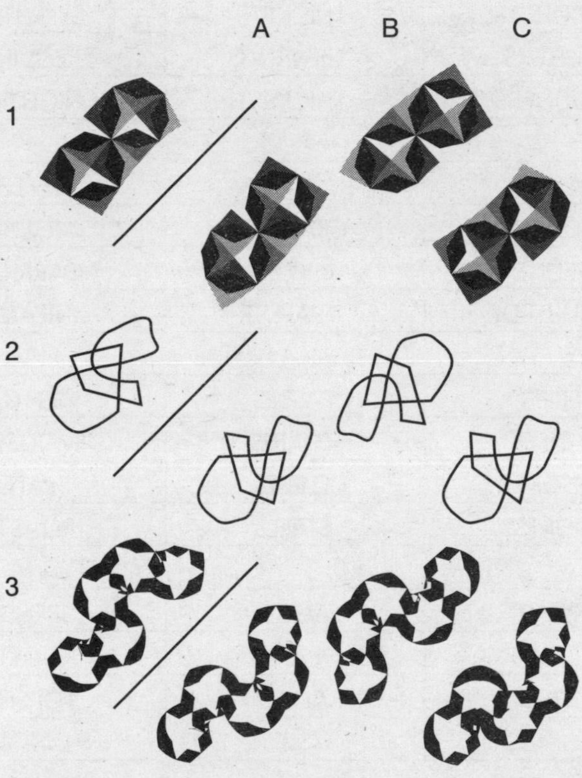

TIME TAKEN:	INCORRECT ANSWERS:
TIME POINTS:	**TOTAL SCORE:**

Odd One Out

Look at each of these sets of words. Can you work out which word is the odd one out in each case?

Butter
Eggs
Cheese
Cream
Yoghurt

Bottlenose
Basking
Reef
Tiger
Hammerhead

Lime
Lemon
Orange
Nectarine
Grapefruit

Netball
Tennis
Volleyball
Football
Basketball

TIME TAKEN:	INCORRECT ANSWERS:
TIME POINTS:	**TOTAL SCORE:**

Shape Dividing

Draw three straight lines in order to divide the shape into four separate areas. Each area must contain precisely one of each size of circle. The three lines may touch but they must not cross.

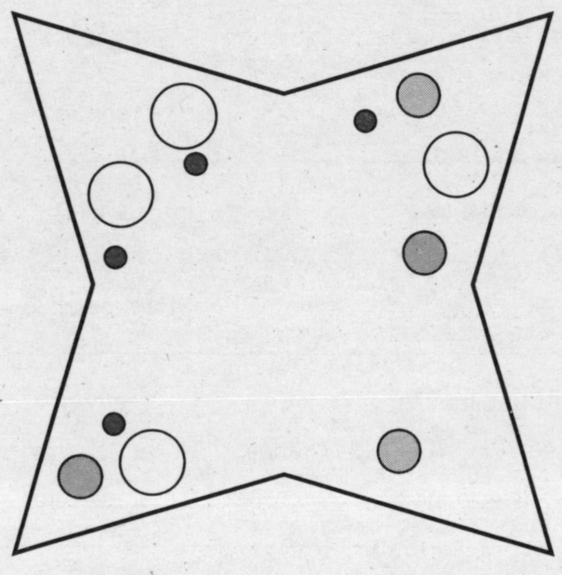

TIME TAKEN:	INCORRECT ANSWERS:
TIME POINTS:	**TOTAL SCORE:**

Time Elapsed

Work out how many hours and minutes have passed between each of these pairs of times.

5:45am to 8:55am =	:	5:10pm to 11:25pm =	:
1:10pm to 1:30pm =	:	12:55pm to 9:35pm =	:
1:50pm to 11:10pm =	:	1:55am to 2:25pm =	:
3:25pm to 7:50pm =	:	7:45pm to 8:35pm =	:
11:05am to 8:15pm =	:	12:30pm to 9:40pm =	:
3:55pm to 4:20pm =	:	10:10pm to 10:35pm =	:
6:10am to 2:25pm =	:	12:50pm to 9:00pm =	:
6:05pm to 6:35pm =	:	12:20am to 3:15pm =	:
7:00am to 9:10am =	:	1:20am to 7:25pm =	:
1:15am to 8:15am =	:	11:15am to 7:25pm =	:
7:40am to 1:40pm =	:	7:10pm to 8:35pm =	:
9:05am to 3:55pm =	:	12:25pm to 7:50pm =	:
3:50pm to 8:55pm =	:	4:25am to 8:00pm =	:
6:40am to 8:40am =	:	7:05am to 9:50pm =	:
7:45am to 11:40pm =	:	4:30am to 8:30pm =	:

TIME TAKEN:	INCORRECT ANSWERS:
TIME POINTS:	**TOTAL SCORE:**

Visual Memory

Spend 1 minute studying this path. Then cover the top half of this page and try to redraw it accurately on the empty grid below.

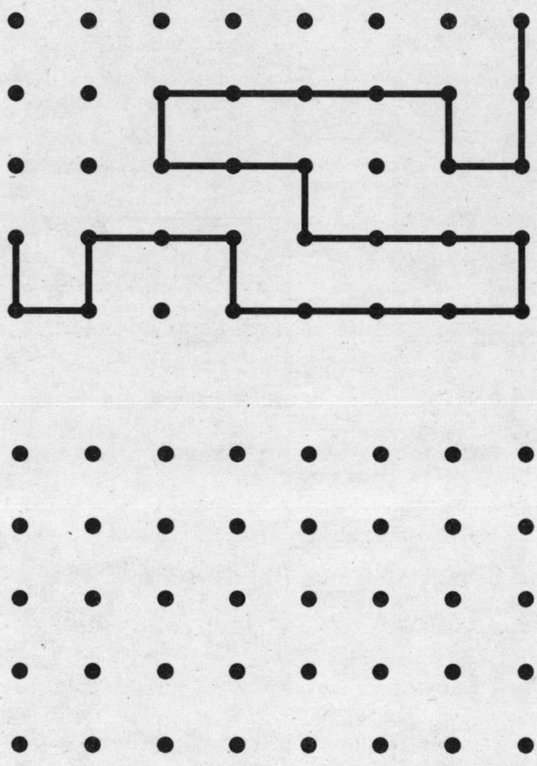

INCORRECT ANSWERS:	TOTAL SCORE:

Missing Signs

Insert the missing sign into each of these arithmetic expressions in order to make the equation true. You will need to add, subtract, multiply or divide.

38 □ 84 = 122	6 □ 3 = 18	121 □ 11 = 11
22 □ 134 = 156	25 □ 63 = 88	8 □ 3 = 24
7 □ 2 = 14	15 □ 2 = 17	58 □ 10 = 48
16 □ 61 = 77	4 □ 5 = 9	112 □ 8 = 14
5 □ 10 = 50	28 □ 67 = 95	11 □ 10 = 110
100 □ 37 = 137	9 □ 47 = 56	38 □ 36 = 2
37 □ 107 = 144	45 □ 36 = 9	39 □ 91 = 130
18 □ 6 = 3	18 □ 2 = 9	3 □ 6 = 18
124 □ 4 = 128	10 □ 49 = 59	14 □ 20 = 34
25 □ 22 = 3	24 □ 2 = 12	49 □ 7 = 7
4 □ 3 = 12	36 □ 6 = 6	2 □ 91 = 93
12 □ 3 = 4	2 □ 4 = 8	102 □ 24 = 78
77 □ 3 = 74	36 □ 4 = 9	8 □ 4 = 2

TIME TAKEN:	INCORRECT ANSWERS:
TIME POINTS:	**TOTAL SCORE:**

Counting and Perception

Spend no more than 10 seconds looking at each group of symbols in each turn, then try to sort them into order of increasing frequency. Write "1" in the "Order" column for the shape that occurs least often, and so on.

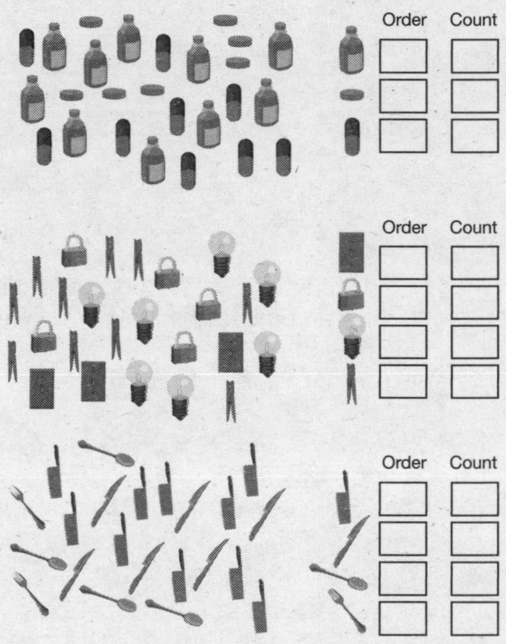

Now take as long as you think you need to write in the second column the precise count of each symbol.

TIME TAKEN:	INCORRECT ANSWERS:
TIME POINTS:	**TOTAL SCORE:**

Logical Puzzlers

Try to solve these problems – each requires only simple logic to solve, but you might find that making notes with a pencil will help!

Reading the display as if it were one continuous number, what is twice the highest value that a 12-hour digital clock displays during the day?

How many times a day does a digital clock display a number in minutes that is a non-zero multiple of six?

If an oak tree drops 40 acorns every day, how long will it take the tree to drop a total of 600 acorns?

TIME TAKEN:	INCORRECT ANSWERS:
TIME POINTS:	**TOTAL SCORE:**

Missing Words

Study each of these 3 lists of words for a total of 2 minutes. Then cover the top half of the page and see if you can identify which word is missing from each list below.

Bhangra	Bluebeat	Hiphop	Jazz
House	Indie	Bop	Boogiewoogie

Suite	Symphony	Trio	Waltz
Toccata	Opera	Overture	Concerto

Romanesque	Saxon	Doric	Edwardian
Elizabethan	Baroque	Byzantine	Moorish

Now try to spot the missing word from each list:

Boogiewoogie, House, Bop, Bhangra, Hiphop, Jazz, Indie

MISSING:

Opera, Overture, Waltz, Symphony, Suite, Concerto, Trio

MISSING:

Byzantine, Moorish, Romanesque, Doric, Edwardian, Saxon, Elizabethan

MISSING:

INCORRECT ANSWERS:	TOTAL SCORE:

Solutions

1: Shape Folding
a

2: Matchstick Thinking

4: Anagrammatic
Set 1: 4 pairs of anagrams:
COMPLIES and POLEMICS
GUNSHOTS and SHOTGUNS
CURTSIES and CRUSTIES
BRIGHTEN and BERTHING
Set 2: 5 pairs of anagrams:
FINGER and FRINGE
RENAME and MEANER
TRUCKS and STRUCK
FODDER and FORDED
TAILED and DILATE
Set 3: 4 pairs of anagrams:
RESIDENT and INSERTED
BRIGADES and ABRIDGES
ROASTING and ORGANIST
MEGATONS and MONTAGES
Set 4: 2 pairs of anagrams:
NAGGED and GANGED
BRAVED and ADVERB

6: Reflective Power
1B, 2C, 3B

7: Odd One Out

Eggs – the rest are milk products
Bottlenose – a type of dolphin, the rest are types of shark
Nectarine – the rest are citrus fruits
Tennis – the rest are always team sports

7: Shape Dividing

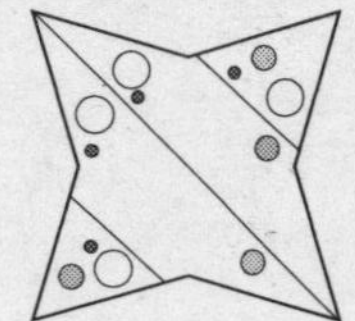

8: Time Elapsed

5:45am to 8:55am =	**3:10**	5:10pm to 11:25pm =	**6:15**
1:10pm to 1:30pm =	**0:20**	12:55pm to 9:35pm =	**8:40**
1:50pm to 11:10pm =	**9:20**	1:55am to 2:25pm =	**12:30**
3:25pm to 7:50pm =	**4:25**	7:45pm to 8:35pm =	**0:50**
11:05am to 8:15pm =	**9:10**	12:30pm to 9:40pm =	**9:10**
3:55pm to 4:20pm =	**0:25**	10:10pm to 10:35pm =	**0:25**
6:10am to 2:25pm =	**8:15**	12:50pm to 9:00pm =	**8:10**
6:05pm to 6:35pm =	**0:30**	12:20am to 3:15pm =	**14:55**
7:00am to 9:10am =	**2:10**	1:20am to 7:25pm =	**18:05**
1:15am to 8:15am =	**7:00**	11:15am to 7:25pm =	**8:10**
7:40am to 1:40pm =	**6:00**	7:10pm to 8:35pm =	**1:25**
9:05am to 3:55pm =	**6:50**	12:25pm to 7:50pm =	**7:25**
3:50pm to 8:55pm =	**5:05**	4:25am to 8:00pm =	**15:35**
6:40am to 8:40am =	**2:00**	7:05am to 9:50pm =	**14:45**
7:45am to 11:40pm =	**15:55**	4:30am to 8:30pm =	**16:00**

10: Missing Signs

90 [−] 30 = 60	79 [−] 28 = 51	31 [+] 61 = 92
12 [×] 3 = 36	4 [×] 4 = 16	5 [×] 11 = 55
38 [+] 84 = 122	6 [×] 3 = 18	121 [÷] 11 = 11
22 [+] 134 = 156	25 [+] 63 = 88	8 [×] 3 = 24
7 [×] 2 = 14	15 [+] 2 = 17	58 [−] 10 = 48
16 [+] 61 = 77	4 [+] 5 = 9	112 [÷] 8 = 14
5 [×] 10 = 50	28 [+] 67 = 95	11 [×] 10 = 110
100 [+] 37 = 137	9 [+] 47 = 56	38 [−] 36 = 2
37 [+] 107 = 144	45 [−] 36 = 9	39 [+] 91 = 130
18 [÷] 6 = 3	18 [÷] 2 = 9	3 [×] 6 = 18
124 [+] 4 = 128	10 [+] 49 = 59	14 [+] 20 = 34
25 [−] 22 = 3	24 [÷] 2 = 12	49 [÷] 7 = 7
4 [×] 3 = 12	36 [÷] 6 = 6	2 [+] 91 = 93
12 [÷] 3 = 4	2 [×] 4 = 8	102 [−] 24 = 78
77 [−] 3 = 74	36 [÷] 4 = 9	8 [÷] 4 = 2

11: Counting and Perception

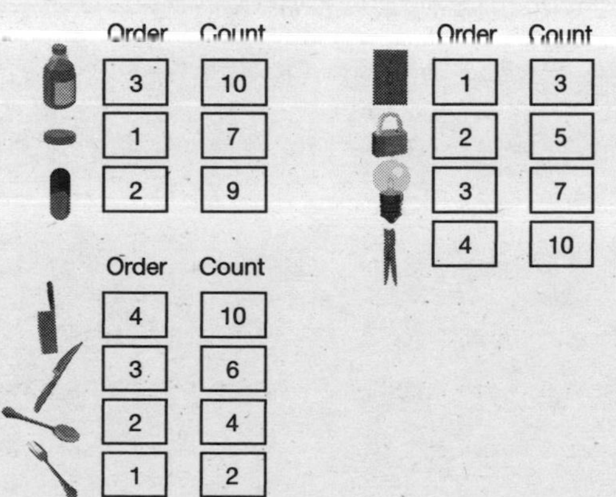

12: Logical Puzzlers

2,518 – which is twice 1,259. Should your digital clock display seconds too then 251,918 (which is twice 125,959) is also an acceptable answer!

216, or 24 times 11.

15 days.

DAY
24

Anagrammatic

Look at each of these sets of 12 words. How many pairs of anagrams can you spot in each set, and what are they?

BERTHING	ANTIQUES	SHOTGUNS
CRUSTIES	STOICISM	COMPLIES
GUNSHOTS	MOUNTAIN	CURTSIES
BRIGHTEN	BALDNESS	POLEMICS

CASTES	FRINGE	TRUCKS
SHORTS	FORDED	RENAME
STRUCK	MEANER	DILATE
TAILED	FINGER	FODDER

FREELOAD	ROASTING	MEGATONS
ORGANIST	MAGICIAN	BRIGADES
ABRIDGES	RESIDENT	AMENDING
INSERTED	MONTAGES	SWATHING

HIGHER	MASCOT	FIGHTS
WINCES	NAGGED	SUITOR
BRAVED	LODGED	GANGED
COSTLY	ADVERB	REDDER

TIME TAKEN:	INCORRECT ANSWERS:
TIME POINTS:	**TOTAL SCORE:**

Reflective Power

Look at the three figures on the left-hand side . If each of these was reflected in the diagonal "mirror" adjacent to it, which of the figures on the right would be the result?

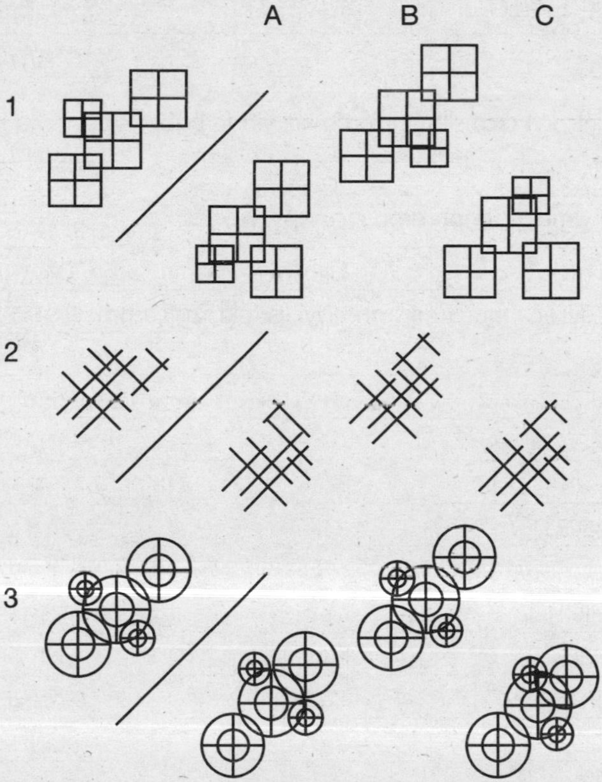

A B C

1

2

3

TIME TAKEN:	INCORRECT ANSWERS:
TIME POINTS:	**TOTAL SCORE:**

Cryptogram

Decode each of these quotations by replacing A with Z, B with A, C with B, and so on, through to replacing Y with X and Z with Y.

G yjuywq yppgtc jyrc yr rfc mddgac, zsr G kyic sn dmp gr zw jcytgle cypjw.

Afypjcq Jykz.

Mljw mlc kyl ctcp slbcpqrmmb kc, ylb fc bgbl'r slbcpqrylb kc.

E.U. Fcecj

Ufyr'q ylmrfcp umpb dmp rfcqyspsq?

Qrctcl Upgefr

Rpccq aysqc kmpc nmjjsrgml rfyl ysrmkmzgjcq bm.

Pmlyjb Pcyeyl

TIME TAKEN:	INCORRECT ANSWERS:
TIME POINTS:	**TOTAL SCORE:**

Word List

Try to memorize these 24 types of cocktail.

After 2 minutes cover the table and write as many as you can in the boxes below. You do not need to remember the correct order.

Long Island tea	Sangria	Screwdriver	Buck's fizz
Highball	Gin sling	Swizzle	Spritzer
White lady	Zombie	Cooler	Eggnog
Daiquiri	Manhattan	Margarita	Snowball
Pink gin	Mojito	Cold duck	Bloody Mary
Black velvet	Americano	Stinger	Kir

Now try to recall as many as you can:

INCORRECT ANSWERS:	TOTAL SCORE:

Shape Dividing

Draw three straight lines in order to divide the shape into four separate areas. Each area must contain precisely one of each size of circle. The three lines may touch but they must not cross.

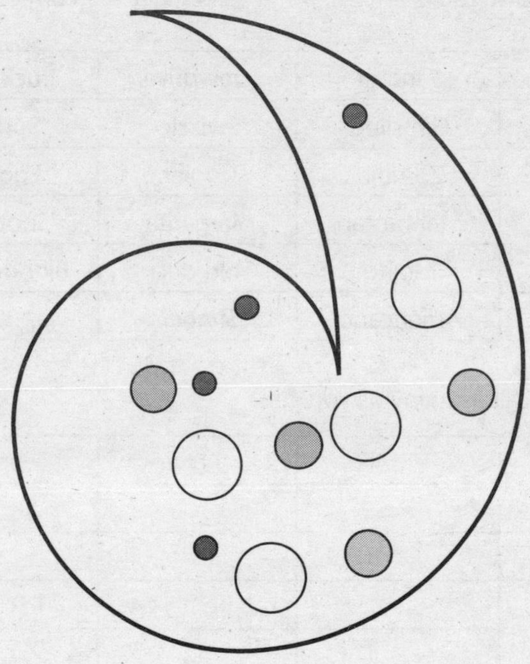

TIME TAKEN:	INCORRECT ANSWERS:
TIME POINTS:	**TOTAL SCORE:**

Rotation

If you were to rotate each of these three pictures as indicated by the arrow beneath, which of the figures below would be the result?

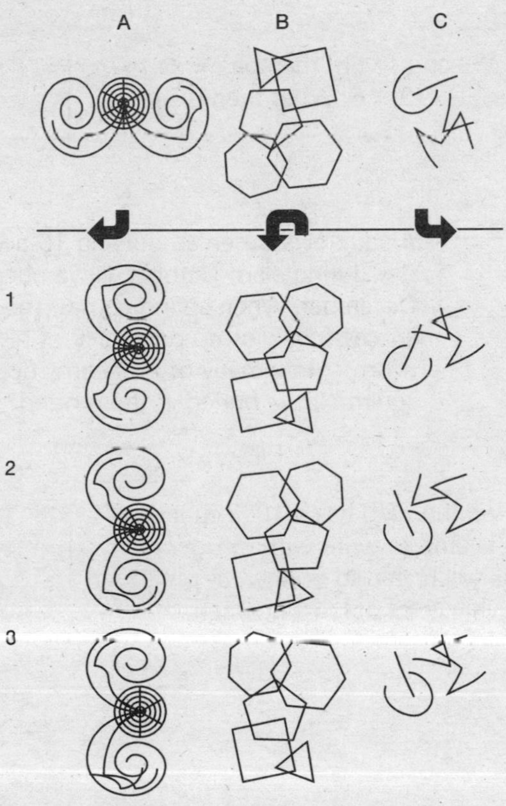

TIME TAKEN:	INCORRECT ANSWERS:
TIME POINTS:	**TOTAL SCORE:**

Logical Puzzlers

Try to solve these problems – each requires only simple logic to solve, but you might find that making notes with a pencil will help!

If a=1, b=2, c=3 and so on, then baa = 2+1+1 = 4 and cab = 3+1+2 = 6. What then is the value of 'two'?

A squirrel is observed burying 10 acorns every day during all of October, November, and December. When spring comes, the squirrel successfully digs up only 75% of his buried acorns. How many of his acorns does the squirrel leave buried in the ground?

The pen I'm writing with has a 10% chance of failing when I come to write with it. How many of these pens will I need to bring with me to have a 99% chance of at least one pen working?

TIME TAKEN:	INCORRECT ANSWERS:
TIME POINTS:	**TOTAL SCORE:**

Visual Memory

Spend 1 minute studying this path. Then cover the top half of this page and try to redraw it accurately on the empty grid below.

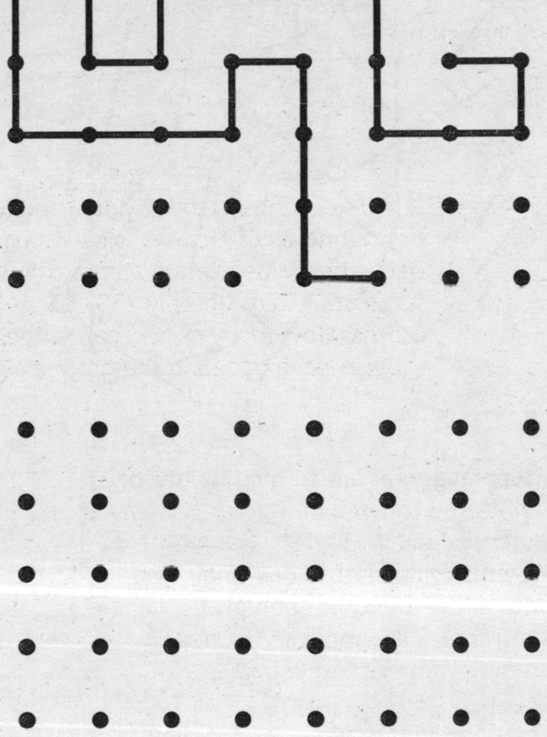

INCORRECT ANSWERS:	TOTAL SCORE:

Observation and Counting

Look at these lines and see how long it takes you to answer the observation questions below.

How many separate areas are formed by the lines?

Can you draw the whole figure in a single pen-stroke without either lifting the pen off the paper or going over a line more than once? You may cross over an existing line.

How many straight lines do you need to draw this figure?

TIME TAKEN:	INCORRECT ANSWERS:
TIME POINTS:	**TOTAL SCORE:**

Speed Arithmetic

Complete the following set of arithmetic equations as quickly as possible. You should be able to do them all in your head without using a calculator or making notes.

95 − 8 =	12 + 88 =	92 + 6 =
81 − 4 =	16 + 16 =	13 + 11 =
7 × 11 =	72 − 14 =	64 − 15 =
12 + 66 =	13 + 14 =	19 + 51 =
4 + 23 =	100 + 1 =	6 × 3 =
7 + 51 =	12 × 5 =	11 × 2 =
8 × 4 =	1 + 1 =	64 + 17 =
7 × 6 =	4 × 7 =	13 + 97 =
9 × 4 =	57 + 4 =	10 + 15 =
61 − 9 =	86 − 11 =	89 − 13 =
20 + 4 =	2 × 3 =	17 − 14 =
5 × 7 =	7 + 75 =	8 × 9 =
11 + 36 =	12 × 2 =	16 + 77 =

TIME TAKEN:	INCORRECT ANSWERS:
TIME POINTS:	**TOTAL SCORE:**

Creative Thinking

See if you can solve each of the following conundrums. If you get stuck then try thinking laterally – they all have logical solutions, but the logic might not be what you expect!

If you place a coin on the table and then another identical one touching it, how many times will the second coin turn through a complete revolution when you hold the first coin still and roll the second once around the outside of the first coin? Try to work it out without using coins first!

We can all agree that one comes before two, but how can two come after three and four before one?

TIME TAKEN:	INCORRECT ANSWERS:
TIME POINTS:	**TOTAL SCORE:**

Missing Words

Study each of these 3 lists of words for 2 minutes. Then cover the top half of the page and see if you can identify which word is missing from each list below.

Lemon	Poplar	Lilac	Lime
Quince	Lind	Raffia	Linden

Anteater	Iguana	Newt	Frog
Gorilla	Ape	Giraffe	Llama

Skiing	Skating	Canoeing	Windsurfing
Badminton	Tennis	Croquet	Snooker

Now try to spot the missing word from each list:

Raffia, Linden, Poplar, Lilac, Lime, Quince, Lemon

MISSING:

Newt, Gorilla, Llama, Ape, Anteater, Giraffe, Iguana

MISSING:

Skiing, Canoeing, Croquet, Skating, Windsurfing, Tennis, Badminton

MISSING:

INCORRECT ANSWERS:	TOTAL SCORE:

Time Elapsed

Work out how many hours and minutes have passed between each of these pairs of times.

10:05am to 4:20pm =	:	2:25am to 2:55am =	:
1:50am to 9:25pm =	:	5:30pm to 6:40pm =	:
8:35pm to 11:05pm =	:	3:20am to 2:25pm =	:
6:35pm to 9:00pm =	:	9:05pm to 11:05pm =	:
10:05am to 8:40pm =	:	7:45am to 8:30am =	:
1:20pm to 11:55pm =	:	8:50am to 4:10pm =	:
4:45am to 10:50am =	:	10:40am to 1:30pm =	:
12:00am to 3:40am =	:	12:50pm to 6:35pm =	:
9:05am to 7:25pm =	:	8:00am to 8:50pm =	:
6:10am to 1:35pm =	:	11:10am to 8:55pm =	:
12:45am to 12:10pm =	:	6:05am to 9:20am =	:
4:15am to 9:40pm =	:	6:05am to 8:45am =	:
12:05am to 3:05pm =	:	5:50am to 4:05pm =	:
7:05am to 9:15pm =	:	2:30am to 10:55am =	:
3:20am to 4:35pm =	:	3:30pm to 3:40pm =	:

TIME TAKEN:	INCORRECT ANSWERS:
TIME POINTS:	**TOTAL SCORE:**

Solutions

1: Anagrammatic

Set 1: 4 pairs of anagrams:
SIMMERING and IMMERSING
ESPRESSOS and REPOSSESS
BACKWARDS and DRAWBACKS
CORSETING and ESCORTING
Set 2: 4 pairs of anagrams:
DEVIATES and SEDATIVE
CREATING and REACTING
RETRACES and CATERERS
INTENDED and INDENTED
Set 3: 2 pairs of anagrams:
PURSES and SUPERS
BINDER and INBRED
Set 4: 4 pairs of anagrams:
GRATERS and GARRETS
DELIGHT and LIGHTED
PLEASES and ELAPSES
STRAITS and ARTISTS

2: Reflective Power

1A, 2A, 3B

3: Cryptogram

I always arrive late at the office, but I make up for it by leaving early.
Charles Lamb.

Only one man ever understood me, and he didn't understand me.
G.W. Hegel

What's another word for thesaurus?
Steven Wright

Trees cause more pollution than automobiles do.
Ronald Reagan

5: Shape Dividing

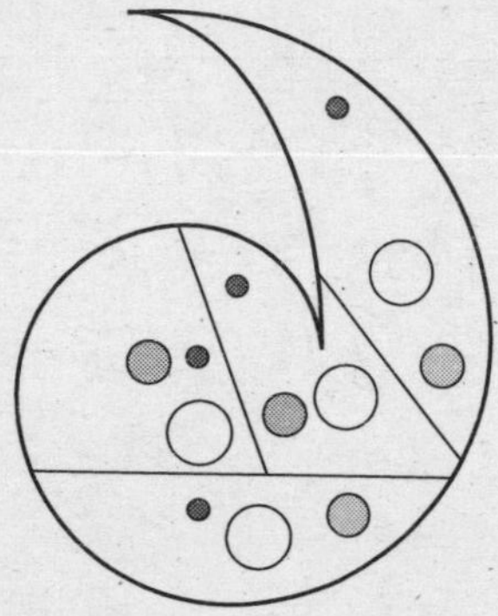

6: Rotation
A2, B1, C3

7: Logical Puzzlers
58, which is 20 (t) + 23 (w) + 15 (o).

230 acorns.

2 pens. The chance of both failing is 10% of 10%, or 1% – which means there is a 99% chance of this not happening, or, in other words, at least one working.

9: Observation and Counting
26 separate areas are formed by these lines.

Yes, you can draw it in a single stroke.

33 straight lines are needed to draw this figure.

10: Speed Arithmetic

95 − 8 = **87**	12 + 88 = **100**	92 + 6 = **98**
81 − 4 = **77**	16 + 16 = **32**	13 + 11 = **24**
7 × 11 = **77**	72 − 14 = **58**	64 − 15 = **49**
12 + 66 = **78**	13 + 14 = **27**	19 + 51 = **70**
4 + 23 = **27**	100 + 1 = **101**	6 × 3 = **18**
7 + 51 = **58**	12 × 5 = **60**	11 × 2 = **22**
8 × 4 = **32**	1 + 1 = **2**	64 + 17 = **81**
7 × 6 = **42**	4 × 7 = **28**	13 + 97 = **110**
9 × 4 = **36**	57 + 4 = **61**	10 + 15 = **25**
61 − 9 = **52**	86 − 11 = **75**	89 − 13 = **76**
20 + 4 = **24**	2 × 3 = **6**	17 − 14 = **3**
5 × 7 = **35**	7 + 75 = **82**	8 × 9 = **72**
11 + 36 = **47**	12 × 2 = **24**	16 + 77 = **93**

11: Creative Thinking

The outer coin will perform two full revolutions.

They do in a dictionary!

13: Time Elapsed

10:05am to 4:20pm =	**6:15**	2:25am to 2:55am =	**0:30**
1:50am to 9:25pm =	**19:35**	5:30pm to 6:40pm =	**1:10**
8:35pm to 11:05pm =	**2:30**	3:20am to 2:25pm =	**11:05**
6:35pm to 9:00pm =	**2:25**	9:05pm to 11:05pm =	**2:00**
10:05am to 8:40pm =	**10:35**	7:45am to 8:30am =	**0:45**
1:20pm to 11:55pm =	**10:35**	8:50am to 4:10pm =	**7:20**
4:45am to 10:50am =	**6:05**	10:40am to 1:30pm =	**2:50**
12:00am to 3:40am =	**3:40**	12:50pm to 6:35pm =	**5:45**
9:05am to 7:25pm =	**10:20**	8:00am to 8:50pm =	**12:50**
6:10am to 1:35pm =	**7:25**	11:10am to 8:55pm =	**9:45**
12:45am to 12:10pm =	**11:25**	6:05am to 9:20am =	**3:15**
4:15am to 9:40pm =	**17:25**	6:05am to 8:45am =	**2:40**
12:05am to 3:05pm =	**15:00**	5:50am to 4:05pm =	**10:15**
7:05am to 9:15pm =	**14:10**	2:30am to 10:55am =	**8:25**
3:20am to 4:35pm =	**13:15**	3:30pm to 3:40pm =	**0:10**

DAY
25

Missing Numbers

Insert the missing number into each of these arithmetic expressions in order to make the equations true. You should not need a calculator to do this!

☐ + 85 = **90**	☐ + 28 = **30**	100 − ☐ = **81**
17 + ☐ = **81**	☐ + 5 = **11**	8 × ☐ = **72**
3 + ☐ = **44**	☐ − 10 = **9**	☐ + 53 = **57**
17 − ☐ = **6**	☐ − 10 = **24**	☐ + 93 = **101**
12 + ☐ = **58**	☐ × 7 = **63**	4 × ☐ = **48**
65 − ☐ = **61**	☐ − 9 = **58**	5 + ☐ = **46**
85 − ☐ = **73**	☐ + 6 = **52**	40 − ☐ = **25**
84 − ☐ = **69**	17 + ☐ = **28**	10 + ☐ = **28**
65 + ☐ = **84**	42 + ☐ = **47**	☐ × 10 = **60**
☐ − 9 = **13**	☐ + 44 = **49**	☐ − 3 = **76**
9 × ☐ = **99**	7 + ☐ = **21**	59 − ☐ = **52**
☐ + 4 = **83**	☐ × 10 = **100**	28 + ☐ = **44**
☐ − 13 = **47**	☐ + 15 = **42**	☐ − 18 = **12**

TIME TAKEN:	INCORRECT ANSWERS:
TIME POINTS:	**TOTAL SCORE:**

Matchstick Thinking

The picture below shows 12 matchsticks arranged into 1 large and 4 small squares.

Can you move 4 matchsticks only in order to make precisely 3 squares? All matches must be used in making the squares, and you may not overlap matches.

TIME TAKEN:	INCORRECT ANSWERS:
TIME POINTS:	**TOTAL SCORE:**

Logical Puzzlers

Try to solve these problems – each requires only simple logic to solve, but you might find that making notes with a pencil will help!

High tide on the beach at Brighton is at 1pm today. If high tides are at twelve hours and twenty minutes apart from each other, at what time will high tide be two afternoons from now?

If you turn over a three-minute egg-timer and the amount of sand in the top part halves in 45 seconds, how long will it take for the rest of the sand to pass through to the bottom?

If an aeroplane produces 90 decibels of noise at take-off, how loud will it sound to somebody who uses -12 decibels ear-plugs?

TIME TAKEN:	INCORRECT ANSWERS:
TIME POINTS:	**TOTAL SCORE:**

Observation and Counting

Look at these arcs (single curves) and see how long it takes you to answer the observation questions below.

Is it possible to draw the whole figure in a single pen- stroke without lifting the pen off the paper or going over a line more than once? You may cross over an existing line.

How many separate areas are formed between the lines?

What is the minimum number of arcs you would need to draw this figure?

TIME TAKEN:	INCORRECT ANSWERS:
TIME POINTS:	**TOTAL SCORE:**

Visual Memory

Spend 1 minute studying this path. Then cover the top half of this page and try to redraw it accurately on the empty grid below.

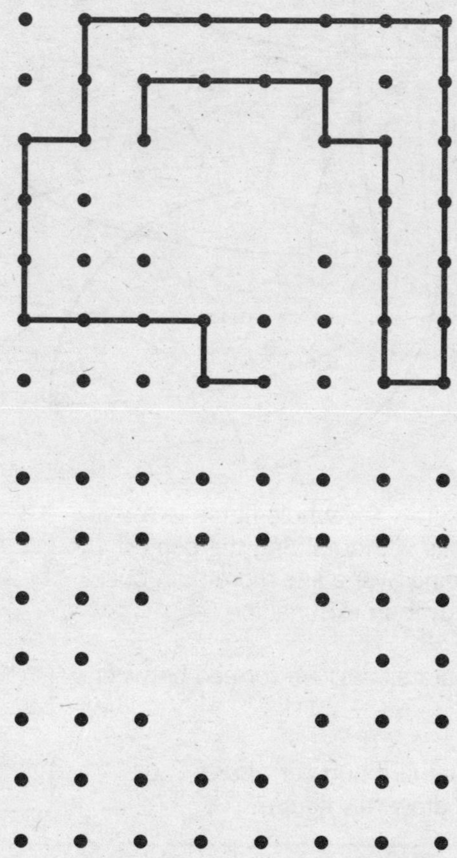

INCORRECT ANSWERS:	TOTAL SCORE:

Number Sequences

Look at each of these number sequences and see if you can deduce which number comes next in the series.

885	875	865	855	845	
334	201	133	68	65	
228	238	267	315	382	
11	22	44	88	176	
403	242	161	81	80	
721	714	707	700	693	
264	186	124	78	48	
9	16	25	41	66	

TIME TAKEN:	INCORRECT ANSWERS:
TIME POINTS:	**TOTAL SCORE:**

Speed Arithmetic

Complete the following set of arithmetic equations as quickly as possible. You should be able to do them all in your head without using a calculator or making notes.

6 × 6 =	17 + 35 =	65 − 14 =
11 × 2 =	105 − 5 =	25 − 4 =
7 × 2 =	7 × 7 =	7 × 6 =
66 − 11 =	17 + 11 =	9 + 96 =
93 − 4 =	81 − 19 =	9 × 6 =
100 + 16 =	12 + 38 =	74 − 19 =
29 − 17 =	19 + 95 =	4 × 9 =
7 × 9 =	10 × 2 =	4 × 10 =
63 + 7 =	95 + 10 =	3 + 88 =
10 × 9 =	45 − 18 =	3 × 11 =
107 − 19 =	5 × 12 =	93 − 16 =
8 × 6 =	68 + 4 =	108 − 5 =
12 × 8 =	84 − 5 =	12 × 2 =

TIME TAKEN:	INCORRECT ANSWERS:
TIME POINTS:	**TOTAL SCORE:**

Creative Thinking

See if you can solve each of the following conundrums. If you get stuck then try thinking laterally – they all have logical solutions, but the logic might not be what you expect!

If I tell you that I know someone who predicts the future, how can it possibly be the case that I am telling the truth?

Which 11-letter word is most commonly pronounced incorrectly?

TIME TAKEN:	INCORRECT ANSWERS:
TIME POINTS:	**TOTAL SCORE:**

Rotation

If you were to rotate each of these three pictures as indicated by the arrow beneath, which of the figures below would be the result?

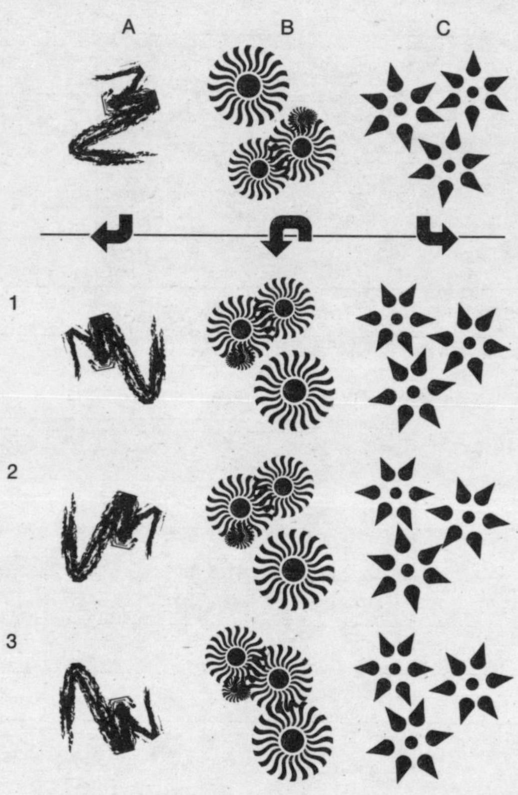

TIME TAKEN:	INCORRECT ANSWERS:
TIME POINTS:	**TOTAL SCORE:**

Word List

Try to memorize these 24 currencies.

After 2 minutes cover the table and write as many as you can in the boxes below. You do not need to remember the correct order.

Dollar	Peso	Pound	Mark
Guilder	Escudo	Franc	Dinar
Duktat	Riel	Lek	Rupee
Lita	Lira	Euro	Rouble
Yen	Yuan	Dong	Krona
Baht	Punt	Peseta	Dirham

Now try to recall as many as you can:

INCORRECT ANSWERS:	TOTAL SCORE:

Missing Words

Study each of these 3 lists of words for a total of 2 minutes. Then cover the top half of the page and see if you can identify which word is missing from each list below.

Bang	Biff	Wham	Whiz
Zang	Zap	Kersplat	Pow

Altocumulus	Altostratus	Cirrocumulus	Cirrostratus
Cirrus	Cumulonimbus	Nimbostratus	Stratocumulus

Avenue	Street	Boulevard	Lane
Bypass	Freeway	Motorway	Passage

Now try to spot the missing word from each list:

Zang, Whiz, Pow, Biff, Wham, Zap, Bang

MISSING:

Cirrocumulus, Cirrostratus, Stratocumulus, Altostratus, Altocumulus, Cirrus, Cumulonimbus

MISSING:

Boulevard, Bypass, Freeway, Avenue, Passage, Street, Lane

MISSING:

INCORRECT ANSWERS:	TOTAL SCORE:

Anagrammatic

Look at each of these sets of 12 words. How many pairs of anagrams can you spot in each set, and what are they?

SIMMERING	PEPPERING	BACKWARDS
ESCORTING	UNDAUNTED	CORSETING
ESPRESSOS	CORPORATE	IMMERSING
GUARDRAIL	DRAWBACKS	REPOSSESS

CREATING	SPECKLED	RETRACES
IMPACTED	INTENDED	SEDATIVE
GRATUITY	REACTING	INDENTED
DEVIATES	CATERERS	BLUBBERS

ENZYME	STATES	BINDER
PURSES	GAFFES	WAKENS
SUPERS	INBRED	DINNED
CROAKS	SIMILE	JABBER

LIGHTED	STRAITS	ELAPSES
ARTISTS	SOBERED	GARRETS
ENAMELS	PAUNCHY	DELIGHT
GRATERS	PAINFUL	PLEASES

TIME TAKEN:	INCORRECT ANSWERS:
TIME POINTS:	**TOTAL SCORE:**

Reflective Power

Look at the three figures on the left-hand side. If each of these was reflected in the diagonal "mirror" adjacent to it, which of the figures on the right would be the result?

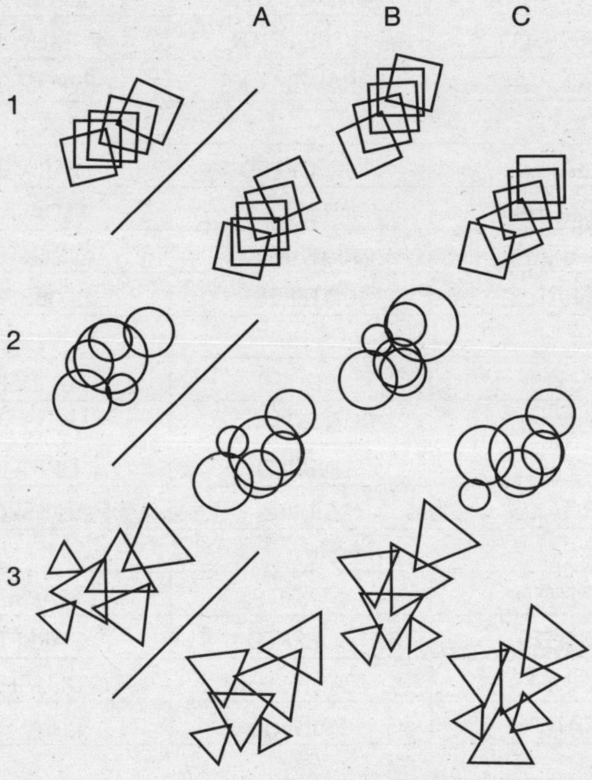

A B C

1

2

3

TIME TAKEN:	INCORRECT ANSWERS:
TIME POINTS:	**TOTAL SCORE:**

Solutions

1: Missing Numbers

[5] + 85 = **90**	[2] + 28 = **30**	100 – [19] = **81**
17 + [64] = **81**	[6] + 5 = **11**	8 × [9] = **72**
3 + [41] = **44**	[19] – 10 = **9**	[4] + 53 = **57**
17 – [11] = **6**	[34] – 10 = **24**	[8] + 93 = **101**
12 + [46] = **58**	[9] × 7 = **63**	4 × [12] = **48**
65 – [4] = **61**	[67] – 9 = **58**	5 + [41] = **46**
85 – [12] = **73**	[46] + 6 = **52**	40 – [15] = **25**
84 – [15] = **69**	17 + [11] = **28**	10 + [18] = **28**
65 + [19] = **84**	42 + [5] = **47**	[6] × 10 = **60**
[22] – 9 = **13**	[5] + 44 = **49**	[79] – 3 = **76**
9 × [11] = **99**	7 + [14] = **21**	59 – [7] = **52**
[79] + 4 = **83**	[10] × 10 = **100**	28 + [16] = **44**
[60] – 13 = **47**	[27] + 15 = **42**	[30] 10 = **12**

2: Matchstick Thinking

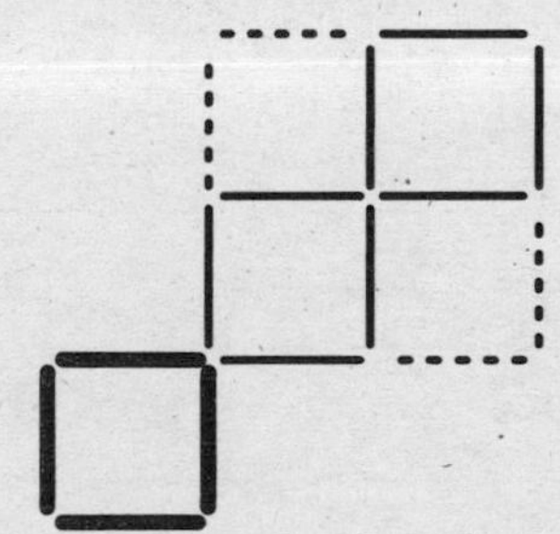

3: Logical Puzzlers
2:20pm.

2 minutes 15 seconds. It doesn't matter that half the height of sand has passed already; you know it's a 3-minute timer and only 45 seconds has elapsed.

78 decibels.

4: Observation and Counting
Yes, you can draw it in a single stroke.

8 separate areas.

17 arcs/curves.

6: Number Sequences
538, 587, 636, 685, 734, **783**
Rule: add 49 to previous number

177, 135, 101, 75, 57, **47**
Rule: difference between numbers decreases by 8 each time

77, 47, 30, 17, 13, **4**
Rule: subtract the previous number from the one before it

852, 805, 758, 711, 664, **617**
Rule: subtract 47 from previous number

436, 449, 467, 490, 518, **551**
Rule: difference between numbers increases by 5 each time

343, 358, 373, 388, 403, **418**
Rule: add 15 to previous number

14, 50, 64, 114, 178, **292**
Rule: add the previous two numbers

12, 57, 69, 126, 195, **321**
Rule: add the previous two numbers

7: Speed Arithmetic

6 × 6 = **36**	17 + 35 = **52**	65 − 14 = **51**
11 × 2 = **22**	105 − 5 = **100**	25 − 4 = **21**
7 × 2 = **14**	7 × 7 = **49**	7 × 6 = **42**
66 − 11 = **55**	17 + 11 = **28**	9 + 96 = **105**
93 − 4 = **89**	81 − 19 = **62**	9 × 6 = **54**
100 + 16 = **116**	12 + 38 = **50**	74 − 19 = **55**
29 − 17 = **12**	19 + 95 = **114**	4 × 9 = **36**
7 × 9 = **63**	10 × 2 = **20**	4 × 10 = **40**
63 + 7 = **70**	95 + 10 = **105**	3 + 88 = **91**
10 × 9 = **90**	45 − 18 = **27**	3 × 11 = **33**
107 − 19 = **88**	5 × 12 = **60**	93 − 16 = **77**
8 × 6 = **48**	68 + 4 = **72**	108 − 5 = **103**
12 × 8 = **96**	84 − 5 = **79**	12 × 2 = **24**

8: Creative Thinking

You can easily be telling the truth; it doesn't mean that their predictions also come true!

That would be the word "incorrectly"!

9: Rotation

A3, B2, C1

12: Anagrammatic

Set 1: 1 pair of anagrams:
LATENTS and TALENTS

Set 2: 6 pairs of anagrams:
SIGNATORY and GYRATIONS
REDEVELOP and DEVELOPER
DIRECTORS and CREDITORS
HEARTIEST and EARTHIEST
REPRISING and SPRINGIER
TRICEPSES and PRECISEST

Set 3: 6 pairs of anagrams:
VERSES and SEVERS
CITRUS and RUSTIC
THESES and SHEETS
GAPING and PAGING
TONING and NOTING
INDENT and TINNED

Set 4: 2 pairs of anagrams:
TESTAMENT and STATEMENT
INSURGENT and UNRESTING

13: Reflective Power

1C, 2C, 3B

DAY
26

Rotation

If you were to rotate each of these three pictures as indicated by the arrow beneath, which of the figures below would be the result?

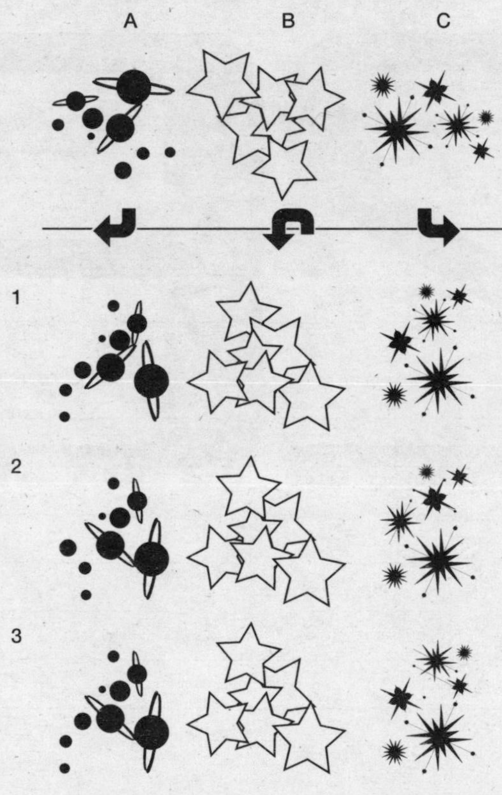

TIME TAKEN:	INCORRECT ANSWERS:
TIME POINTS:	**TOTAL SCORE:**

Word List

Try to memorize these 24 types of fabric.

After 2 minutes, cover the table and write as many as you can in the boxes below. You do not need to remember the correct order.

Cotton	Leather	Linen	Satin
Fleece	Shag	Tartan	Wool
Fur	Dungaree	Mohair	Moleskin
Calico	Denim	Corduroy	Brocade
Baize	Chiffon	Silk	Linen
Tarpaulin	Taffeta	Tweed	Velvet

Now try to recall as many as you can:

INCORRECT ANSWERS:	TOTAL SCORE:

Reflective Power

Look at the three figures on the left-hand side. If each of these was reflected in the diagonal "mirror" adjacent to it, which of the figures on the right would be the result?

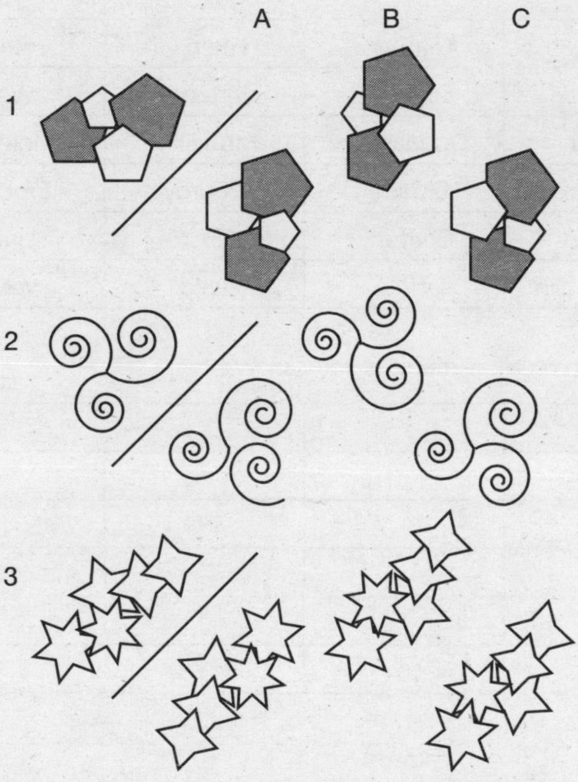

A B C

1

2

3

TIME TAKEN:	INCORRECT ANSWERS:
TIME POINTS:	**TOTAL SCORE:**

Creative Thinking

See if you can solve each of the following conundrums. If you get stuck then try thinking laterally – they all have logical solutions, but the logic might not be what you expect!

In what situation would having quartzes be particularly advantageous?

What occurs once in January and once in February, but then doesn't occur again until June, July, and August?

TIME TAKEN:	INCORRECT ANSWERS:
TIME POINTS:	**TOTAL SCORE:**

Missing Signs

Insert the missing sign into each of these arithmetic expressions in order to make the equation true. You will need to add, subtract, multiply or divide.

54	☐	20	=	34	61	☐	32	=	29	98	☐	7	=	14
59	☐	37	=	22	21	☐	16	=	5	42	☐	9	=	33
18	☐	38	=	56	58	☐	26	=	32	42	☐	17	=	25
15	☐	25	=	40	26	☐	4	=	30	77	☐	33	=	44
11	☐	11	=	1	6	☐	10	=	60	120	☐	12	=	10
29	☐	16	=	13	6	☐	2	=	3	84	☐	12	=	7
8	☐	4	=	2	10	☐	11	=	110	9	☐	8	=	72
106	☐	4	=	102	28	☐	112	=	140	31	☐	68	=	99
12	☐	7	=	84	2	☐	3	=	6	33	☐	11	=	3
48	☐	9	=	57	69	☐	23	=	46	94	☐	35	=	59
71	☐	21	=	50	9	☐	6	=	3	62	☐	33	=	29
34	☐	32	=	2	101	☐	11	=	90	60	☐	5	=	12
73	☐	36	=	37	42	☐	3	=	14	110	☐	11	=	10

TIME TAKEN:	INCORRECT ANSWERS:
TIME POINTS:	**TOTAL SCORE:**

Logical Puzzlers

Try to solve these problems – each requires only simple logic to solve, but you might find that making notes with a pencil will help!

If there are two high tides every day, how many high tides take place in a two-week period?

Half the people in my drama group are happy, but, of those, only a quarter describe themselves as rich. How many of this group of eighty people are both happy and rich?

If a=1, b=2, c=3 and so on,
then baa = 2+1+1 = 4 and cab = 3+1+2 = 6.
What then is the value of 'three'?

TIME TAKEN:	INCORRECT ANSWERS:
TIME POINTS:	**TOTAL SCORE:**

Visual Memory

Spend 1 minute studying this path. Then cover the top half of this page and try to redraw it accurately on the empty grid below.

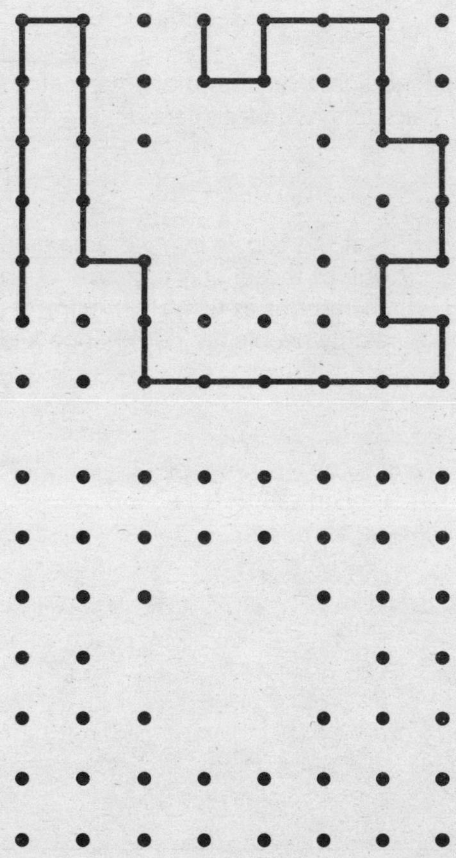

INCORRECT ANSWERS:	**TOTAL SCORE:**

Missing Numbers

Insert the missing number into each of these arithmetic expressions in order to make the equations true. You should not need a calculator to do this!

27 + ☐ = **44**	☐ + 2 = **56**	44 − ☐ = **29**
☐ − 13 = **80**	☐ × 4 = **32**	☐ + 20 = **23**
☐ − 6 = **100**	24 + ☐ = **31**	☐ × 3 = **12**
3 × ☐ = **15**	36 − ☐ = **25**	☐ + 3 = **57**
39 − ☐ = **19**	☐ + 98 = **117**	☐ × 12 = **84**
85 + ☐ = **95**	36 − ☐ = **17**	☐ + 5 = **11**
☐ + 49 = **53**	4 + ☐ = **36**	5 × ☐ = **45**
☐ − 13 = **9**	☐ × 9 = **36**	☐ + 16 = **23**
☐ + 14 = **57**	☐ + 1 = **11**	☐ − 13 = **66**
☐ + 16 = **101**	☐ − 10 = **88**	92 − ☐ = **91**
6 + ☐ = **17**	4 × ☐ = **48**	13 − ☐ = **12**
19 + ☐ = **35**	89 − ☐ = **70**	95 − ☐ = **84**
☐ + 90 = **102**	☐ × 11 = **77**	☐ − 16 = **25**

TIME TAKEN:	INCORRECT ANSWERS:
TIME POINTS:	**TOTAL SCORE:**

Cryptogram

Decode each of these quotations by replacing A with Z, B with A, C with B, and so on, through to replacing Y with X and Z with Y.

Tmetgxtcrt lxiwdji iwtdgn xh qaxcs, qji iwtdgn lxiwdji tmetgxtcrt xh btgt xcitaatrijpa eapn.

Xbpccjta Zpci

Xu lt lpxi udg iwt bdbtci lwtc tktgniwxcv, pqhdajitan tktgniwxcv xh gtpsn, lt hwpaa ctktg qtvxc.

Xkpc Ijgvtctk

Xi xh vdds id wpkt pc tcs id ydjgctn idlpgs; qji xi xh iwt ydjgctn iwpi bpiitgh, xc iwt tcs.

Jghjap At Vjxc

Sd cdi vd lwtgt iwt epiw bpn atps, vd xchitps lwtgt iwtgt xh cd epiw pcs atpkt p igpxa.

Gpaew Lpasd Tbtghdc

TIME TAKEN:	INCORRECT ANSWERS:
TIME POINTS:	**TOTAL SCORE:**

Counting and Perception

Spend no more than 10 seconds looking at each group of symbols in each turn, then try to sort them into order of increasing frequency. Write "1" in the "Order" column for the shape that occurs least often, and so on.

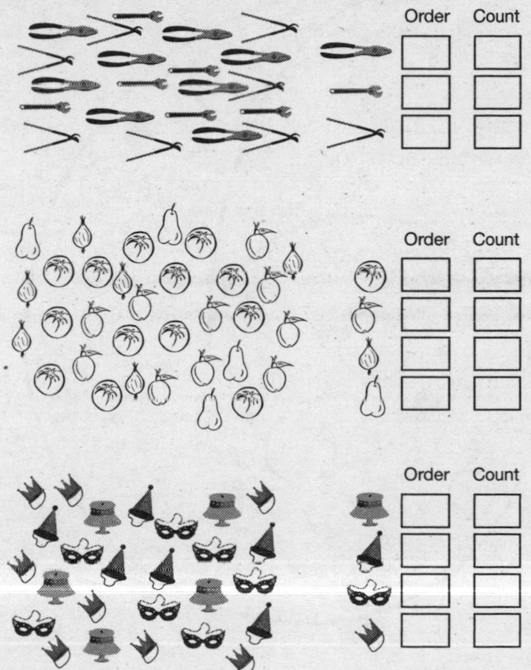

Now take as long as you think you need to write in the second column the precise count of each symbol.

TIME TAKEN:	INCORRECT ANSWERS:
TIME POINTS:	**TOTAL SCORE:**

Shape Dividing

Draw three straight lines in order to divide the shape into four separate areas. Each area must contain precisely one of each size of circle. The three lines may touch but they must not cross.

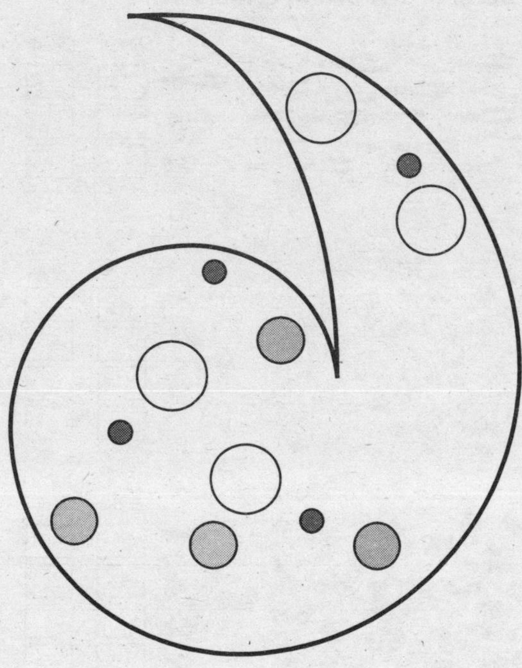

TIME TAKEN:	INCORRECT ANSWERS:
TIME POINTS:	**TOTAL SCORE:**

Missing Words

Study each of these 3 lists of words for a total of 2 minutes. Then cover the top half of the page and see if you can identify which word is missing from each list below.

Bright	Shiny	Glossy	Gleaming
Glowing	Polished	Sleek	Lustrous

Valley	Basin	Tundra	Scree
Loch	Jungle	Lagoon	Cliff

Lake	River	Stream	Watercourse
Pool	Loch	Puddle	Brook

Now try to spot the missing word from each list:

Glossy, Sleek, Glowing, Shiny, Bright, Gleaming, Lustrous

MISSING:

Cliff, Lagoon, Loch, Valley, Scree, Jungle, Tundra

MISSING:

Brook, Puddle, Watercourse, Lake, Loch, Pool, Stream

MISSING:

INCORRECT ANSWERS:	TOTAL SCORE:

Visual Sequences

Can you work out which pattern comes next in each of these two visual sequences?

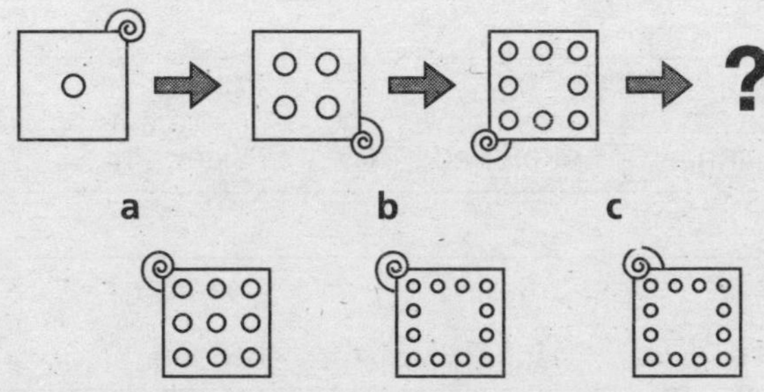

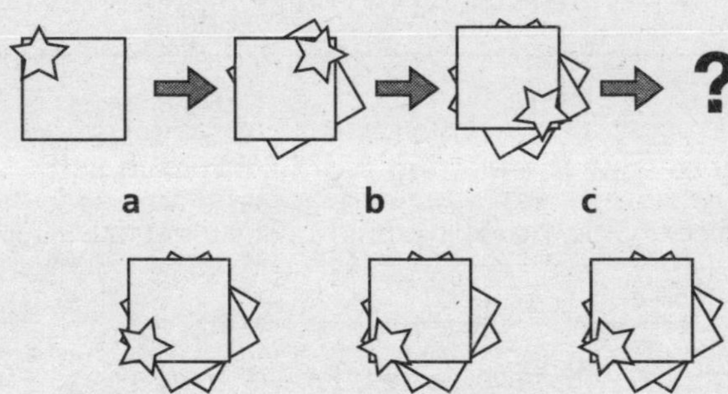

TIME TAKEN:	INCORRECT ANSWERS:
TIME POINTS:	**TOTAL SCORE:**

Solutions

1: Rotation

A2, B3, C1

3: Reflective Power

1B, 2B, 3A

4: Creative Thinking

When playing the board game Scrabble™, where it would be particularly high-scoring!

The letter "u".

5: Missing Signs

54 [–] 20 = 34	61 [–] 32 = 29	98 [÷] 7 = 14
59 [–] 37 = 22	21 [–] 16 = 5	42 [–] 9 = 33
18 [+] 38 = 56	58 [–] 26 = 32	42 [–] 17 = 25
15 [+] 25 = 40	26 [+] 4 = 30	77 [–] 33 = 44
11 [÷] 11 = 1	6 [×] 10 = 60	120 [÷] 12 = 10
29 [–] 16 = 13	6 [÷] 2 = 3	84 [÷] 12 = 7
8 [÷] 4 = 2	10 [×] 11 = 110	9 [×] 8 = 72
106 [–] 4 = 102	28 [+] 112 = 140	31 [+] 68 = 99
12 [×] 7 = 84	2 [×] 3 = 6	33 [÷] 11 = 3
48 [+] 9 = 57	69 [–] 23 = 46	94 [–] 35 = 59
71 [–] 21 = 50	9 [–] 6 = 3	62 [–] 33 = 29
34 [–] 32 = 2	101 [–] 11 = 90	60 [÷] 5 = 12
73 [–] 36 = 37	42 [÷] 3 = 14	110 [÷] 11 = 10

6: Logical Puzzles

28 high tides.

10 people.

56, which is 20 (t) + 8 (h) + 18 (r) + 5 (e) + 5 (e).

8: Missing Numbers

27 + [17] = **44**	[54] + 2 = **56**	44 – [15] = **29**
[93] – 13 = **80**	[8] × 4 = **32**	[3] + 20 = **23**
[106] – 6 = **100**	24 + [7] = **31**	[4] × 3 = **12**
3 × [5] = **15**	36 – [11] = **25**	[54] + 3 = **57**
39 – [20] = **19**	[19] + 98 = **117**	[7] × 12 = **84**
85 + [10] = **95**	36 – [19] = **17**	[6] + 5 = **11**
[4] + 49 = **53**	4 + [32] = **36**	5 × [9] = **45**
[22] – 13 = **9**	[4] × 9 = **36**	[7] + 16 = **23**
[43] + 14 = **57**	[10] + 1 = **11**	[79] – 13 = **66**
[85] + 16 = **101**	[98] – 10 = **88**	92 – [1] = **91**
6 + [11] = **17**	4 × [12] = **48**	13 – [1] = **12**
19 + [16] = **35**	89 – [19] = **70**	95 – [11] = **84**
[12] + 90 = **102**	[7] × 11 = **77**	[41] – 16 = **25**

9: Cryptogram

Experience without theory is blind, but theory without experience is mere intellectual play.

Imannuel Kant

If we wait for the moment when everything, absolutely everything is ready, we shall never begin.

Ivan Turgenev

It is good to have an end to journey toward; but it is the journey that matters, in the end.

Ursula Le Guin

Do not go where the path may lead, go instead where there is no path and leave a trail.

Ralph Waldo Emerson

10: Counting and Perception

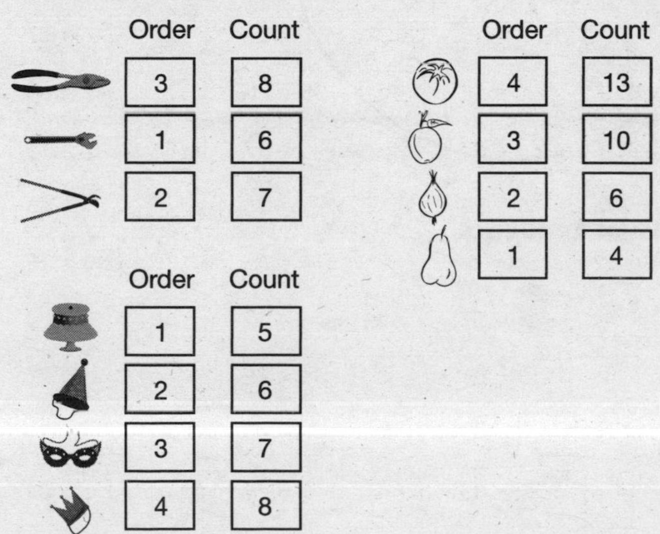

	Order	Count
	3	8
	1	6
	2	7

	Order	Count
	4	13
	3	10
	2	6
	1	4

	Order	Count
	1	5
	2	6
	3	7
	4	8

11: Shape Dividing

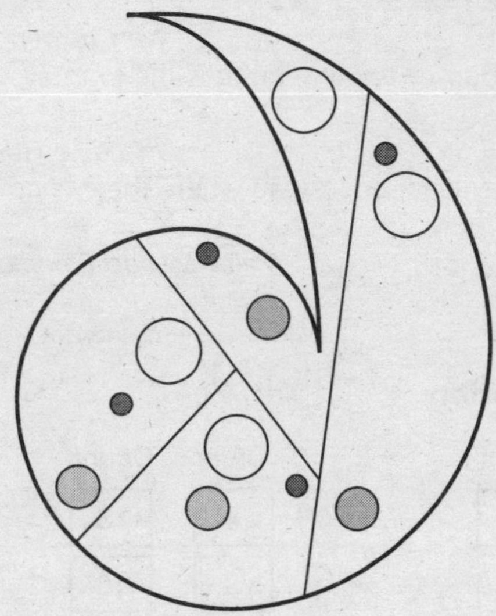

13: Visual Sequence

b, c

DAY
27

Creative Thinking

See if you can solve each of the following conundrums. If you get stuck then try thinking laterally – they all have logical solutions, but the logic might not be what you expect!

In what way can 'No timer day' mistakenly become 'On vines fax'?

What is the easiest way to get down from a horse?

TIME TAKEN:	INCORRECT ANSWERS:
TIME POINTS:	**TOTAL SCORE:**

Visual Memory

Spend 1 minute studying this path. Then cover the top half of this page and try to redraw it accurately on the empty grid below.

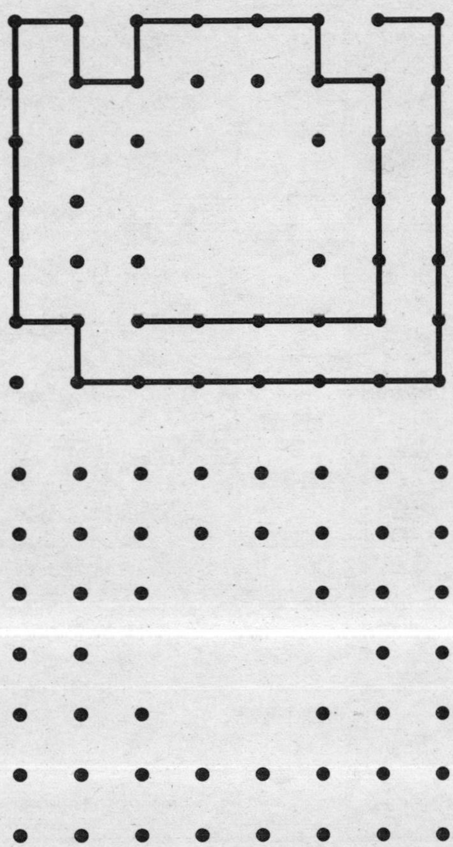

INCORRECT ANSWERS:	**TOTAL SCORE:**

Time Elapsed

Work out how many hours and minutes have passed between each of these pairs of times.

3:25am to 4:55am =	:	3:55am to 5:30pm =	:
5:40am to 8:40pm =	:	8:20am to 10:05pm =	:
7:25pm to 7:55pm =	:	3:35am to 11:35pm =	:
12:35pm to 7:10pm =	:	2:55am to 12:15pm =	:
9:35am to 9:45pm =	:	2:50am to 4:40pm =	:
3:20am to 9:55pm =	:	11:25am to 7:20pm =	:
9:00pm to 11:30pm =	:	2:00am to 9:15am =	:
2:45am to 11:30am =	:	9:30am to 2:55pm =	:
12:05am to 5:20am =	:	3:35pm to 11:35pm =	:
10:00pm to 11:25pm =	:	9:50am to 2:40pm =	:
12:20am to 12:15pm =	:	8:45am to 9:35pm =	:
2:10pm to 2:30pm =	:	8:15pm to 9:50pm =	:
1:15am to 7:00am =	:	8:20am to 11:15pm =	:
7:45am to 2:25pm =	:	4:10am to 11:10am =	:
9:40am to 5:40pm =	:	7:00am to 11:20am =	:

TIME TAKEN:	INCORRECT ANSWERS:
TIME POINTS:	**TOTAL SCORE:**

Logical Puzzlers

Try to solve these problems – each requires only simple logic to solve, but you might find that making notes with a pencil will help!

I had two rabbits as pets, but they bred quickly and produced six baby rabbits almost right away. Each of those six babies then had six more rabbits. How many rabbits do I now have?

My stamp collection has 124 stamps in it. However I have discovered that 16 of them are part of a pair of duplicates. How many distinct stamps do I have in my collection?

If I lose one third of my money, but then find half of what I had lost, how much money will I have of the £6 I started out with?

TIME TAKEN:	INCORRECT ANSWERS:
TIME POINTS:	**TOTAL SCORE:**

Observation and Counting

Look at these squares and triangles and see how long it takes you to answer the observation questions below.

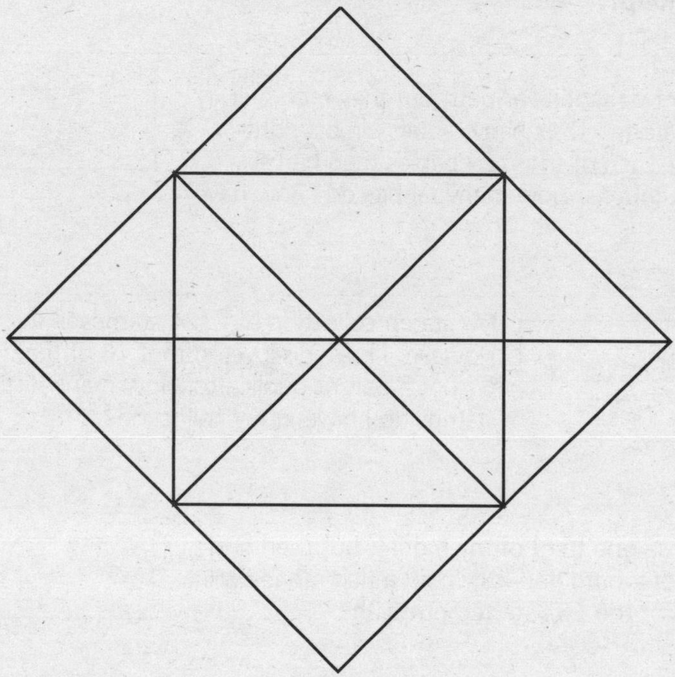

How many squares can you count? ______

How many triangles can you count? ______

TIME TAKEN:	INCORRECT ANSWERS:
TIME POINTS:	**TOTAL SCORE:**

Missing Words

Study each of these 3 lists of words for 2 minutes. Then cover the top half of the page and see if you can identify which word is missing from each list below.

Genial	Affable	Convivial	Friendly
Warm	Hospitable	Kind	Congenial

Red	Read	Ready	Reading
Reader	Redder	Reddish	Reddy

Chest	Bookcase	Cupboard	Table
Dresser	Drawer	Wardrobe	Bureau

Now try to spot the missing word from each list:

Congenial, Affable, Genial, Friendly, Kind, Warm, Convivial

MISSING:

Read, Red, Reddish, Ready, Reddy, Reader, Redder

MISSING:

Drawer, Chest, Bookcase, Dresser, Bureau, Table, Cupboard

MISSING:

INCORRECT ANSWERS:	TOTAL SCORE:

Balancing

Looking at these two weighing scales, can you say which of these three objects is the heavier?

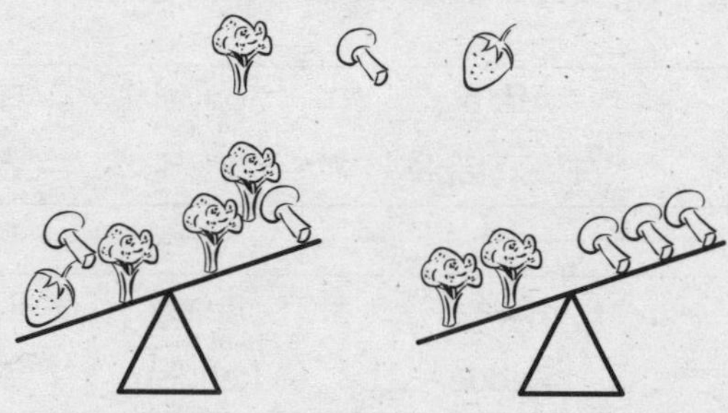

And which of these three objects is the heaviest?

TIME TAKEN:	INCORRECT ANSWERS:
TIME POINTS:	**TOTAL SCORE:**

Reflective Power

Look at the three figures on the left-hand side. If each of these was reflected in the diagonal "mirror" adjacent to it, which of the figures on the right would be the result?

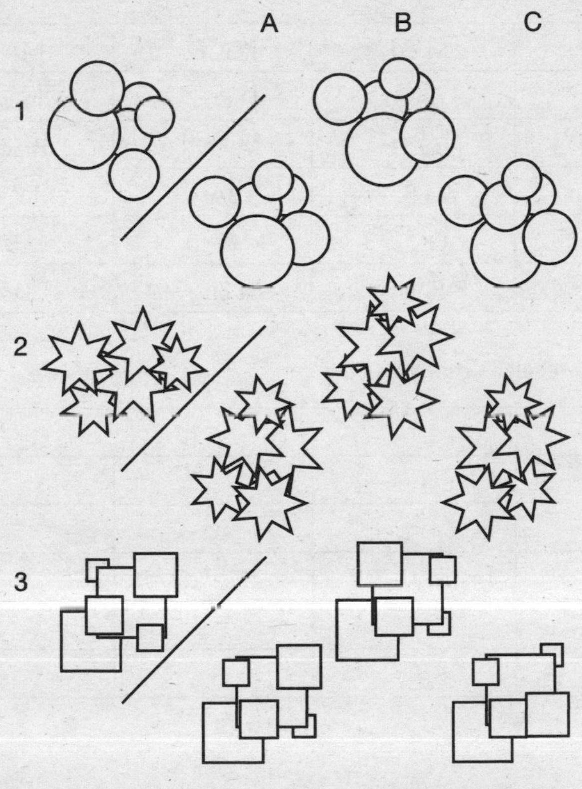

TIME TAKEN:	INCORRECT ANSWERS:
TIME POINTS:	**TOTAL SCORE:**

Word List

Try to memorize these 24 educational degree types.

After 2 minutes, cover the table and write as many as you can in the boxes below. You do not need to remember the correct order.

Ph.D	M.Ed	PGCE	MA
B.Eng	OND	D.Phil	Dip.Ed
HND	B.Litt	M.Phil	B.Sc
M.Mus	M.Sc	BA	M.Ch
M.Litt	ONC	M.Tech	LLB
HNC	B.Pharm	M.Eng	DDS

Now try to recall as many as you can:

INCORRECT ANSWERS:	**TOTAL SCORE:**

Matchstick Thinking

The picture below shows 3 matchsticks.

How can you rearrange these 3 matchsticks in order to make 6? You may not break any matchsticks into pieces!

TIME TAKEN:	INCORRECT ANSWERS:
TIME POINTS:	**TOTAL SCORE:**

Speed Arithmetic

Complete the following set of arithmetic equations as quickly as possible. You should be able to do them all in your head without using a calculator or making notes.

9 × 9 =	61 + 12 =	87 + 20 =
11 × 7 =	12 × 11 =	2 × 2 =
64 + 10 =	9 + 16 =	8 + 82 =
48 + 16 =	101 − 8 =	99 − 18 =
11 + 90 =	6 × 10 =	59 − 19 =
89 − 19 =	86 − 3 =	11 × 10 =
9 × 10 =	7 + 26 =	6 + 31 =
75 − 2 =	86 + 19 =	16 + 22 =
14 + 12 =	4 × 10 =	23 − 8 =
12 − 1 =	8 × 6 =	107 − 6 =
67 − 15 =	9 × 8 =	19 + 55 =
66 + 8 =	2 × 7 =	93 − 14 =
3 × 10 =	6 × 5 =	70 − 6 =

TIME TAKEN:	INCORRECT ANSWERS:
TIME POINTS:	**TOTAL SCORE:**

Visual Inference

Two symbols each with a following symbol are shown. Can you work out the rule being applied in order to deduce which of the last three symbols should replace each question mark?

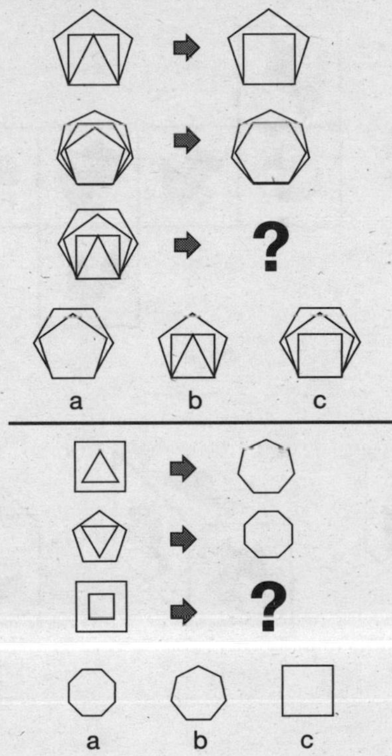

TIME TAKEN:	INCORRECT ANSWERS:
TIME POINTS:	**TOTAL SCORE:**

Shape Folding

If you were to cut out this shape and fold it into a cube, which of the three pictures below would be the result?

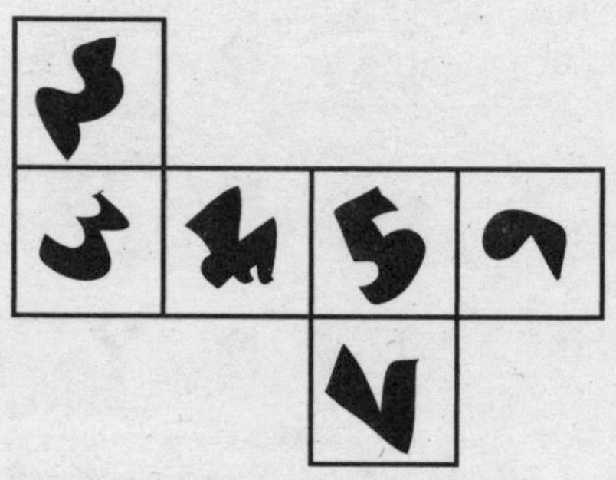

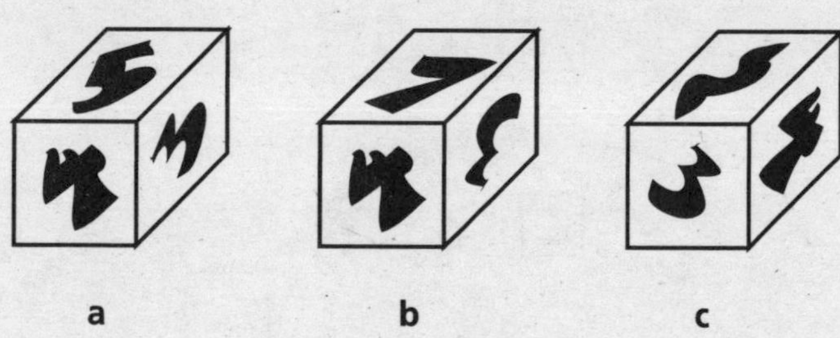

a **b** **c**

TIME TAKEN:	INCORRECT ANSWERS:
TIME POINTS:	**TOTAL SCORE:**

Solutions

1: Creative Thinking

If you type it on a phone using predictive text, the system can create these alternative words from the key-press sequence of 66 84637 329.

You get down for making quilts, etc from a duck or goose or other feathered animal, not a horse.

3: Time Elapsed

3:25am to 4:55am =	**1:30**	3:55am to 5:30pm =	**13:35**
5:40am to 8:40pm =	**15:00**	8:20am to 10:05pm =	**13:45**
7:25pm to 7:55pm =	**0:30**	3:35am to 11:35pm =	**20:00**
12:35pm to 7:10pm =	**6:35**	2:55am to 12:15pm =	**9:20**
9:35am to 9:45pm =	**12:10**	2:50am to 4:40pm =	**13:50**
3:20am to 9:55pm =	**18:35**	11:25am to 7:20pm =	**7:55**
9:00pm to 11:30pm =	**2:30**	2:00am to 9:15am =	**7:15**
2:45am to 11:30am =	**8:45**	9:30am to 2:55pm =	**5:25**
12:05am to 5:20am =	**5:15**	3:35pm to 11:35pm =	**8:00**
10:00pm to 11:25pm =	**1:25**	9:50am to 2:40pm =	**4:50**
12:20am to 12:15pm =	**11:55**	8:45am to 9:35pm =	**12:50**
2:10pm to 2:30pm =	**0:20**	8:15pm to 9:50pm =	**1:35**
1:15am to 7:00am =	**5:45**	8:20am to 11:15pm =	**14:55**
7:45am to 2:25pm =	**6:40**	4:10am to 11:10am =	**7:00**
9:40am to 5:40pm =	**8:00**	7:00am to 11:20am =	**4:20**

4: Logical Puzzlers
44 rabbits. 2 + 6 + (6x6) = 44.

116 stamps.

£5.

5:Observation and Counting
6 squares in total.

26 triangles.

7: Balancing

The heaviest items are:

8: Reflective Power
1C, 2C, 3C

9: Matchstick Thinking

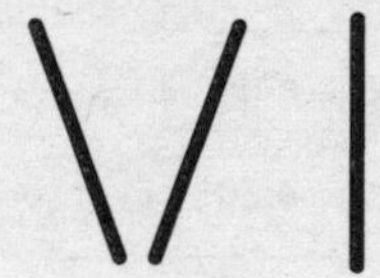

11: Speed Arithmetic

9 × 9 = **81**	61 + 12 = **73**	87 + 20 = **107**
11 × 7 = **77**	12 × 11 = **132**	2 × 2 = **4**
64 + 10 = **74**	9 + 16 = **25**	8 + 82 = **90**
48 + 16 = **64**	101 − 8 = **93**	99 − 18 = **81**
11 + 90 = **101**	6 × 10 = **60**	59 − 19 = **40**
89 − 19 = **70**	86 − 3 = **83**	11 × 10 = **110**
9 × 10 = **90**	7 + 26 = **33**	6 + 31 = **37**
75 − 2 = **73**	86 + 19 = **105**	16 + 22 = **38**
14 + 12 = **26**	4 × 10 = **40**	23 − 8 = **15**
12 − 1 = **11**	8 × 6 = **48**	107 − 6 = **101**
67 − 15 = **52**	9 × 8 = **72**	19 + 55 = **74**
66 + 8 = **74**	2 × 7 = **14**	93 − 14 = **79**
3 × 10 = **30**	6 × 5 = **30**	70 − 6 = **64**

12: Visual Inference

c

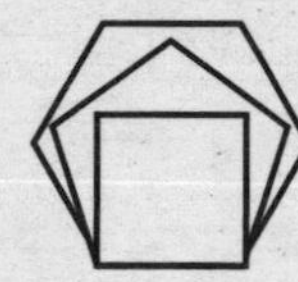

a

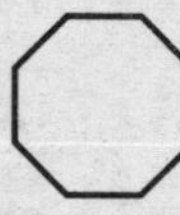

13: Shape Folding

b

DAY
28

Missing Words

Study each of these 3 lists of words for a total of 2 minutes. Then cover the top half of the page and see if you can identify which word is missing from each list below.

A	Rearranged	Correctly	This
Could	If	Sentence	Be

All	Any	Aware	After
Appoint	Aside	Ark	Ante

Sign	Approve	Complete	Contract
Enscribe	Sanction	Seal	Confirm

Now try to spot the missing word from each list:

Correctly, Could, Rearranged, Be, This, Sentence, A

MISSING:

All, Any, Appoint, Aware, Ark, Ante, After

MISSING:

Seal, Enscribe, Approve, Complete, Contract, Sanction, Confirm

MISSING:

INCORRECT ANSWERS:	TOTAL SCORE:

Speed Arithmetic

Complete the following set of arithmetic equations as quickly as possible. You should be able to do them all in your head without using a calculator or making notes.

56 − 6 =	42 − 15 =	16 + 51 =
87 − 9 =	76 − 15 =	10 × 8 =
5 × 4 =	9 + 79 =	12 + 73 =
6 × 10 =	33 − 4 =	18 − 1 =
15 + 29 =	79 − 6 =	15 − 7 =
2 × 4 =	8 − 5 =	54 − 6 =
10 × 4 =	95 + 13 =	18 + 99 =
9 × 12 =	95 + 8 =	14 + 83 =
17 + 14 =	99 − 13 =	80 + 7 =
64 − 17 =	79 − 12 =	43 + 12 =
108 − 5 =	5 + 16 =	17 + 7 =
99 − 10 =	3 + 5 =	82 − 11 =
9 + 31 =	48 + 14 =	19 − 14 =

TIME TAKEN:	INCORRECT ANSWERS:
TIME POINTS:	**TOTAL SCORE:**

Reflective Power

Look at the three figures on the left-hand side. If each of these was reflected in the diagonal "mirror" adjacent to it, which of the figures on the right would be the result?

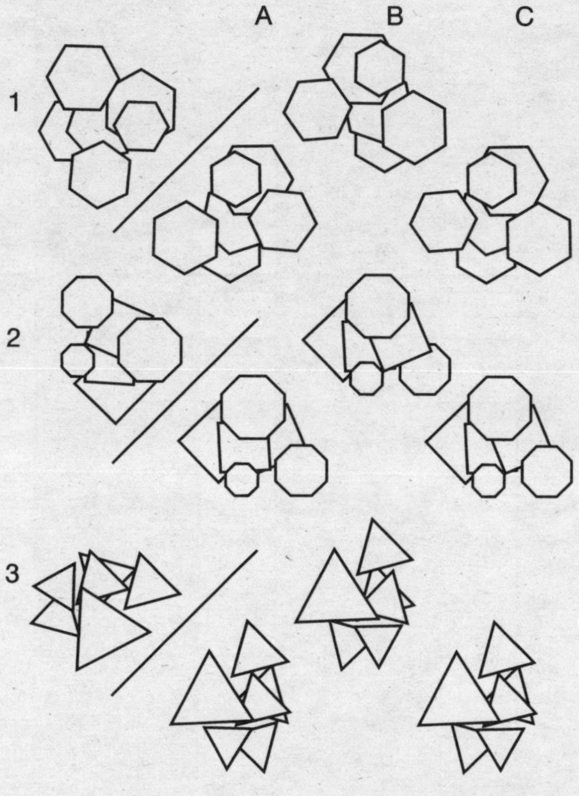

A B C

1

2

3

TIME TAKEN:	INCORRECT ANSWERS:
TIME POINTS:	**TOTAL SCORE:**

Odd One Out

Look at each of these sets of words. Can you work out which word is the odd one out in each case?

Silverside
Tenderloin
Topside
Rump
Bottomtail

Anubis
Hermes
Eros
Nike
Poseidon

Waterfront
Quay
Dock
Wharf
Jetty

Othello
Hamlet
Coriolanus
Macbeth
Cymbeline

TIME TAKEN:	INCORRECT ANSWERS:
TIME POINTS:	**TOTAL SCORE:**

Creative Thinking

See if you can solve each of the following conundrums. If you get stuck then try thinking laterally – they all have logical solutions, but the logic might not be what you expect!

Before sunrise I got up 120 times, and yet I managed to sleep over 7 hours between each time I got up. How can this be true?

There is something which is so fragile that simply speaking its name breaks it. What is that something?

TIME TAKEN:	INCORRECT ANSWERS:
TIME POINTS:	**TOTAL SCORE:**

Observation and Counting

Look at these different shapes and see how long it takes you to answer the observation questions below.

How many of each of the following can you count?

Stars [ ] Squares [ ]

Hexagons (six-sided shapes) [ ]

Triangles [ ] Arcs/curves [ ]

How many separate areas are formed by these shapes?

[ ]

TIME TAKEN:	INCORRECT ANSWERS:
TIME POINTS:	**TOTAL SCORE:**

Anagrammatic

Look at each of these sets of 12 words. How many pairs of anagrams can you spot in each set, and what are they?

DEVALUE	TALENTS	CLOSING
WARFARE	RECEIPT	GUTTING
LATENTS	MINORED	PATRIOT
JELLIES	GOVERNS	OUTPOST

SIGNATORY	CREDITORS	REDEVELOP
GYRATIONS	PRECISEST	REPRISING
DEVELOPER	EARTHIEST	DIRECTORS
HEARTIEST	SPRINGIER	TRICEPSES

SEVERS	PAGING	THESES
INDENT	VERSES	GAPING
RUSTIC	SHEETS	NOTING
TONING	CITRUS	TINNED

DRENCHING	STATEMENT	UNRESTING
BOUNCIEST	INSURGENT	TESTAMENT
MALTREATS	MOODINESS	BOHEMIANS
EQUIPPING	SPEECHING	SAINTLIER

TIME TAKEN:	INCORRECT ANSWERS:
TIME POINTS:	**TOTAL SCORE:**

Visual Memory

Spend 1 minute studying this path. Then cover the top half of this page and try to redraw it accurately on the empty grid below.

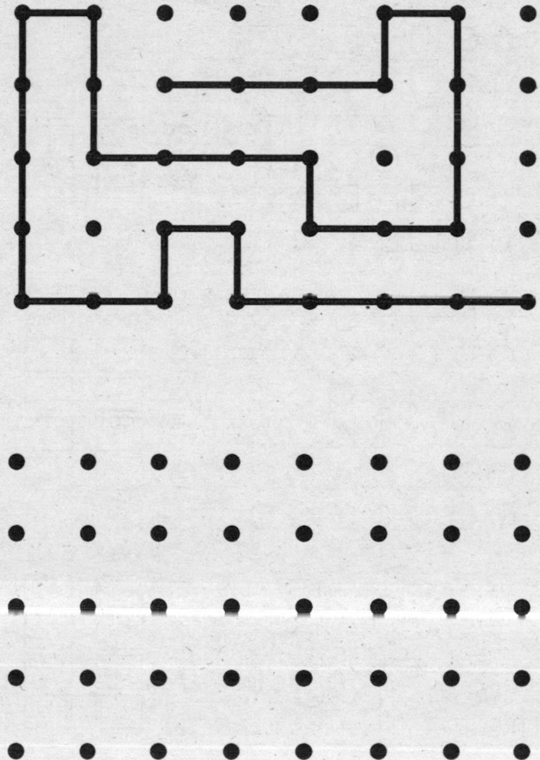

INCORRECT ANSWERS:	TOTAL SCORE:

Counting and Perception

Spend no more than 10 seconds looking at each group of symbols in each turn, then try to sort them into order of increasing frequency. Write "1" in the "Order" column for the shape that occurs least often, and so on.

	Order	Count
□		
○		
☆		

	Order	Count
◇		
△		
Hexagon		
Heptagon		

	Order	Count
Large circle		
Small circle		
Vertical oval		
Horizontal oval		

Now take as long as you think you need to write in the second column the precise count of each symbol.

TIME TAKEN:	INCORRECT ANSWERS:
TIME POINTS:	**TOTAL SCORE:**

Time Elapsed

Work out how many hours and minutes have passed between each of these pairs of times.

12:35am to 4:35pm =	:	8:10am to 8:20am =	:
7:05am to 8:10am =	:	3:00am to 2:00pm =	:
11:10am to 7:00pm =	:	9:55am to 1:35pm =	:
1:00am to 1:30am =	:	3:25pm to 7:15pm =	:
5:30am to 6:35pm =	:	10:25pm to 10:30pm =	:
1:35am to 4:45am =	:	6:30am to 1:55pm =	:
12:15am to 6:50am =	:	12:40pm to 1:20pm =	:
4:25pm to 8:05pm =	:	10:30am to 12:10pm =	:
5:25am to 11:45pm =	:	4:25am to 2:30pm =	:
1:15am to 7:10pm =	:	3:00am to 8:45pm =	:
3:45am to 3:25pm =	:	2:15am to 9:15am =	:
4:10pm to 9:45pm =	:	2:40am to 11:00pm =	:
1:55am to 10:15pm =	:	8:45am to 3:40pm =	:
1:55am to 11:45pm =	:	2:55am to 9:10am =	:
10:25am to 12:45pm =	:	4:30am to 2:15pm =	:

TIME TAKEN:	INCORRECT ANSWERS:
TIME POINTS:	**TOTAL SCORE:**

Logical Puzzlers

Try to solve these problems – each requires only simple logic to solve, but you might find that making notes with a pencil will help!

Bob is pleased with the fact that he is two inches taller than Dave, but Simon isn't so pleased that he's four inches shorter than Dave. If Bob is five foot ten inches, then how tall is Simon?

A windmill power-generator turns 10 times every minute, but twice as fast when it's windy. If it's windy for an hour then how many revolutions will the windmill make?

If every hundredth person in the world owned a brain workout book, and there are 6.6 billion inhabitants of the Earth, write out in figures how many brain workout books that would be.

TIME TAKEN:	INCORRECT ANSWERS:
TIME POINTS:	**TOTAL SCORE:**

Shape Dividing

Draw three straight lines in order to divide the shape into four separate areas. Each area must contain precisely one of each size of circle. The three lines may touch but they must not cross.

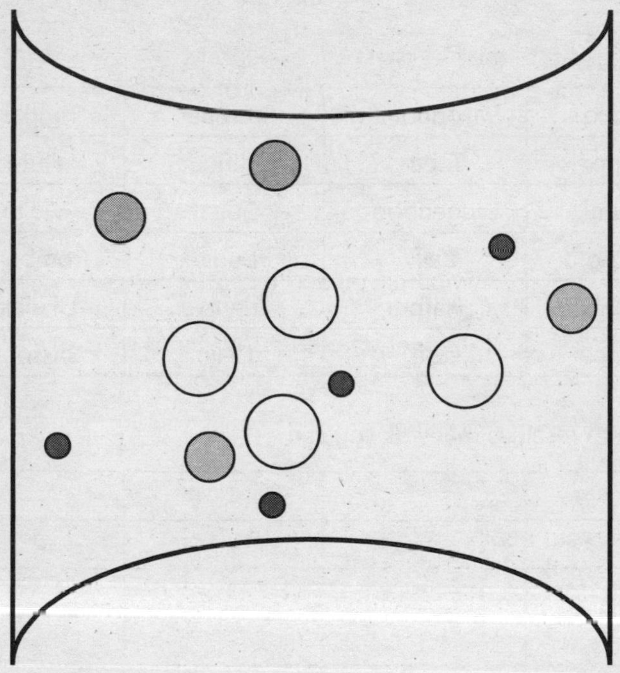

TIME TAKEN:	INCORRECT ANSWERS:
TIME POINTS:	**TOTAL SCORE:**

Word List

Try to memorize these 24 musical instruments.

After 2 minutes, cover the table and write as many as you can in the boxes below. You do not need to remember the correct order.

Piccolo	Saxophone	Trumpet	Timpani
Piano	Tuba	Clarinet	Flute
Drum	Didgeridoo	Guitar	Violin
Clavichord	Bell	Bugle	Trombone
Euphonium	Harp	Triangle	Ukulele
Ocarina	Lute	Cello	Bassoon

Now try to recall as many as you can:

INCORRECT ANSWERS:	**TOTAL SCORE:**

Solutions

2: Speed Arithmetic

56 − 6 = **50**	42 − 15 = **27**	16 + 51 = **67**
87 − 9 = **78**	76 − 15 = **61**	10 × 8 = **80**
5 × 4 = **20**	9 + 79 = **88**	12 + 73 = **85**
6 × 10 = **60**	33 − 4 = **29**	18 − 1 = **17**
15 + 29 = **44**	79 − 6 = **73**	15 − 7 = **8**
2 × 4 = **8**	8 − 5 = **3**	54 − 6 = **48**
10 × 4 = **40**	95 + 13 = **108**	18 + 99 = **117**
9 × 12 = **108**	95 + 8 = **103**	14 + 83 = **97**
17 + 14 = **31**	99 − 13 = **86**	80 + 7 = **87**
64 − 17 = **47**	79 − 12 = **67**	43 + 12 = **55**
108 − 5 = **103**	5 + 16 = **21**	17 + 7 = **24**
99 − 10 = **89**	3 + 5 = **8**	82 − 11 = **71**
9 + 31 = **40**	48 + 14 = **62**	19 − 14 = **5**

3: Reflective Power

1A, 2B, 3C

4: Odd One Out

Bottomtail – not a cut of beef
Anubis – the only Egyptian god; the rest are Greek gods
Waterfront – the rest you can fasten a boat to
Cymbeline – the rest are Shakespearean tragedies;
Cymbeline is a comedy

5: Creative Thinking

I must be living at the Arctic or Antarctic, where during winter there is no daylight!

Silence.

6: Observation and Counting

There are the following counts:
Stars **1** Squares **1**
Hexagons (six-sided shapes) **3** Triangles **3** Arcs/curves **5**

14 separate areas are formed by these shapes.

7: Anagrammatic

Set 1: 1 pair of anagrams:
RESINS and SIRENS

Set 2: 3 pairs of anagrams:
ENLISTED and LISTENED
LESSENED and NEEDLESS
PROTEINS and POINTERS

Set 3: 4 pairs of anagrams:
AWNING and WANING
CARESS and SCARES
GUILED and UGLIED
EARNER and NEARER

Set 4: 4 pairs of anagrams:
REISSUED and RESIDUES
ENLISTED and LISTENED
CLEANERS and CLEANSER
WREATHES and WEATHERS

9: Counting and Perception

	Order	Count
□	2	12
○	1	10
☆	3	20

	Order	Count
◇	3	15
△	2	6
⬡	1	5
heptagon	4	16

	Order	Count
◯	3	10
∘	4	13
0	1	7
⬭	2	8

10: Time Elapsed

12:35am to 4:35pm =	**16:00**	8:10am to 8:20am =	**0:10**
7:05am to 8:10am =	**1:05**	3:00am to 2:00pm =	**11:00**
11:10am to 7:00pm =	**7:50**	9:55am to 1:35pm =	**3:40**
1:00am to 1:30am =	**0:30**	3:25pm to 7:15pm =	**3:50**
5:30am to 6:35pm =	**13:05**	10:25pm to 10:30pm =	**0:05**
1:35am to 4:45am =	**3:10**	6:30am to 1:55pm =	**7:25**
12:15am to 6:50am =	**6:35**	12:40pm to 1:20pm =	**0:40**
4:25pm to 8:05pm =	**3:40**	10:30am to 12:10pm =	**1:40**
5:25am to 11:45pm =	**18:20**	4:25am to 2:30pm =	**10:05**
1:15am to 7:10pm =	**17:55**	3:00am to 8:45pm =	**17:45**
3:45am to 3:25pm =	**11:40**	2:15am to 9:15am =	**7:00**
4:10pm to 9:45pm =	**5:35**	2:40am to 11:00pm =	**20:20**
1:55am to 10:15pm =	**20:20**	8:45am to 3:40pm =	**6:55**
1:55am to 11:45pm =	**21:50**	2:55am to 9:10am =	**6:15**
10:25am to 12:45pm =	**2:20**	4:30am to 2:15pm =	**9:45**

11. Logical Puzzlers

Simon is 5 foot 4 inches tall.

1,200 times.

66,000,000 (66 million).

12: Shape Dividing

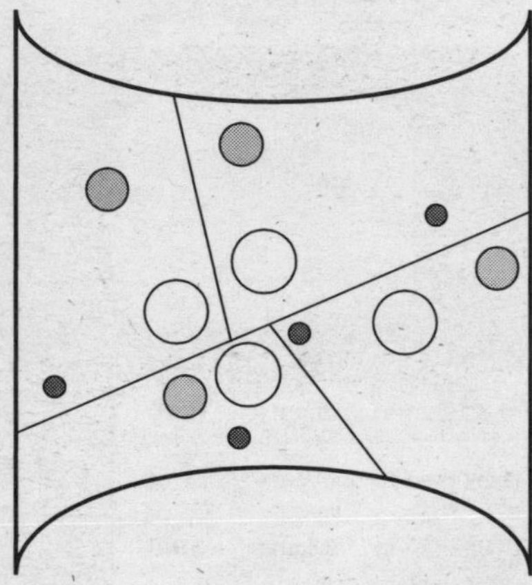

DAY
29

Number Sequences

Look at each of these number sequences and see if you can deduce which number comes next in the series.

175	106	69	37	32	
520	314	206	108	98	
640	642	657	685	726	
948	906	871	843	822	
2627	2227	1827	1427	1027	
477	290	187	103	84	
694	697	700	703	706	
951	966	981	996	1011	

TIME TAKEN:	INCORRECT ANSWERS:
TIME POINTS:	**TOTAL SCORE:**

Observation and Counting

Look at these different circles and spirals and see how long it takes you to answer the observation questions below.

How many circles can you count?

And how many spirals can you count?

If you were to colour in each area so that no two areas of the same colour touched on any side, how many colours would you need?

TIME TAKEN:	INCORRECT ANSWERS:
TIME POINTS:	**TOTAL SCORE:**

Cryptogram

Decode each of these quotations by replacing A with N, B with O, C with P, and so on, through to replacing Y with L and Z with M.

Rfcpc gq lmrfgle upmle ugrf Ykcpgay rfyr ayllmr zc aspcb ugrf ufyr gq pgefr gl Ykcpgay.

Zgjj Ajglrml

Uc fytc mlc amslrpw, mlc amlqrgrsrgml ylb mlc dsrspc.

Ecmpec U Zsqf

Nmjgrgaq gq lmr y zyb npmdcqqgml. Gd wms qsaaccb, rfcpc ypc kylw pcuypbq; gd wms bgqepyac wmspqcjd, wms ayl yjuywq upgrc y zmmi.

Pmlyjb Pcyeyl osmrc

Mpbcp ugrfmsr jgzcprw ylb jgzcprw ugrfmsr mpbcp ypc cosyjjw bcqrpsargtc.

Rfcmbmpc Pmmqctcjr

TIME TAKEN:	INCORRECT ANSWERS:
TIME POINTS:	**TOTAL SCORE:**

Speed Arithmetic

Complete the following set of arithmetic equations as quickly as possible. You should be able to do them all in your head without using a calculator or making notes.

11 × 8 =	44 + 4 =	85 − 17 =
70 − 14 =	16 + 61 =	32 − 5 =
90 − 14 =	99 + 6 =	83 − 13 =
21 + 19 =	22 + 1 =	5 × 11 =
84 − 6 =	7 + 66 =	59 + 5 =
2 + 51 =	4 × 9 =	10 + 2 =
9 × 4 =	4 × 10 =	11 − 3 =
24 − 7 =	3 × 8 =	19 + 7 =
27 − 7 =	3 × 4 =	68 + 11 =
24 − 5 =	12 × 3 =	35 − 13 =
47 − 17 =	37 − 19 =	6 + 16 =
50 + 5 =	91 − 15 =	72 + 2 =
101 − 12 =	71 − 2 =	14 + 71 =

TIME TAKEN:	INCORRECT ANSWERS:
TIME POINTS:	**TOTAL SCORE:**

Word List

Try to memorize these 24 elements.

After 2 minutes, cover the table and write as many as you can in the boxes below. You do not need to remember the correct order.

Tungsten	Barium	Gallium	Arsenic
Phosphorous	Carbon	Helium	Iridium
Mercury	Gold	Chromium	Hydrogen
Iodine	Xenon	Chlorine	Gallium
Zinc	Iron	Manganese	Lead
Plutonium	Neptunium	Radon	Silver

Now try to recall as many as you can:

INCORRECT ANSWERS:	**TOTAL SCORE:**

Matchstick Thinking

The picture below shows 10 matchsticks arranged into the *invalid* Roman numeral equation 11 – 1 = 6.

Can you move 2 matchsticks only in order to make a *valid* Roman numeral equation? You may not overlap any matches that are not already overlapping.

XI – I = VI

TIME TAKEN:	INCORRECT ANSWERS:
TIME POINTS:	**TOTAL SCORE:**

Logical Puzzlers

Try to solve these problems – each requires only simple logic to solve, but you might find that making notes with a pencil will help!

A train enters a 5km tunnel travelling at 60km/hour. For what period of time is any part of the train in the tunnel, given that the train is 1km long?

If 50% of inspiration is perspiration, but inspiration is 80% luck, what percentage of luck is perspiration?

On a traditional circular clock-face, how many times does the minute hand overlap the hour hand in the 12 hours from 12 o'clock to 12 o'clock?

TIME TAKEN:	INCORRECT ANSWERS:
TIME POINTS:	**TOTAL SCORE:**

Counting and Perception

Spend no more than 10 seconds looking at each group of symbols in each turn, then try to sort them into order of increasing frequency. Write "1" in the "Order" column for the shape that occurs least often, and so on.

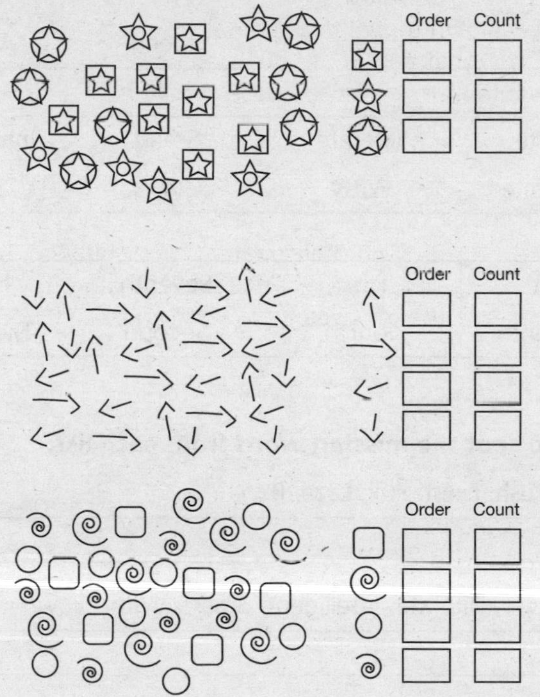

Now take as long as you think you need to write in the second column the precise count of each symbol.

TIME TAKEN:	INCORRECT ANSWERS:
TIME POINTS:	**TOTAL SCORE:**

Missing Words

Study each of these 3 lists of words for a total of 2 minutes. Then cover the top half of the page and see if you can identify which word is missing from each list below.

Exert	Push	Try	Pull
Laze	Run	Speed	Walk

Erudite	Illiterate	Smart	Intelligent
Uneducated	Witty	Clever	Slow

First	Fifth	Seventh	Ninth
Thirteenth	Fourth	Second	Twentieth

Now try to spot the missing word from each list:

Try, Walk, Push, Exert, Pull, Laze, Run

MISSING:

Erudite, Clever, Illiterate, Intelligent, Smart, Witty, Slow

MISSING:

Second, Thirteenth, First, Twentieth, Seventh, Ninth, Fifth

MISSING:

INCORRECT ANSWERS:	**TOTAL SCORE:**

Missing Numbers

Insert the missing number into each of these arithmetic expressions in order to make the equations true. You should not need a calculator to do this!

95 − ☐ = **84**	☐ + 79 = **82**	☐ × 11 = **33**
☐ − 16 = **3**	3 × ☐ = **27**	12 × ☐ = **108**
66 − ☐ = **50**	13 − ☐ = **10**	84 − ☐ = **70**
☐ × 4 = **12**	80 − ☐ = **64**	4 × ☐ = **20**
☐ + 7 = **27**	☐ − 4 = **67**	☐ + 6 = **63**
☐ × 10 = **40**	☐ − 17 = **58**	32 − ☐ = **21**
3 × ☐ = **9**	☐ × 8 = **24**	3 + ☐ = **77**
12 + ☐ = **55**	10 + ☐ = **17**	☐ − 1 = **70**
☐ + 3 = **86**	84 − ☐ = **73**	☐ + 4 = **7**
47 − ☐ = **35**	81 − ☐ = **62**	☐ − 12 = **2**
☐ + 38 = **42**	☐ − 18 = **61**	☐ − 18 = **11**
☐ − 9 = **14**	15 + ☐ = **81**	43 − ☐ = **24**
9 × ☐ = **45**	☐ + 9 = **79**	☐ − 4 = **82**

TIME TAKEN:	INCORRECT ANSWERS:
TIME POINTS:	**TOTAL SCORE:**

Shape Dividing

Draw three straight lines in order to divide the shape into four separate areas. Each area must contain only one of each size of circle. The three lines may touch but they must not cross.

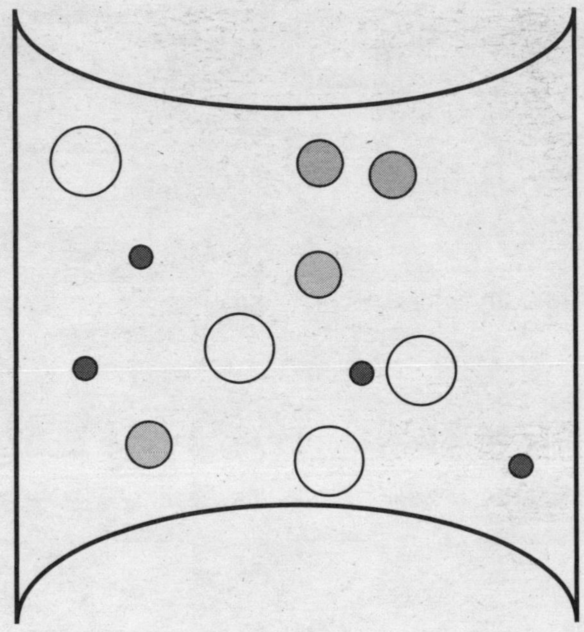

TIME TAKEN:	INCORRECT ANSWERS:
TIME POINTS:	**TOTAL SCORE:**

Rotation

If you were to rotate each of these three pictures as indicated by the arrow beneath, which of the figures below would be the result?

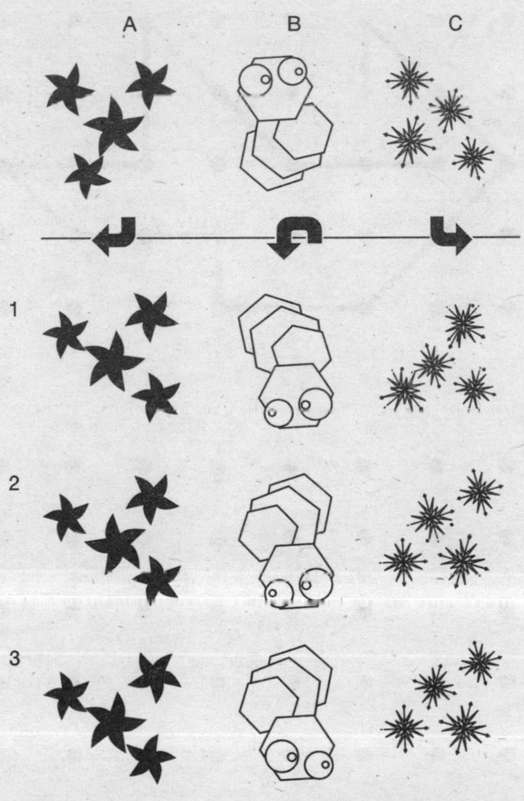

TIME TAKEN:	INCORRECT ANSWERS:
TIME POINTS:	**TOTAL SCORE:**

Visual Memory

Spend 1 minute studying this path. Then cover the top half of this page and try to redraw it accurately on the empty grid below.

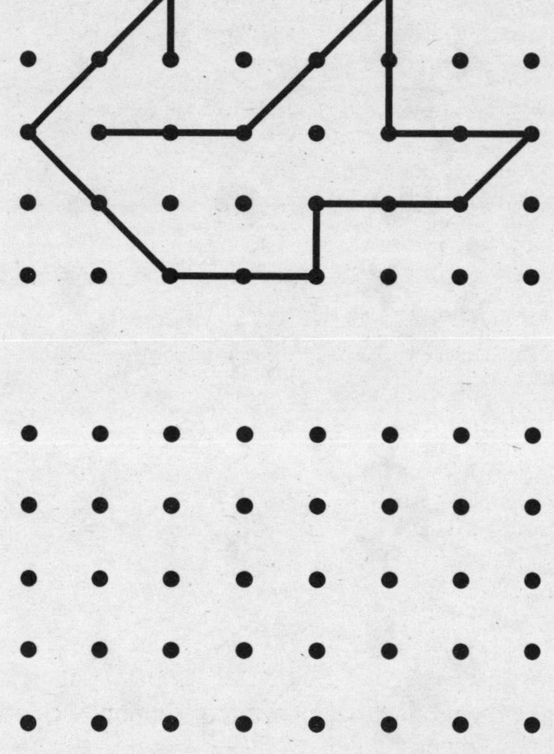

INCORRECT ANSWERS:	**TOTAL SCORE:**

Solutions

1: Number Sequences

10, 38, 48, 86, 134, **220**
Rule: add the previous two numbers

12, 60, 72, 132, 204, **336**
Rule: add the previous two numbers

314, 302, 290, 278, 266, **254**
Rule: subtract 12 from previous number

800, 805, 822, 851, 892, **945**
Rule: difference between numbers increases by 12 each time

5001, 4146, 3291, 2436, 1581, **726**
Rule: subtract 855 from previous number

11, 19, 30, 49, 79, **128**
Rule: add the previous two numbers

293, 303, 322, 350, 387, **433**
Rule: difference between numbers increases by 9 each time

886, 879, 872, 865, 858, **851**
Rule: subtract 7 from previous number

2: Observation and Counting

4 circles in total.

3 spirals in total.

3 colours are needed.

3: Cryptogram

There is nothing wrong with America that cannot be cured with what is right in America.

Bill Clinton

We have one country, one constitution and one future.

George W Bush

Politics is not a bad profession. If you succeed, there are many rewards; if you disgrace yourself, you can always write a book.

Ronald Reagan

Order without liberty and liberty without order are equally destructive.

Theodore Roosevelt

4: Speed Arithmetic

11 × 8 = **88**	44 + 4 = **48**	85 − 17 = **68**
70 − 14 = **56**	16 + 61 = **77**	32 − 5 = **27**
90 − 14 = **76**	99 + 6 = **105**	83 − 13 = **70**
21 + 19 = **40**	22 + 1 = **23**	5 × 11 = **55**
84 − 6 = **78**	7 + 66 = **73**	59 + 5 = **64**
2 + 51 = **53**	4 × 9 = **36**	10 + 2 = **12**
9 × 4 = **36**	4 × 10 = **40**	11 − 3 = **8**
24 − 7 = **17**	3 × 8 = **24**	19 + 7 = **26**
27 − 7 = **20**	3 × 4 = **12**	68 + 11 = **79**
24 − 5 = **19**	12 × 3 = **36**	35 − 13 = **22**
47 − 17 = **30**	37 − 19 = **18**	6 + 16 = **22**
50 + 5 = **55**	91 − 15 = **76**	72 + 2 = **74**
101 − 12 = **89**	71 − 2 = **69**	14 + 71 = **85**

6: Matchstick Thinking

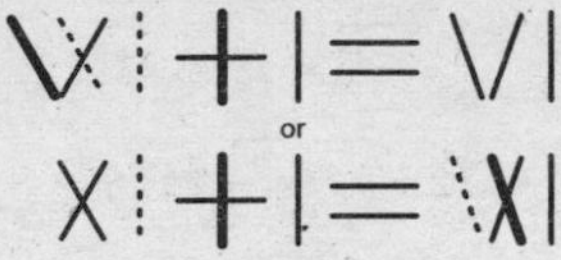

or

7: Logical Puzzlers

6 minutes, given that the tunnel length is 5km and the train is 1km, so the train must travel 6km from the point it enters the tunnel until the point it leaves it.

40% luck.

13 times.

8: Counting and Perception

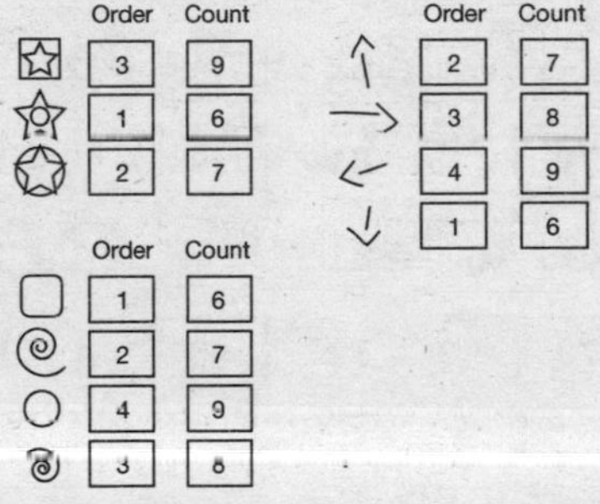

10: Missing Numbers

95 – 11 = **84**	3 + 79 = **82**	3 × 11 = **33**
19 – 16 = **3**	3 × 9 = **27**	12 × 9 = **108**
66 – 16 = **50**	13 – 3 = **10**	84 – 14 = **70**
3 × 4 = **12**	80 – 16 = **64**	4 × 5 = **20**
20 + 7 = **27**	71 – 4 = **67**	57 + 6 = **63**
4 × 10 = **40**	75 – 17 = **58**	32 – 11 = **21**
3 × 3 = **9**	3 × 8 = **24**	3 + 74 = **77**
12 + 43 = **55**	10 + 7 = **17**	71 – 1 = **70**
83 + 3 = **86**	84 – 11 = **73**	3 + 4 = **7**
47 – 12 = **35**	81 – 19 = **62**	14 – 12 = **2**
4 + 38 = **42**	79 – 18 = **61**	29 – 18 = **11**
23 – 9 = **14**	15 + 66 = **81**	43 – 19 = **24**
9 × 5 = **45**	70 + 9 = **79**	86 – 4 = **82**

11: Shape Dividing

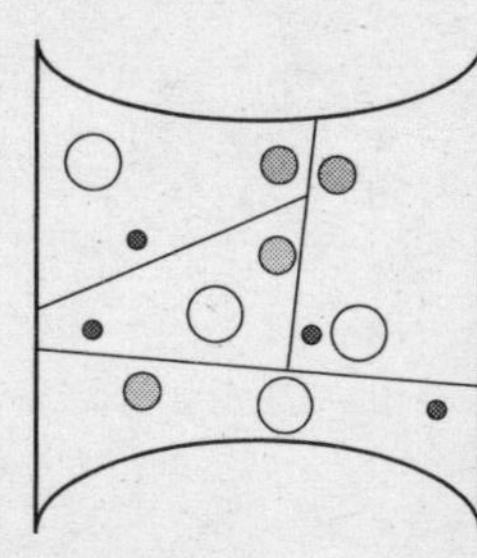

12: Rotation

A1, B2, C3

DAY
30

Odd One Out

Look at each of these sets of words. Can you work out which word is the odd one out in each case?

Rebecca
Victoria
Anne
Elizabeth
Mary

Rowing
Running
Football
Cycling
Swimming

Polo
Dressage
Steeplechase
Show-jumping
Aerobatics

Skiing
Skeleton
Bobsleigh
Toboggan
Luge

TIME TAKEN:	INCORRECT ANSWERS:
TIME POINTS:	**TOTAL SCORE:**

Shape Dividing

Draw three straight lines in order to divide the shape into four separate areas. Each area must contain only one of each size of circle. The three lines may touch but they must not cross.

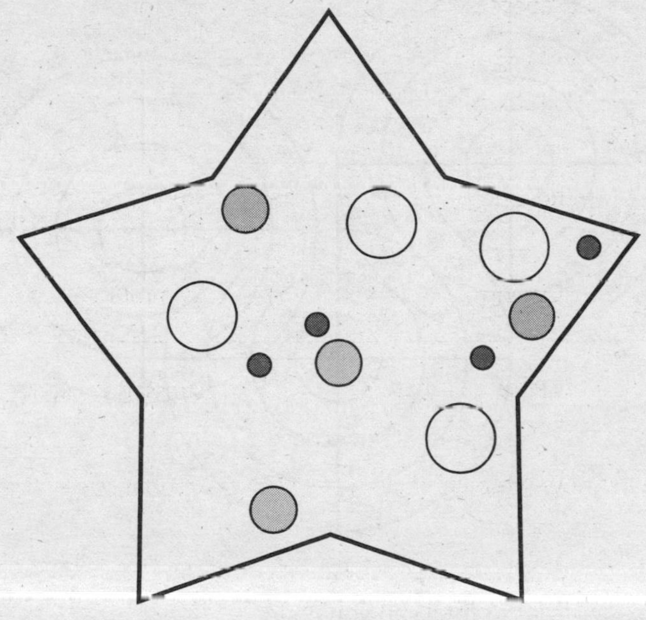

TIME TAKEN:	INCORRECT ANSWERS:
TIME POINTS:	**TOTAL SCORE:**

Observation and Counting

Look at these different target patterns and see how long it takes you to answer the observation questions below.

How many circles in total can you count?

How many quarter pie segments can you count, like this shape: ◿ ?

TIME TAKEN:	INCORRECT ANSWERS:
TIME POINTS:	**TOTAL SCORE:**

Visual Memory

Spend 1 minute studying this path. Then cover the top half of this page and try to redraw it accurately on the empty grid below.

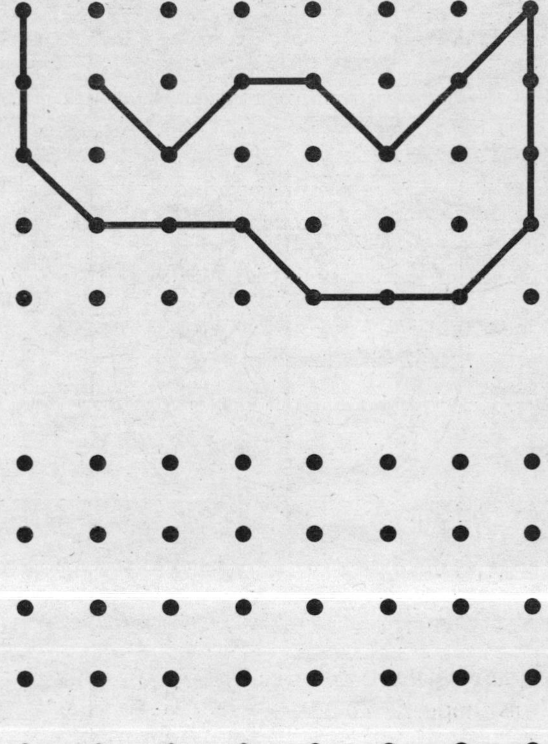

INCORRECT ANSWERS:	**TOTAL SCORE:**

Time Elapsed

Work out how many hours and minutes have passed between each of these pairs of times.

7:25am to 9:25pm =	:	6:10am to 7:05am =	:
3:35am to 1:00pm =	:	6:10pm to 9:25pm =	:
9:30am to 5:30pm =	:	2:20am to 8:00am =	:
3:50am to 11:15am =	:	4:15am to 1:45pm =	:
4:15am to 1:00pm =	:	4:35am to 5:00pm =	:
1:55pm to 2:25pm =	:	4:50pm to 9:10pm =	:
7:00pm to 8:00pm =	:	10:25am to 1:30pm =	:
7:10am to 8:55pm =	:	1:05am to 4:30am =	:
8:00am to 8:10am =	:	6:00pm to 10:15pm =	:
8:00am to 4:25pm =	:	1:10am to 10:10pm =	:
3:45pm to 3:50pm =	:	9:45pm to 9:55pm =	:
4:45am to 6:20pm =	:	12:00am to 4:15pm =	:
8:15am to 7:10pm =	:	8:25am to 11:25pm =	:
6:00am to 11:50am =	:	4:20am to 8:40pm =	:
11:35am to 11:15pm =	:	11:05am to 11:20pm =	:

TIME TAKEN:	INCORRECT ANSWERS:
TIME POINTS:	**TOTAL SCORE:**

Creative Thinking

See if you can solve each of the following conundrums. If you get stuck then try thinking laterally – they all have logical solutions, but the logic might not be what you expect!

Whilst wearing my trousers, how can I put my left hand in my right trouser pocket and my right hand in my left trouser pocket without crossing my arms?

The day before yesterday I was 18 years old. Next year I'm going to be 21 years old. How can this be?

TIME TAKEN:	INCORRECT ANSWERS:
TIME POINTS:	**TOTAL SCORE:**

Reflective Power

Look at the three figures on the left-hand side. If each of these was reflected in the diagonal "mirror" adjacent to it, which of the figures on the right would be the result?

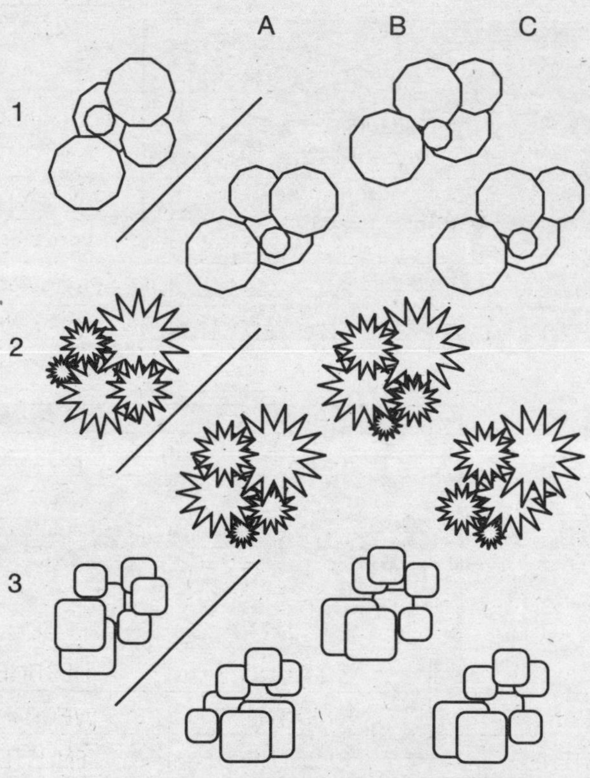

TIME TAKEN:	INCORRECT ANSWERS:
TIME POINTS:	**TOTAL SCORE:**

Anagrammatic

Look at each of these sets of 12 words. How many pairs of anagrams can you spot in each set, and what are they?

VACUUM	BULLED	PULSED
SIRENS	PETROL	FROSTS
KLUTZY	TRENDS	DEPLOY
JOCKED	SPONGE	RESINS

SAUNTERS	POINTERS	LISTENED
DECISION	NEEDLESS	LESSENED
JAYWALKS	INTERVAL	OUTWEIGH
PROTEINS	ENLISTED	POIGNANT

NEARER	EARNER	AWNING
EMBALM	WHEWED	DORSAL
WANING	SCARES	HAMLET
CARESS	GUILED	UGLIED

PRODUCED	RETAINER	RESIDUES
CLEANSER	STEALING	DESTINED
CLEANERS	WREATHES	WEATHERS
LISTENED	REISSUED	ENLISTED

TIME TAKEN:	INCORRECT ANSWERS:
TIME POINTS:	**TOTAL SCORE:**

Missing Signs

Insert the missing sign into each of these arithmetic expressions in order to make the equation true. You will need to add, subtract, multiply or divide.

81	☐	33	=	114	33	☐	99	=	132	88	☐	39	=	49
8	☐	4	=	2	36	☐	16	=	52	89	☐	32	=	57
93	☐	9	=	102	63	☐	3	=	60	7	☐	5	=	35
9	☐	10	=	90	5	☐	5	=	1	3	☐	6	=	18
25	☐	36	=	61	26	☐	12	=	38	10	☐	4	=	40
70	☐	37	=	33	16	☐	4	=	4	42	☐	6	=	7
6	☐	9	=	54	82	☐	32	=	114	12	☐	8	=	96
10	☐	5	=	2	30	☐	117	=	147	126	☐	6	=	132
11	☐	56	=	67	57	☐	25	=	82	60	☐	12	=	5
11	☐	11	=	121	10	☐	3	=	30	91	☐	2	=	89
7	☐	12	=	84	10	☐	9	=	90	3	☐	10	=	13
97	☐	1	=	96	27	☐	9	=	3	48	☐	12	=	4
6	☐	6	=	36	22	☐	63	=	85	115	☐	18	=	133

TIME TAKEN:	INCORRECT ANSWERS:
TIME POINTS:	**TOTAL SCORE:**

Word List

Try to memorize these 24 soft drinks.

After 2 minutes, cover the table and write as many as you can in the boxes below. You do not need to remember the correct order.

Orangeade	Soda Pop	Tonic	Water
Cream soda	Cherryade	Limeade	Lemonade
Milk	Coffee	Apple Juice	Orange juice
Ginger ale	Tea	Tomato Juice	Cola
Soda water	Lassi	Cocoa	Root beer
Sherbet	Smoothie	Slush puppy	Herbal tea

Now try to recall as many as you can:

INCORRECT ANSWERS:	TOTAL SCORE:

Rotation

If you were to rotate each of these three pictures as indicated by the arrow beneath, which of the figures below would be the result?

TIME TAKEN:	INCORRECT ANSWERS:
TIME POINTS:	**TOTAL SCORE:**

Logical Puzzlers

Try to solve these problems – each requires only simple logic to solve, but you might find that making notes with a pencil will help!

Five pigs, seven sheep and four cows are eating in a barn. If each sheep eats half of what each cow eats, but three times as much as a pig, how many kilograms of food is eaten. Assume that all the pigs together eat 10 kilograms a day.

If 75% of 800 recording artists are in the music industry for the love of music, but two thirds of these later change their mind, how many of all the recording artists are not doing it for the love of music?

My printer uses 55 sheets of paper a day, but I only print on 5% of each sheet. My ink cartridge lasts for 100 sheets of 100% ink. How many sheets of paper can I print at my usual rate before my ink cartridge runs out?

TIME TAKEN:	INCORRECT ANSWERS:
TIME POINTS:	**TOTAL SCORE:**

Missing Words

Study each of these 3 lists of words for 2 minutes. Then cover the top half of the page and see if you can identify which word is missing from each list below.

Zed	Ell	Em	Ay
Bee	Dee	Aitch	Zee

Pound	Dollar	Euro	Yen
Pence	Cents	Lira	Mark

Devour	Eat	Consume	Absorb
Engorge	Stuff	Fill	Overpower

Now try to spot the missing word from each list:

Ell, Aitch, Zee, Em, Bee, Zed, Dee

MISSING:

Euro, Pence, Lira, Mark, Pound, Dollar, Cents

MISSING:

Overpower, Absorb, Engorge, Devour, Fill, Stuff, Eat

MISSING:

INCORRECT ANSWERS:	TOTAL SCORE:

Solutions

1: Odd One Out

Future – the rest may all be only in the mind
Siamese – the rest are types of dog; this is a cat
Vaulting – the rest are combat sports
Plate – the rest are forms of cutlery

2: Shape Dividing

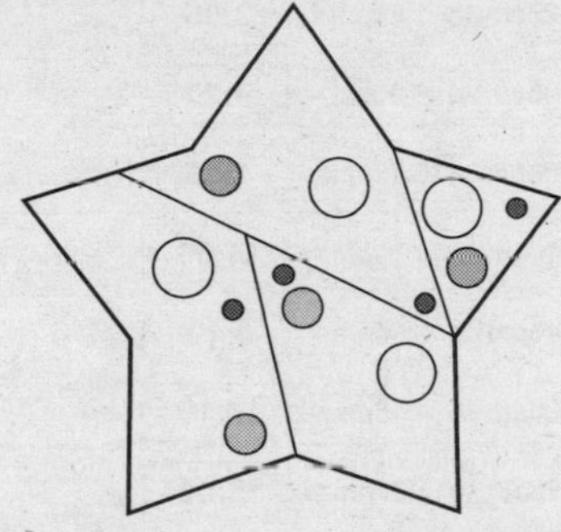

3: Observation and Counting

12 circles in total.

64 quarter pie segments.

5: Time Elapsed

7:25am to 9:25pm =	**14:00**	6:10am to 7:05am =	**0:55**
3:35am to 1:00pm =	**9:25**	6:10pm to 9:25pm =	**3:15**
9:30am to 5:30pm =	**8:00**	2:20am to 8:00am =	**5:40**
3:50am to 11:15am =	**7:25**	4:15am to 1:45pm =	**9:30**
4:15am to 1:00pm =	**8:45**	4:35am to 5:00pm =	**12:25**
1:55pm to 2:25pm =	**0:30**	4:50pm to 9:10pm =	**4:20**
7:00pm to 8:00pm =	**1:00**	10:25am to 1:30pm =	**3:05**
7:10am to 8:55pm =	**13:45**	1:05am to 4:30am =	**3:25**
8:00am to 8:10am =	**0:10**	6:00pm to 10:15pm =	**4:15**
8:00am to 4:25pm =	**8:25**	1:10am to 10:10pm =	**21:00**
3:45pm to 3:50pm =	**0:05**	9:45pm to 9:55pm =	**0:10**
4:45am to 6:20pm =	**13:35**	12:00am to 4:15pm =	**16:15**
8:15am to 7:10pm =	**10:55**	8:25am to 11:25pm =	**15:00**
6:00am to 11:50am =	**5:50**	4:20am to 8:40pm =	**16:20**
11:35am to 11:15pm =	**11:40**	11:05am to 11:20pm =	**12:15**

6: Creative Thinking

Just put the trousers on backwards, with your right leg in the left trouser leg and vice-versa!

Today is the 1st of January, and my birthday is on the 31st of December.

7: Reflective Power

1B, 2B, 3A

8: Anagrammatic

Set 1: 4 pairs of anagrams:
TRUEST and UTTERS
BORING and ROBING
STATED and TASTED
LADDER and LARDED

Set 2: 1 pair of anagrams:
LOGARITHM and ALGORITHM

Set 3: 4 pairs of anagrams:
MEDICATES and DECIMATES
SCALLOPED and COLLAPSED
FORESTING and FOSTERING
BACTERIAL and CALIBRATE

Set 4: 1 pair of anagrams:
LECTURES and CRUELEST

9: Missing Signs

81	+	33 = 114	33	+	99 = 132	88	–	39 = 49
8	÷	4 = 2	36	+	16 = 52	89	–	32 = 57
93	+	9 = 102	63	–	3 = 60	7	×	5 = 35
9	×	10 = 90	5	÷	5 = 1	3	×	6 = 18
25	+	36 = 61	26	+	12 = 38	10	×	4 = 40
70	–	37 = 33	16	÷	4 = 4	42	÷	6 = 7
6	×	9 = 54	82	+	32 = 114	12	×	8 = 96
10	÷	5 = 2	30	+	117 = 147	126	+	6 = 132
11	+	56 = 67	57	+	25 = 82	60	÷	12 = 5
11	×	11 = 121	10	×	3 = 30	91	–	2 = 89
7	×	12 = 84	10	×	9 = 90	3	+	10 = 13
97	–	1 = 96	27	÷	9 = 3	48	÷	12 = 4
6	×	6 = 36	22	+	63 = 85	115	+	18 = 133

11: Rotation

A2, B2, C3

12: Logical Puzzlers

100kg, since each pig eats 2kg, sheep 6kg and cow 12kg. That's (5x2kg) + (7x6kg) + (4x12kg) = 10kg + 42kg + 48kg = 100kg.

600 recording artists.

2,000 sheets. The fact that I usually print 55 a day is irrelevant to the question asked.

DAY
31

Word List

Try to memorize these 24 types of animal.

After 2 minutes, cover the table and write as many as you can in the boxes below. You do not need to remember the correct order.

Pig	Sheep	Bear	Badger
Kangaroo	Camel	Leopard	Lion
Cat	Elk	Fox	Wolf
Horse	Rabbit	Seal	Whale
Mole	Monkey	Otter	Beaver
Elephant	Rabbit	Guinea pig	Tiger

Now try to recall as many as you can:

INCORRECT ANSWERS:	**TOTAL SCORE:**

Reflective Power

Look at the three figures on the left-hand side. If each of these was reflected in the diagonal "mirror" adjacent to it, which of the figures on the right would be the result?

A B C

1

2

3

TIME TAKEN:	INCORRECT ANSWERS:
TIME POINTS:	**TOTAL SCORE:**

Logical Puzzlers

Try to solve these problems – each requires only simple logic to solve, but you might find that making notes with a pencil will help!

If a=1, b=2, c=3 and so on,
then baa = 2+1+1 = 4 and cab = 3+1+2 = 6.
Given this, which has the highest value: "one", "two" or "three"?

Looking in my wallet I find I have 3 coins, which I tip out onto the desk. What is the likelihood that only 1 of them is heads-up?

If a red, a white, and a blue flag are each tied up with either a red, a white, or a blue cord, but no flag is tied up with a cord of the same colour, and the red flag is not tied with a white cord, what colour cord is used on each flag?

TIME TAKEN:	INCORRECT ANSWERS:
TIME POINTS:	**TOTAL SCORE:**

Missing Words

Study each of these 3 lists of words for 2 minutes. Then cover the top half of the page and see if you can identify which word is missing from each list below.

Defy	Deplane	Describe	Deify
Destiny	Despot	Demur	Delay

Hot	Steaming	Fired	Cool
Warm	Freezing	Boiling	Sweltering

Monitor	Keyboard	Hub	Printer
Mouse	Switch	Drive	Stand

Now try to spot the missing word from each list:

Demur, Deplane, Delay, Deify, Destiny, Despot, Defy

MISSING:

Cool, Steaming, Warm, Hot, Boiling, Freezing, Fired

MISSING:

Drive, Printer, Switch, Stand, Keyboard, Hub, Monitor

MISSING:

INCORRECT ANSWERS:	TOTAL SCORE:

Observation and Counting

Look at this grid and the diagonal lines and see how long it takes you to answer the observation question below. It is quite tricky!

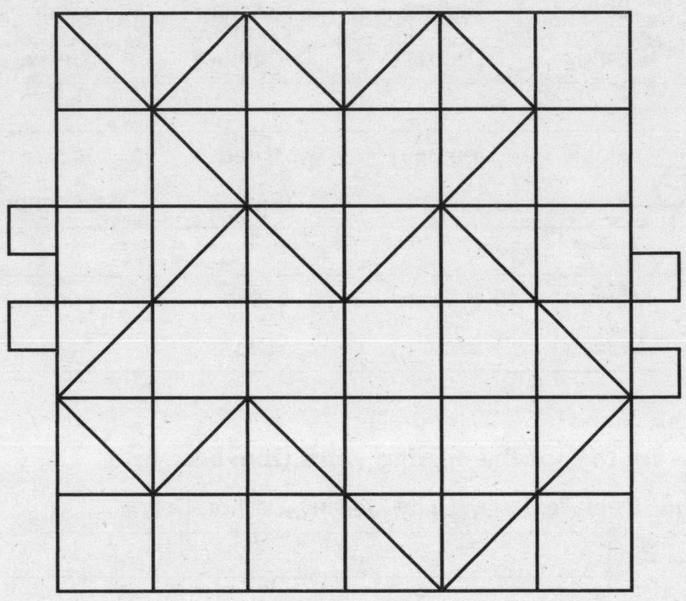

How many triangles can you count?

TIME TAKEN:	INCORRECT ANSWERS:
TIME POINTS:	**TOTAL SCORE:**

Matchstick Thinking

The picture below shows 9 matchsticks arranged into the *invalid* Roman numeral equation 6 – 1 = 2.

Can you move 2 matchsticks only in order to make a *valid* Roman numeral equation? You must find 2 different solutions in order to complete this challenge!

TIME TAKEN:	INCORRECT ANSWERS:
TIME POINTS:	**TOTAL SCORE:**

Time Elapsed

Work out how many hours and minutes have passed between each of these pairs of times.

5:45am to 4:20pm =	:	1:30pm to 6:10pm =	:
4:50pm to 5:35pm =	:	11:05pm to 11:10pm =	:
4:50am to 1:35pm =	:	7:20am to 10:05pm =	:
2:25am to 6:50am =	:	6:00am to 6:50pm =	:
9:00am to 9:20am =	:	5:35pm to 8:50pm =	:
7:20am to 3:30pm =	:	9:40am to 2:30pm =	:
4:15am to 7:20am =	:	3:00pm to 10:00pm =	:
5:20am to 12:50pm =	:	11:05am to 10:10pm =	:
3:10am to 11:40am =	:	12:40pm to 12:45pm =	:
3:45pm to 9:20pm =	:	2:10am to 5:05pm =	:
2:30pm to 3:35pm =	:	5:10pm to 8:55pm =	:
6:25pm to 11:25pm =	:	2:30am to 12:20pm =	:
3:25am to 11:15am =	:	11:50am to 4:20pm =	:
3:05pm to 3:35pm =	:	12:25am to 6:55pm =	:
2:40pm to 3:05pm =	:	11:05am to 2:10pm =	:

TIME TAKEN:	INCORRECT ANSWERS:
TIME POINTS:	**TOTAL SCORE:**

Shape Folding

If you were to cut out this shape and fold it into a cube, which of the three pictures below would be the result?

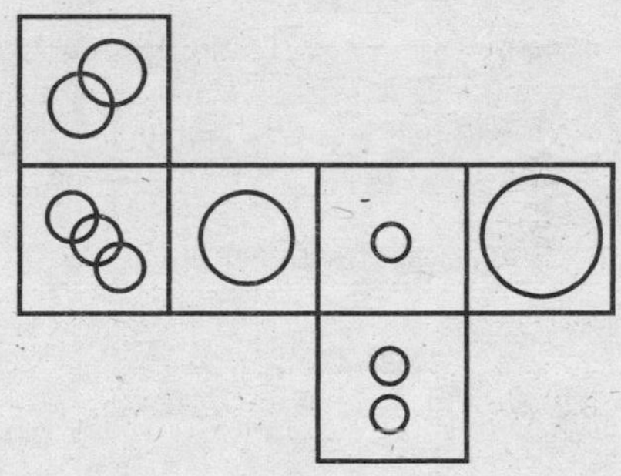

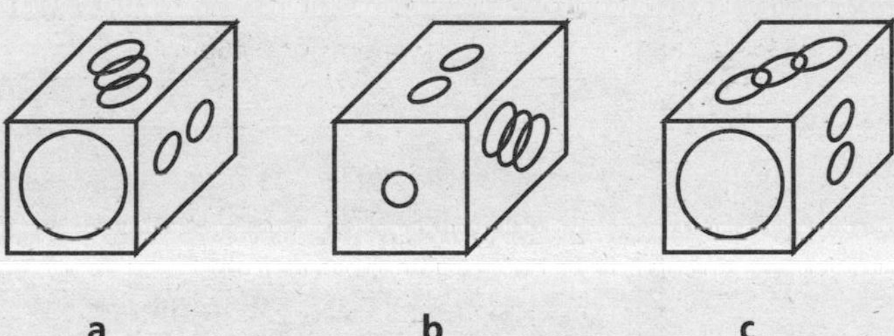

a **b** **c**

TIME TAKEN:	INCORRECT ANSWERS:
TIME POINTS:	**TOTAL SCORE:**

Creative Thinking

See if you can solve each of the following conundrums. If you get stuck then try thinking laterally – they all have logical solutions, but the logic might not be what you expect!

What is made by light, and yet contains no light?

"Each set of crates has a central caster on which it rolls – this reacts to the weight and caters for all possibilities". What can you find traces of in this sentence?

TIME TAKEN:	INCORRECT ANSWERS:
TIME POINTS:	**TOTAL SCORE:**

Cryptogram

Decode each of these quotations by replacing A with D, B with E, C with F, and so on, through to replacing Y with B and Z with C.

Sgd adrs zqftldms zfzhmrs cdlnbqzbx hr z ehud-lhmtsd bnmudqrzshnm vhsg sgd zudqzfd unsdq.

Vhmrsnm Bgtqbghkk

H zl dwsqznqchmzqhkx ozshdms, oqnuhcdc H fds lx nvm vzx hm sgd dmc.

Lzqfzqds Sgzsbgdq

Xnt nmkx qdpthqd svn sghmfr hm khed: xntq rzmhsx zmc xntq vhed.

Snmx Akzhq

Mdbdrrhsx hr sgd okdz cnq dudqx hmeqhmfdldms ne gtlzm eqddcnl: hs hr sgd zqftldms ne sxqzmsr; hs hr sgd bqddc ne rkzudr.

Vhkkhzl Ohss

TIME TAKEN:	INCORRECT ANSWERS:
TIME POINTS:	**TOTAL SCORE:**

Visual Memory

Spend 1 minute studying this path. Then cover the top half of this page and try to redraw it accurately on the empty grid below.

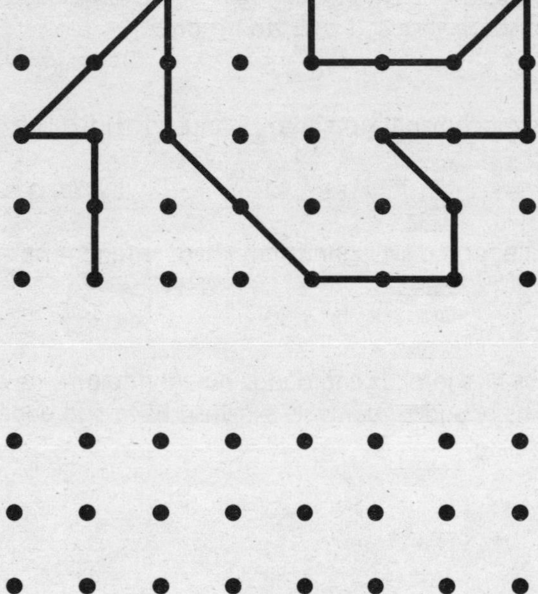

INCORRECT ANSWERS:	**TOTAL SCORE:**

Speed Arithmetic

Complete the following set of arithmetic equations as quickly as possible. You should be able to do them all in your head without using a calculator or making notes.

9 – 3 =	11 × 2 =	89 + 3 =
53 – 18 =	21 + 15 =	85 – 17 =
60 – 7 =	96 – 11 =	7 × 6 =
90 – 19 =	85 – 12 =	2 + 3 =
20 + 85 =	53 – 17 =	51 – 15 =
74 – 8 =	39 + 13 =	6 × 4 =
6 × 5 =	5 × 2 =	6 + 16 =
20 + 1 =	32 + 14 =	3 + 57 =
3 × 10 =	6 × 10 =	1 + 11 =
8 × 6 =	7 + 0 =	101 – 1 =
63 – 8 =	2 × 8 =	19 + 10 =
58 + 10 =	33 + 17 =	9 + 82 =
17 + 1 =	79 – 20 =	93 – 12 =

TIME TAKEN:	INCORRECT ANSWERS:
TIME POINTS:	**TOTAL SCORE:**

Balancing

Looking at these weighing scales, can you say which of these four objects is the heaviest?

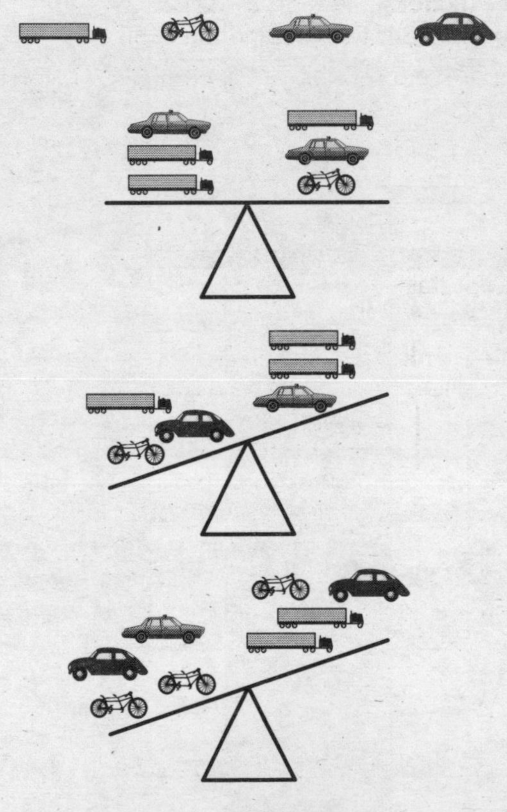

TIME TAKEN:	INCORRECT ANSWERS:
TIME POINTS:	**TOTAL SCORE:**

Solutions

2: Reflective Power
1A, 2C, 3B

3: Logical Puzzlers
"two", since one=34, two=58 and three=56.

3 in 8, since of the 8 possible outcomes (HHH, HHT, HTH, THH, HTT, THT, TTH, TTT) there are 3 which have only 1 head up.

Red flag with a blue cord; White flag with a red cord; Blue flag with a white cord.

5: Observation and Counting
78 triangles in total.

Matchstick Thinking

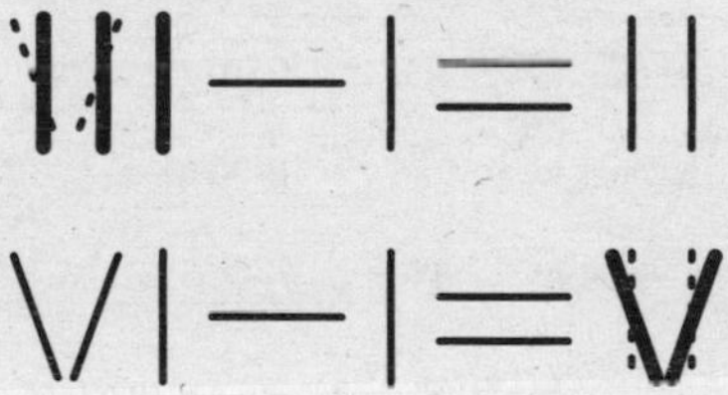

III – I = II

VI – I = V

7: Time Elapsed

5:45am to 4:20pm =	10:35	1:30pm to 6:10pm =	4:40
4:50pm to 5:35pm =	0:45	11:05pm to 11:10pm =	0:05
4:50am to 1:35pm =	8:45	7:20am to 10:05pm =	14:45
2:25am to 6:50am =	4:25	6:00am to 6:50pm =	12:50
9:00am to 9:20am =	0:20	5:35pm to 8:50pm =	3:15
7:20am to 3:30pm =	8:10	9:40am to 2:30pm =	4:50
4:15am to 7:20am =	3:05	3:00pm to 10:00pm =	7:00
5:20am to 12:50pm =	7:30	11:05am to 10:10pm =	11:05
3:10am to 11:40am =	8:30	12:40pm to 12:45pm =	0:05
3:45pm to 9:20pm =	5:35	2:10am to 5:05pm =	14:55
2:30pm to 3:35pm =	1:05	5:10pm to 8:55pm =	3:45
6:25pm to 11:25pm =	5:00	2:30am to 12:20pm =	9:50
3:25am to 11:15am =	7:50	11:50am to 4:20pm =	4:30
3:05pm to 3:35pm =	0:30	12:25am to 6:55pm =	18:30
2:40pm to 3:05pm =	0:25	11:05am to 2:10pm =	3:05

8: Shape Folding

C

9: Creative Thinking

A shadow.

There are traces of the word traces! There are 4 anagrams of traces: reacts, caters, crates and caster.

10: Cryptogram

The best argument against democracy is a five-minute conversation with the average voter.

Winston Churchill

I am extraordinarily patient, provided I get my own way in the end.

Margaret Thatcher

You only require two things in life: your sanity and your wife.

Tony Blair

Necessity is the plea for every infringement of human freedom: it is the argument of tyrants; it is the creed of slaves.

William Pitt

11: Speed Arithmetic

9 − 3 = **6**	11 × 2 = **22**	89 + 3 = **92**
53 − 18 = **35**	21 + 15 = **36**	85 − 17 = **68**
60 − 7 = **53**	96 − 11 = **85**	7 × 6 = **42**
90 − 19 = **71**	85 − 12 = **73**	2 + 3 = **5**
20 + 85 = **105**	53 − 17 = **36**	51 − 15 = **36**
74 − 8 = **66**	39 + 13 = **52**	6 × 4 = **24**
6 × 5 = **30**	5 × 2 = **10**	6 + 16 = **22**
20 + 1 = **21**	32 + 14 = **46**	3 + 57 = **60**
3 × 10 = **30**	6 × 10 = **60**	1 + 11 = **12**
8 × 6 = **48**	7 + 9 = **16**	101 − 1 = **100**
63 − 8 = **55**	2 × 8 = **16**	19 + 10 = **29**
58 + 10 = **68**	33 + 17 = **50**	9 + 82 = **91**
17 + 1 = **18**	79 − 20 = **59**	93 − 12 = **81**

13: Balancing

The heaviest item is: